Allan Aubrey **Boesak**   Wendell L. **Griffen**

PARABLES, POLITICS, AND PROPHETIC FAITH

Hope and Perseverance
in Times of Peril

© 2023
Allan Aubrey Boesak
Wendell L. Griffen
Published in the United States by Nurturing Faith, Macon, GA.
Nurturing Faith is a book imprint of Good Faith Media (goodfaithmedia.org).
Library of Congress Cataloging-in-Publication Data is available.

ISBN: 978-1-63528-229-0

All rights reserved. Printed in the United States of America.

Scripture quotations marked NRSV are from the Revised Standard Version of the Bible, copyright © 1946, 1952, and 1971 National Council of the Churches of Christ in the United States of America. Used by permission. All rights reserved worldwide.

Scripture quotations marked (NIV) are taken from the Holy Bible, New International Version®, NIV®. Copyright © 1973, 1978, 1984, 2011 by Biblica, Inc.™ Used by permission of Zondervan. All rights reserved worldwide. www.zondervan.com The "NIV" and "New International Version" are trademarks registered in the United States Patent and Trademark Office by Biblica, Inc.™

Scripture quotations marked (DRB) are taken from the 1899 DOUAY-RHEIMS BIBLE, public domain.

Scripture quotations marked (ESV) are from the ESV® Bible (The Holy Bible, English Standard Version®), © 2001 by Crossway, a publishing ministry of Good News Publishers. Used by permission. All rights reserved. The ESV text may not be quoted in any publication made available to the public by a Creative Commons license. The ESV may not be translated in whole or in part into any other language.

Scripture quotations marked (NLT) are taken from the Holy Bible, New Living Translation, copyright ©1996, 2004, 2015 by Tyndale House Foundation. Used by permission of Tyndale House Publishers, Carol Stream, Illinois 60188. All rights reserved.

Scripture quotations marked (NASB) taken from the (NASB®) New American Standard Bible®, Copyright © 1960, 1971, 1977, 1995, 2020 by The Lockman Foundation. Used by permission. All rights reserved. lockman.org

Scriptures marked (KJV) are taken from the KING JAMES VERSION (KJV): KING JAMES VERSION, public domain.

Cover color image by Majid Shahid from Pixabay.

For Dirkie Smit

With admiration and deep gratitude for the brilliant work he has done and the example he has set,

And to the memory of Vuyani Vellem

With praise and thanksgiving to God for his life, our friendship, and the enduring legacy he left behind.

For Iva E. Carruthers, Angela Y. Davis, Emilie M. Townes,

and to the memory of James H. Cone

Whose faithful disciplined critique of empire, imperialist religion, and white supremacist nationalism and patriarchy inspire, challenge, and encourage prophetic denunciation of religious conformity to and complicity with oppression, and revolutionary effort to unmask its disguises, condemn it, and combat it.

Contents

Foreword..1
    Dr. Jeremiah A Wright Jr.

Preface...9
    Dr. Teresa Smallwood

Introduction: "Utter Chaos Under the Heavens"................................11
    Allan Aubrey Boesak and Wendell L. Griffen

Chapter 1: A Cloud the Size of a Human Hand
    On Manufactured Scarcity, Kairos, and the Abundance of Grace (I).........23
    Allan Aubrey Boesak

Chapter 2: A Cloud the Size of a Human Hand
    On Manufactured Scarcity, Kairos, and the Abundance of Grace (II)........35
    Allan Aubrey Boesak

Chapter 3: A Cloud the Size of a Human Hand
    On Manufactured Scarcity, Kairos, and the Abundance of Grace (III).......47
    Allan Boesak

Chapter 4: Calling Zacchaeus
    On Repentance, Reparations, and Black Theology (I).................55
    Wendell Griffen

Chapter 5: Calling Zacchaeus
    On Repentance, Reparations, and Black Theology (II)................65
    Wendell Griffen

Chapter 6: Grapes, Thorns, Figs, and Thistles
    On the "Hateful Faithful"..75
    Wendell Griffen

Chapter 7: Wolves, Shepherds, and Hirelings
    On the Power of Combative Love..83
    Allan Boesak

Chapter 8: Shiphrah, Puah, Rahab, and the Magi
    On Epiphany, Empire, and Prophetic Resistance.....................101
    Wendell Griffen

Chapter 9: "Only Don't Go Too Far Away"
   On the Perils of Negotiating with Pharaoh 117
   Allan Boesak

Chapter 10: Missing Micaiah
   On Prophetic Integrity about Haiti 139
   Wendell Griffen

Chapter 11: Paying Homage to the Bramble
   On Democracy Born of Disastrous Decisions 149
   Allan Boesak

Chapter 12: Briers, Thorns, and Scorpions
   On Prophetic Perseverance and Hope for a Desperate World 167
   Wendell Griffen

Epilogue 179

Notes 181

The Authors 190

Foreword

Dr. Jeremiah A Wright Jr.

In the opening chapters of his historic book, *The Destruction of Black Civilization: Great Issues of a Race from 4500 B.C. to 2000 A.D.*, Dr. Chancellor Williams records the conversation between a traveler in West Africa and one of the region's famed griots.

The traveler asked, "Whatever became of the people of Sumer? Legend has it that they were Black!"

The griot thought for a moment then said, "Ah! They forgot their story and so they died!"

African pedagogy demonstrates just how important storytelling is in preserving the culture, the history, and the legacy of a people. Africans used and still use storytelling to make a point, to teach a lesson, or to demonstrate a truth. Jesus was cut from the same cultural cloth as all other Africans. He knew the stories of Moses, Joshua, Deborah, Anna, Miriam, Samuel and the judges, David and the kings. He knew the stories of his people.

The same is true all over Africa. In South Africa alone, Afrikaans, English, Pedi, Sotho, Ndebele, Swazi, Tsonga, and Tswana are the official languages (in addition to English) of the people. In each of those languages, children are taught the stories of their people. They are passed on from generation to generation. They do not forget their stories!

I included English and Afrikaans because they are listed as two of the "official" languages of the country. The stories they represent as colonizers, however, point to one of the problems with which South African theologians wrestle today. Including stories in Afrikaans as the true stories of a people (such as the *Voortrekkers*) is problematic because colonizers do not tell the truth about any of the indigenous African people. More drastically, moreover, almost no South African knows the story of the Khoi and San people. "They forgot their story and so they died!"

In a private conversation with Dr. Allan Boesak, one of the authors of this fascinating book, I asked him if he knew of anyone in his family who could speak Khoi or San. I asked because I was taught in elementary school that to learn a foreign language, one had to think in that language.

To think in a foreign language means to embrace not only the phonics, the semantics, the grammar, the pragmatics, the syntax, and the other elements of the linguistics concerning that particular language; it also means thinking in that language. One had to think like a Khoi. One had to think like a San. One had to embrace the culture of the people whose language he or she was trying to master. To learn their language is to learn an entire history of a people.

Dr. Boesak told me that his brother could still speak Khoi and some words of San, but he could not speak them fluently because he had no one with whom he could converse in those languages. "They forgot their story and so they died!"

The matter of decolonizing becoming more complex in this area of language and linguistics has been illustrated by two different authors, Cornel West and Jerome Ross. Mitri Raheb should also be added to the list of scholars who "muddy these waters."

Cornel West argues that no matter how steeped in the culture of African peoples African Americans may become when trying to decolonize the racist thought, racist teachings, and racist understandings of the world we inherited, African Americans can learn Ibo, Yoruba, Xhosa, Zulu, Fon, Ashanti, Ga, or whatever, but they will still "dream in the English language!" The fact of being born in a particular settler colonial project and learning the language of the colonizer in infancy will make the problem or task of decolonizing that individual's thinking (and beliefs) even more difficult.

I reference Cornel West and Jerome Ross. I would be remiss, however, if I did not mention at least one or two of my sisters in the theological education community, Madipoane Masenya's work in the Old Testament wisdom literature, African biblical hermeneutics, and Hebrew Bible is one such sister. Dr. Masenya's insights did not come alive for me because of my association with her at the University of South Africa. They came alive and heightened or underscored the whole issue of decolonizing the thought patterns of South Africans (and African Americans) as she relayed her story about riding on a bus to go facilitate a women's retreat with females of the First Congregational Church of Groutville. She was on the bus carrying the women and seated next to a colleague of hers who also taught at the University of South Africa. Seated behind them on the bus were two women who were church leaders of the First Congregational Church, and they were talking to each other in Zulu.

During a lull in Dr. Masenya and her colleague's conversation, she overheard one of the women say to the other, "I sure hope these professors lead their workshops in Zulu so we can understand what it is they are saying."

That one sentence caught Dr. Masenya off guard and caught me off guard. The assumption in South Africa is that the "official language" of English is taught in the school system. The underlying assumption there, however, is that all citizens of South Africa go to elementary school and secondary school.

The assumption never takes into account the vast—overwhelmingly vast!—number of South African citizens who are not privileged to have any kind of education given their rural living conditions.

Dr. Musa Dube-Shomanah of Botswana put an exclamation point behind this issue when she pointed out to me that the Bible when translated into English, Spanish, or Portuguese is not the same as the word of God in their (Botswanan) native language (Tswana). For members of the church in her context, hearing the Bible in Tswana in many instances is diametrically opposed to what the European translations are saying. The word "demon," for instance, means "ancestor" in her native language. It has no negative connotations or denotations.

To say, then, that Jesus went about casting demons out of poor people is to say that their ancestors were evil! Language is all important. Language as a part of culture must be taken into consideration and deep study when talking about decolonization of theology, theological education, and the everyday language of the people in whose culture one works. Dr. Musa Dube's book, *Postcolonial Feminist Interpretations of the Bible*, offers another female voice that enters the conversation concerning decolonization and language.

Jerome Ross, Professor of Hebrew Bible at the Samuel DeWitt Proctor School of Theology at Virginia Union University, makes the matter even more complicated in his essay, "The Cultural Affinity Between the Ancient Yahwists and the African-Americans: A Hermeneutic for Homiletics." (That article can be found in Samuel Roberts's book, *Born to Preach*, a festschrift in honor of the ministry of Drs. Henry and Ella Mitchell.) Among the many fascinating things that Dr. Ross points out in showing the cultural similarities between the writers of scripture whom we know as the Yahwists and the African Americans, Dr. Ross says every word in the sacred text that we honor as the Holy Scriptures was written during six different kinds of oppression and consequently six different periods of oppression: Egyptian, Assyrian, Babylonian, Persian, Greek, and Roman. The entire New Testament was written under Roman oppression!

Those six different kinds of oppression produced six different cultural realities. Being enslaved in the first chronological period of oppression is quite different from being under oppression in diaspora (starting with the Babylonian diaspora up through the Greco-Roman diaspora). A cursory reading of Acts 2 gives the reader a glimpse of just how many languages the diasporic Jewish community claimed as "home" and their "native languages." Decolonization becomes almost an insurmountable task when it comes to those different cultures, those different ways of thinking, those different ways of our differing belief systems and of knowing.

Both Boesak and Griffen introduce the reader to the problems involved at this level of decolonizing the thought patterns and belief systems of the African American community, the Euro-American community, the South African community—both Black and white—and the white supremacists' construct of beliefs and belief systems.

As I read this text, I thought about a text written by Samuel, the last of the judges in the Hebrew faith, and Solomon, the king described as the greatest of thinkers in the Hebrew Bible and indeed in sacred history. Samuel was a judge, and Wendell Griffen is a judge. Samuel also was called by God to perform the offices of priest and pastor. Wendell Griffen is a pastor of a church in Little Rock, Arkansas.

Samuel performed his ministry while under the oppression of the Assyrians. Solomon was the king of Israel during the reign of the Persians and the Greeks. The biblical judge and the biblical pastor lived and ministered under oppression. The twenty-first-century judge Wendell Griffen and the South African politician and pastor Allan Boesak are both contemporary prophets who carry out their ministries under harsh oppression. Griffen performs his ministry under the umbrella of 400 years of white supremacy, white racism, and American "exceptionalism." Allan Boesak performs his ministry under white oppression—the ideology and practice of apartheid and the harsh heel of a revolution gone bad. I speak of the "new pharaoh" who looks like us—the African National Congress that made errors when they signed the "negotiated settlement" to set Mandela free and attempted futilely to make membership in the ANC contingent upon the color of one's skin.

To the reader of this very important volume, that last sentence may come as a surprise to you. Yet it is true, sadly enough. The ANC, after freedom came to Black Africans, wanted to make membership in the ANC all Black. That insane position would cause Allan Boesak to be sent to prison on trumped-up charges! Boesak wanted the United Democratic Front (UDF) to be the incarnation of the freedom charter, a multiracial, multicultural, interfaith body of persons who wanted freedom, justice, peace, and what was best for all South Africans, no matter their color or creed. The UDF was gaining so much popularity that the leading members of the ANC saw it as a threat to their power, so they created false charges against Boesak and sent him to prison.

Not only was the ANC not pleased with Boesak's position on race and his popularity among the masses; they were also not happy concerning his challenge to their position on violence. None less than Madiba himself posited that there comes a point in time when nonviolence does not work and threw his support behind the MK (uMkhonto we Sizwe). But one of Boesak's mentors, Albert

Luthuli, had a strong stance against violence. Along with that, Boesak's desire for the UDF not only to be nonracial but also to be nonviolent was disturbing to the ANC.

Albert Luthuli was a deacon at the Congregational Church of Groutville and also chief of the ANC and the first South African to win a Nobel Peace Prize. During his acceptance speech for the Nobel Peace Prize, he wore his traditional ANC chieftain's kufi. (The day of his acceptance speech also marked the first property bombing that the MK carried out in its attempt to hasten the end of apartheid.) Many commentators reflect on the seeming disparity while reporting that the bombing took place during Chief Luthuli's acceptance speech.

Boesak carries Dr. Martin Luther King and Archbishop Tutu's position on violence begetting only violence a step further:

> The greatest myth about violence is not that it is controllable, but that it is redemptive. The most visceral reality of violence is not that it begets violence [*pace* Dr. King!], but that it is idolatrous. The most tragic thing about violence is not that it is toxic, but that it is intoxicating. The most devastating truth about violence is not its horrors, but its delusions.

Those complicated issues that are illustrated in the following pages and Judge Griffen's insistence that the enemies against whom we fight are not "monsters" demonstrate how these two twenty-first-century prophetic pastors are in lockstep with each other theologically and sociologically. They are literally birds (the doves of peace) of a feather!

Judge Griffen believes that the teachings of Jesus outweigh the teachings of the "state," and he acted out that belief in front of the courthouse in Little Rock, Arkansas, one Good Friday. He had the audacity to lie in state on the sidewalk in front of the Arkansas Governor's Mansion for ninety minutes on Good Friday (April 15, 2017) to demonstrate the insanity, the inhumanity, and the brutal practice of the death penalty. The "gatekeepers" had apoplexy when this Black judge dared to challenge the hallowed belief of killing being the perfect display of punishment, a bedrock on which this racist country is built.

Where Boesak was sent to prison in his context, Griffen came under attack in his context. Griffen's enemies tried to strip him of his judicial status and even tried to disbar him as a lawyer in the State of Arkansas and in the United States of America.

If you can imagine a book being co-authored by Solomon and Samuel, then you get a glimpse of what a book co-authored by Boesak and Griffen is like. Most intriguing to me about this important work, however, is not their shared prophetic vision from different contexts that speaks to the *zeitgeist* of the twenty-first century. Nor is it their dogged determination to preach hope amid hopeless situations—Griffen in the wake of the Tulsa, Oklahoma, and Elaine, Arkansas, massacres and Boesak in the wake of the Sharpeville massacre (under the old pharaoh) and the Marikana massacre (under the new pharaoh who looks just like us).

Most intriguing to me is the prophetic boldness with which both of these men of God address the illegal state of Israel/Zionism and its vicious, inhumane treatment of the Palestinians from the Nakba in 1948 to Gaza in 2023. These two Christian pastors write parables of hope that parallel the writings of Jewish thinkers like Marc Ellis in *Judaism Does Not Equal Israel* and Ilan Pappe in *The Ethnic Cleansing of Palestine*. Boesak and Griffen's prophetic vision on this matter and every justice matter they address gives me a glimpse of the global dimension that justice ministry has taken and continues to take.

This powerful volume flies in the face of Audre Lorde's maxim that says you cannot destroy the master's house using the master's tools. Griffen and Boesak are both trained jurists and theologians. Their formal training, however, was at the master's hands. They take those tools and masterfully (pardon the pun) proceed to destroy the master's house in this volume that they have co-authored.

What Audre Lorde did not take into account in her maxim, however, was the "extra-judicial" (pardon the pun again) training that both Griffen and Boesak received at the hands of their people—not at the hands of the master, not at the master's institutions of higher learning, and not inside the walls of the racist institutions of settler colonialism. What Griffen got at the kitchen table of the Griffen household and what Boesak got flowing in the waves of the Camissa River that runs down from Table Mount underneath the city of Cape Town are not the master's tools. They are the combined wisdom of enslaved Africans who fought for their own freedom and the Khoi San who never bought into the lies of the white invaders of their sacred grounds.

That fascinating combination helped produce the volume you hold in your hands. It is our prayer that the parables told by Jesus and the parables that these two men of faith have woven together will bless your lives and cause you to answer their question addressed to us in the Epilogue in the affirmative.

Parables were the primary pedagogy of the African and African American way of teaching important lessons. Just like the spirituals created by the enslaved Africans in the United States, parables function on many different levels. Parables are like onions. The more you peel away layer after layer, the stronger the smell of the onion becomes and the more powerful its ability to change the taste of the food in which it is used as seasoning. So it was with the parables of Jesus, and so it is with the parables told by Boesak and Griffen.

Since we are talking about the "taste," let me close with a parable of my own. Dr. Charles H. Long, the preeminent African American professor of the History of Religions, shared this parable with his students at the University of Chicago Divinity School.

Suppose you are to bake a cake and you mix up all of the ingredients perfectly: flour, milk, butter, baking powder, vanilla extract, cinnamon, and nutmeg. Then, you preheat the oven to the desired temperature while you mix the ingredients in a mixing bowl.

Next, you pour the ingredients from the bowl into a baking pan, put that pan in the oven, and let it bake for the accurate amount of time. Then, you pull the cake out of the oven, place it on a wooden baking board, and prepare to add icing when you suddenly realize you have forgotten to put the sugar in with the initial ingredients.

There is no way you can pour sugar on the top of the concoction you just pulled out of the oven and make it a cake. It can never be a cake. The constituting elements determine that it is something less than a cake!

It can be what Black Virginians will recognize as hot water cornbread, but it can't be a cake! Why? Because you forgot one of the constituting elements—sugar.

You cannot pour sugar on the top of that concoction and call it "cake." All you have to do is scrape the sugar off the top, and you will have what you had at the beginning of this concoction, which is missing the most important ingredient for it to be a cake. You cannot put icing on the mess you have made and call it cake. You are missing one of the constituting elements.

It is the same with the Constitution of the United States of America. The constituting elements of this document determined that Africans were never full citizens of the United States. You cannot put sugar on top of that mess. The Thirteenth, Fourteenth, and Fifteenth Amendments are sugar on the top of an imperfectly constituted mess. All you have to do is scrape those amendments off, scrape the sugar off, and the resulting mess will be as it was in 1787. It remains a mess. With Roe v. Wade having been removed, scraped off, can the Nineteenth Amendment be far behind? Can the Thirteenth, Fourteenth, and Fifteenth Amendments be far behind the Nineteenth Amendment?

The answer is an unequivocal no! The framers of the Constitution—the new framers—have to do what they did in South Africa. The South Africans had to build on the Freedom Charter. They had to construct a whole new constitution, this time including the sugar that was omitted in the first concoction.

The new constitution needed in the United States must include the "brown sugar" of Africans as citizens, LGBTQ people as citizens, the right of a woman to choose what happens to her own body—all of this must be part of the sugar that was omitted in the first 1787 concoction. Otherwise, we will end up with the same old mess, rearranging the furniture on the *Titanic*.

Boesak and Griffen have laid out the ingredients for a new cake—this time with the sugar included as one of the constituting elements. The new meal has been prepared. "Oh taste and see that the Lord is good. Blessed is the one who trusts in God!"

Enjoy the meal. The table is set.

Rev. Dr. Jeremiah A. Wright, Jr.
Pastor Emeritus, Trinity United Church of Christ, Chicago, Illinois
Co-Founder, Samuel DeWitt Proctor Conference, Chicago, Illinois

Preface

Dr. Teresa Smallwood

Some kairos moments come when exigencies present conditions so dire that God must lift holy actors to usher in crucial correctives, change, or direction to bring alignment between God and God's people. Such a prophetic mandate is evident in this manuscript. It is a venerable response to Dr. Martin Luther King Jr.'s pronouncement of "the fierce urgency of now" because it relates to the triple evils that Dr. King wrote about in his final manuscript *Where Do We Go from Here: Chaos or Community?* This volume provides a roadmap to reparations, biblical exigency, cultural competency, and political expediency.

The authors evaluate the failures of world systems as well as purported faith-based initiatives in specific regions related to racism, poverty, and militarism. Racism and its cousin xenophobia continue to shroud humanity with the death clothes of incarceration, economic insufficiency, cultural exploitation, old and new Jim Crow. Racist governance is so palpable that truth appears to have been overcome by lies—the very manifestation of evil operating as an "angel of light" (2 Corinthians 11:14, NRSV). Poverty continues to ravage people all over the world. Efforts to deal with hunger and houselessness are meager and ineffective. Militarism continues in the interstices of Myanmar, Afghanistan, Ukraine, Russia, North America (particularly in the streets of the USA through the "bloodletting" of police brutality), South America, Asia, and Africa. Reminiscent of the holy anger of *David Walker's Appeal*, the political resolve of the Black Manifesto, the sobering reasoning of the Belhar Confession, and the spiritual prowess of the ancestors, this book comes at a time when the world needs credible, godly witnesses, witnesses who commune with God, who speak for God as true prophets sent by God.

One born and raised in South Africa and the other born and raised in North America—brothers, nonetheless, in Spirit, discernment, integrity, and prophetic power—Allan Boesak and Wendell Griffen bring cosmic, holy insight for the scriptural exegete and the Bible aficionado as well as the skeptic. Leaving no stones unturned, the authors confront the issues of the present world, and while "standing in awe of the mystery, [they] embrace the prophetic." This volume is replete with example upon example of where we went wrong in the last fifty-five years since the death of Rev. Dr. Martin Luther King Jr.

The prophetic has been used to describe those who speak and act as representatives of God. That general definition, however, has been coopted by those who present themselves as sheep but are literally wolves in sheep's clothing. This point is treated in the following pages with an ardent and precise analysis that will enlighten the most erudite scholarly minds. This book aims to fill the void in the intellectual as well as the spiritual study of biblical exegesis by separating the "marrow from the bone" in critical, cultural interpretation from stories about Moses and the burning bush to stories about the midwives, Shiphrah and Puah. This volume explicates the wise counsel of God in strategically employing women in the work of God's kin(g)dom. No other volume confronts false prophets the way this work does by identifying the insidious shackles placed upon the church through slavish mentalities sold out to "imperialism, racism, capitalism, authoritarianism, sexism, militarism, technocentrism, religious nationalism, and xenophobia."

This manuscript will ably support students of theology as it examines a plethora of political events through the insightful use of scripture. It will enhance scholarly research with its in-depth and keen reflection on key sociopolitical events germane to the rise of nationalism, populism, greed, and avarice around the world. It is an invaluable resource for the clerical body, especially those who are pastoring, because it will serve as a standard bearer to awaken those who have been lulled to sleep by the opiate of prosperity. It is also a consummate checkpoint for those in elected positions who have adopted the meaning of "under God" with the solipsistic notion of a self-absorbed nimbus. This is a manuscript to equip God's people for *prophetic activism*.

Rev. Dr. Teresa Smallwood
James Franklin Kelly and Hope Eyster Kelly Associate Professor of Public Theology
United Lutheran Seminary

Introduction

"Utter Chaos Under the Heavens"

As 2022 was limping towards its end, Irish Minister of Foreign Affairs Simon Coveney, at the end of Ireland's stint on the UN Security Council and looking back at that year, observed, "The world is a crazy and tragic place."[1] Those words caught all sorts of headlines because they struck a chord with people all over the world. Just more than half a century ago, amid the turbulent sixties, Mao Tse Tung, the father of the Chinese Revolution, saw it and said it better. Mao observed the situation in China, appraised the historic moment, and reportedly said this: "Under the heavens, everything is utter chaos." Then he added, "The situation is excellent."[2]

This is a book about parables for our times. We work with selected passages of Scripture, reading and interpreting them as parables as we attempt to understand and discern the signs of our times that we may now, perhaps too benignly, describe as times of great upheaval and confusion. The climate crisis alone, with floods, hurricanes, tornadoes, heat waves, and cold spells that broke every previous record, not to speak of the life-threatening situations in certain parts of our planet, has removed any doubt about how serious that crisis really is. The rising tides of panic on many Pacific islands, for instance, do not even begin to match the ferocity of the rising tides of the ocean that will now certainly, sooner rather than later, swallow them up and wipe them out.

However, it is the apparent combination of inability, shortsightedness, incomprehensible incompetence, and stubborn lack of political will, again on display at the most recent climate conference in Cairo, *even now*, that really reveals the depths of the crisis. The stunningly reckless abandon with which the still unseemly powerful, neo-liberal capitalist forces are wreaking havoc on what is left of the global economy and on the lives of the world's most vulnerable humans is another. COVID-19, with the appearance of new variants just as we thought we might be getting out of the woods, remains a stubborn, death-dealing menace. But we begin with the observations of two political leaders as each were pondering their own times. Might it be that the words of these two world leaders, uttered at such different times, are in themselves a parable for our times?

Mr. Simon Coveney was speaking at the United Nations—to the whole world, in other words—and for him, the "craziness" and "tragedy" of this world mostly meant the war in Ukraine, invaded by Russia, and the consequences for all of Europe. He also spoke about the ongoing crisis in Syria and the failure of the Security Council to secure peace, allowing the never-ending influx of refugees into European countries. A solution there was possible, he says, "but it's all up to Russia," whose veto on the Security Council blocks every possible exit from this treadmill of horrors.

Mr. Coveney is correct about the stranglehold the right to veto any Security Council resolution by the five major powers—the US, Russia, the UK, China, and France—has over the efficacy of such resolutions. He is also right that Russia has stepped in repeatedly to protect Syria. Mr. Coveney knows, too, that at this moment a significant portion of North Eastern Syria, with its rich oil reserves, is being militarily occupied by the United States, while the US is literally stealing Syria's oil for itself—an average of 66,000 barrels per day, according to sources—which is a war crime. Russia does protect Syria and its present leadership. But selective forgetfulness does not make the world a less crazy place. In fact, it adds to the tragedy of world politics at the moment.

Simon Coveney did not mention Yemen, and he did not admonish the United States for its role in that genocidal war driven by Saudi Arabia, who was not mentioned either. Not a word about the forty years of failure of the Security Council on Israel, the Nakba, the occupation, and the question of justice and freedom for Palestinians, worse in 2022 than ever before. He did not mention "Israeli apartheid" and the tragedies it is causing the Palestinian people, while Europe, washing its hands like Pontius Pilate, looks on, supports it, and profits from it, while the US blocks every effort at the UN to hold Israel to account.

The Irish Minister of Foreign Affairs spoke much about the war in Ukraine, and that war, as every war, is a tragedy, no question. Russia's invasion of Ukraine is a contravention of international law. But it is even more tragic if we hear not a word about the craziness that got that war started. US military experts like Scott Ritter, who also served as UN inspector on the Iraq weapons of mass destruction investigation, and retired Colonel Douglass McGregor, to mention only two, along with respected academics such as Noam Chomsky, John Mearsheimer, and Jeffrey Sachs have all exhaustively explained the reasons for what has become the NATO/US/war against Russia in Ukraine.[3] They explained the foolish determination of NATO expansion toward the borders of Russia, totally ignoring the legitimate security concerns of Russia, or the rush toward war, eschewing every path to diplomatic solutions. The point they unfailingly make is that this is a war that could have been prevented. It was truly bewildering to see Boris Johnson, then Prime Minister of the UK, rush to Kyiv, not once but at least twice, to stop Volodymir Zelensky from even thinking about any peace talks with Russia, who seemed to be ready for it. And as this is being written, Johnson, now an ordinary UK Member of Parliament, is in Ukraine again, and nobody knows why. If one has to go on his record, though, it can only be to make sure that peace talks are ruled out, and the war is prolonged. And what to say of Democratic Congressman Adam Schiff's now infamous words from December 20, 2022, "We'll fight them [the Russians] until the last Ukrainian"? On which Senator Lindsey Graham doubled down on a recent visit to Ukraine: "Russians are dying and it's the best money we've ever spent."[4] The despicable absurdity of such intentions may have escaped the senator's war-mongering mind, but it certainly will not have escaped the mind of the mothers and families of those soldiers in Ukraine. In perfect accord with US Congress spending patterns and allocations, year after year, the most money is in any case always spend on war and death—never on health care, education, infrastructure or student debt relief. But to boast, in the company of the Ukrainian leadership, that these amounts are actually the "best" money ever spent because it kills Russians, even if Ukrainian soldiers die in vastly disproportionate numbers in this war gone so horribly wrong for Ukraine—is that not unspeakably "tragic" and "crazy"? That Senator Graham's remark passed without much public comment, let alone public indignation, is perhaps in itself a parable for our times.

Meanwhile, we have learned about the even more foolish and dangerous goal of "regime change" in Russia that slipped out of President Biden's mouth in his infamous speech in Poland.[5] Not a word about the craziness of European governments plunging headlong into US-driven sanctions of Russia that turned out to be devastating to those same European countries as one sanctions package after another proved an utter failure and in fact backfired on Europe. Or what we know now: that the West used the Minsk Agreements, which were meant to prevent the war in the first place, as mere "delaying tactics" according to former German Chancellor Angela Merkel, at last coming clean in her now famous interview in *Der Spiegel*. And before the week was over, this was confirmed by former French president Francois Hollande.[6] All of which leads us to yet another, perhaps even more disturbing question. Does this mean that what has become known as "the collective West" not only shuns diplomacy as it almost instinctively leans towards war but is also now incapable of diplomacy—that it has, in its captivity to its military-industrial complexes and imperialistic, ideological blindness, lost completely the art of diplomacy? That would be tragic indeed.

Not a word about the tragedy of the war because the West is pouring billions of dollars into the most corrupt country in Europe, shunning every attempt to demand accountability for all those weapons and money. Not a word either about one of the most disturbing facts of all: that the proudly liberal, democratic

Western nations are backing a dictator in Ukraine who in turn is backed by Nazis who revere the infamous Stefan Bandera as a national icon; backing a government who is banning opposition news channels, throwing opposition leaders in prison, supporting the publication of a "kill list" on the internet of those who dissent, and suppressing people's language and cultural rights in the Donbass, Donetsk, and Luhansk. President Zelensky is persecuting a Christian church in the Ukraine, locking up its priests, and confiscating its properties. It is tragic that while everybody else, certainly in the Global South, knows all this, the Western media barely ever mention it, suppress the truth about it even as they discover that truth, and denounce those who do raise these issues as "Putin puppets." That epithet alone has the power to shut off all rational discussion, it seems. And because the all-powerful Western media do not mention it, it does not exist. Making mature, informed debate on issues of such global importance impossible while so much is at stake—is that not "crazy" and "tragic"?

Are Russia's troops committing war crimes in Ukraine? Are Ukrainian troops committing war crimes in the Donbass? No war is without crimes, and every war is a crime. So Mr. Putin may very well be a war criminal. But so is every Western leader who has ever backed the United States in its illegal, never-ending wars in the Third World, and who has not had the courage to engage in a single meaningful act against Israel's occupation and the war crimes it is committing on a daily basis. Instead, they parade Mr. Zelensky from world stage to world stage, pronouncing him "the closest thing to Churchill we have ever seen." And again, from a Third World point of view, they may not be entirely wrong. The denunciation of Russia sounds utterly hollow if it comes from the mouth of someone like Ms. Victoria Nuland, US Under Secretary of State for Political Affairs, an open, warmongering neo-conservative and a key architect of the 2014 Maidan coup in Ukraine. So, as one weeps for the tragedy befalling the suffering people of Ukraine, one should rise up in outrage at the hypocrisy, egotism, and greed that make it possible and acceptable in the eyes of far too many in the Western world, for they believe their leaders in this war, like Mao in the Cultural Revolution, have some "higher" goal in mind.

Perhaps the craziness and tragedy is not that Mr. Coveney is right about our world but that he is deliberately only halfway right, and he knows it. It is crazy to bemoan the tragedies of a proxy war that could have been prevented were it not for imperialist greed, egotism, and political foolishness on a scale unheard of in modern history. The tragedy is not only that Third World people are suffering unimaginable consequences from a war they did not start, have nothing to do with, and have no interest to maintain. It is also that the Third World in the Rich North, the poor, powerless, and unprivileged, the people of colour, the have-nots and the never-will-haves, have no say in any of this. Despite living in proudly proclaimed "democracies," they have no way to influence the debates, no power to stop the carnage done to others in their name, no choice but to swallow the lies told in their name, no say in this bleak future being created for their children in their name.

Except if they flood the streets in their thousands, disrupt the workings of their captured democracies so that genuine democracy may stand a chance; except if, through their righteous anger, they dismantle the death-dealing systems that rule over them so that they may save their lives. The tragedy is that almost nowhere in the world do we see signs of the wisdom of that great African American scholar/intellectual/activist, W. E. B. Du Bois, as he searched for what he called the politics of decency, honesty, integrity, courage, and virtue, the immortal wisdom of which we will return to again and again in the chapters that follow. Meanwhile, the real, and only, winners in the war in Ukraine, or Yemen, or Mali, or the Congo, are the arms manufacturing companies in the US who, restless and dissatisfied after the end of the war in Afghanistan, are now once again posting record profits. And of course the politicians who line up to do their bidding.

To say that Mao Tse-tung saw it better is not at all to say that the Chinese Cultural Revolution was "better," less bloody, less tragic, or that the situation in 1960s China was less chaotic than our global situation right now. Far from it. The deaths of 500,000 to one million Chinese citizens in the brutal purges just about everywhere in society, with students taking the lead in a zeal whose lethality still stuns the mind, can never be justified. That, on top of the millions who perished through bad policy decisions, famine, and bloodshed, not even counting the ruination of the lives of millions more during the preceding "Great Leap Forward" of the late 1950s, is beyond tragic. Mao is not wiser because of his belief that "power comes out of the barrel of a gun," even though those same Western leaders who despise him so much have clung ferociously to that belief for as long as anyone can remember.[7]

But sometimes human beings, even in their utter sinfulness, as though they cannot help it, have insights of wisdom that can influence others, with the advantage of hindsight, to gain a deeper understanding of our own situations. Such wisdom from Mao lies in the four words he adds to his observation: "The situation is excellent." For Mao, it might have meant that chaos, in and of itself, is "excellent," and that what he wanted to achieve is more easily achieved by the chaos his cultural revolution had created. In light of the historical evidence, that might be partly true. However, what we in our own times may learn from what Mao said is that when the chaos in any situation is too obvious to ignore, too devastating to be disowned, or downplayed, and when the tragedies piling up because of misrule and greed and abuse of power can no longer be trivialized, people have no choice but to open their eyes and see the truth of it all. Denial of that truth is no longer possible, and people realize not only that too much is at stake but also that they are the ones to do something about it. That is why the situation is "excellent." It is not the chaos by itself that is excellent. It is the realization of the *causes* of that chaos—that it is not divinely appointed or ordained and that human beings have it in their power to change the situation in which they find themselves. That is the situation that is excellent. So Mao, as I read him, is teaching us that in utter, undeniable chaos, humankind may find their most hopeful potential.

But here is the rub. Mao knew, as our modern politicians know, that people always crave hope. The more desperate the situation, the more desperate we are for hope. With death and destruction all around, hope is a force that gives us life. Politicians have always relentlessly exploited that deeply implanted, inescapable human desire. What Mao did with that inextinguishable hope as potential for change that would save China and serve humankind is the tragedy of his times. Perhaps one reason for China's spectacular success today is that they have learned from their mistakes. Perhaps the mistakes of Mao are also read as a parable for the China we encounter today, a global power to be reckoned with. What our modern politicians are doing with the still living hope of the masses is the tragedy we are facing right now, and it is exactly what comes under critique in this book. That is why the words of these two leaders are a parable for our times.

But even half-right, Mr. Coveney is not completely wrong, as a cursory glance at our global situation will verify. Gender-based violence, in its never-ending and ever-growing horrors, was a pandemic long before COVID-19. Apart from the ongoing devastation of the COVID pandemic, two scientists have now warned, in an article published by Al Jazeera, that the new pandemic is hunger.[8] Oxfam continues to point out that global socioeconomic, gender, and racial inequalities, as well as inequality that exists between countries, "are tearing our world apart."[9] This, Oxfam goes on to say, is not by chance or accident but by choice: "economic violence is perpetrated when structural policy choices are made for the benefit of the richest and most powerful people." Another Oxfam report from 2022 makes the point precisely and graphically: socioeconomic inequalities all by themselves—not pandemics or natural disasters or war—are costing the lives of 21,000 people globally every day. That is one person dying every four seconds.

In Afghanistan, one year after the US lost the war there and left, the US is continuing the war through other means—almost, one is compelled to conclude, out of sheer spite, belligerence, and wounded pride. The US has placed punishing sanctions on the country, including on medicines and medical aid, and has frozen the country's assets, crippling the economy. Six million Afghans are now at risk of famine. Groups even more extreme than the Taliban continue the terrors perpetrated on the people for so many decades now, and the most recent bombing of a school as we write this left dozens dead. Most were girls.[10]

In Yemen, on top of the war, the naval blockade, the internal strife, and deadly political uncertainties, the people have to cope with yet another kind of disaster. Because of the sanctions, medicines are very hard to come by. Smuggled-in, contaminated medicines have just killed at least ten children.[11] The Horn of Africa is facing yet another famine, Libya's slave markets are still thriving, and Sudan, Burkina Faso, Mali, Guinea Bissau, and Guinea have all suffered military coup d'etats in the last year or two.[12]

In South Africa, the hopes and dreams of the people who have struggled so hard for so long have been betrayed in indescribable ways. We are a people severely diminished by politics without principles, leadership without vision, policies without commitment, and hence by failure after failure. We are drowning in corruption and lies and cover-ups. We are plagued by deceit and confounded by subterfuge. Our disastrous choices in economic policies have deepened the generational impoverishment of our people while creating new millionaires every second week, it seems, making us the most unequal society in the world today. Just how far have we sunk when the president hides millions of dollars in his mattress while the colonialist, white-controlled media tell us to look the other way; the Reserve Bank, the South African Revenue Service, and the National Prosecuting Authority seem to have lost their collective tongue; and those in parliament who demand accountability are ignored, outvoted, shouted down, and suspended? South Africa is one of the most tragic examples of how a noble struggle for freedom can lose its way.

In the United States, the signs of fascism masquerading in the words and symbols of religious nationalism and white supremacist nativism continue to grow. White people who call themselves evangelical Christians began moving towards authoritarianism in opposition to the New Deal social safety net policies of the Franklin D. Roosevelt presidency and the action by Roosevelt's successor, Harry S. Truman, to desegregate the US military in 1948. Billy Graham and other white religious leaders rejected appeals by Martin Luther King Jr. and other civil rights leaders to join calls for an end to Jim Crow segregation. In 1948, Southern politicians led by South Carolina Senator Strom Thurmond broke from the Democratic Party to form a splinter group known as the Dixiecrats. Although their efforts to defeat Truman in 1948 failed, Thurmond's Dixiecrats grew numerically and in political strength after the 1954 US Supreme Court decision in *Brown v. Board of Education* declared racial segregation in public education unconstitutional.

Southern white Democratic politicians opposed public school desegregation, voting rights, equal rights for women, collective bargaining efforts by workers, anti-poverty initiatives proposed during the Lyndon Johnson presidency, and Medicare. Their stance was almost never challenged by white Protestant, Catholic, and Jewish clergy of any faith, a fact made clear by Martin Luther King Jr.'s now famous "Letter from Birmingham City Jail." Religious nationalism was not obvious, however. Rather, white religious leaders led by Billy Graham became cheerleaders for US military adventures in Southeast Asia, South America, and the Caribbean. They cheered pro-Zionist policies in Palestine and supported the white apartheid regime in South Africa.

White religious tolerance for authoritarianism rose to new levels when Ronald Reagan ran for the US presidency in 1980 against then President Jimmy Carter. Carter's reelection bid ended in defeat because white voters and their religious leaders embraced Reagan's pro-capitalist Cold War nationalism and militarism; his opposition to racial justice, voting rights, and equal rights for women; his support for Israeli expansion in Palestine; and his support (with British Prime Minister Margaret Thatcher) of the white apartheid regime in South Africa. The so-called "war on drugs" begun during the presidency of Richard Nixon continued during the Reagan presidency but took on new meaning as news unfolded that the Reagan Administration used Central American drug-smuggling operations to finance illegal arms deals in what became known as the Iran-Contra Scandal.

As cocaine smuggled into the US during and after the Reagan presidency made its way to urban streets, Reagan and US presidents after him increased militarization of local law enforcement agencies. The result of that militarization was that the "war on drugs" became a frontal attack on civil liberties, especially in indigenous, Black, and Latinx communities. Thanks to those efforts, the increased voting strength of Black persons in the US brought about by the Voting Rights Act of 1965 was undercut. Mass incarceration in the US, the nation whose national anthem boasts of being the "land of the free," is now higher than anywhere else in the world.

Militarization of law enforcement, voter suppression, and intimidation against the people whose ancestors were enslaved were joined by repression against recognition of the rights of women and girls to exercise autonomy over their reproductive choices. Those oppressive efforts combined with bigotry and discrimination against gay, lesbian, bisexual, transgender, intersex, and queer persons. The generation of white religious people who were in grade school during the civil rights gains of the 1960s did not become more affirming, welcoming, or accepting of human diversity, pluralism, and autonomy. Instead, neo-fundamentalist, white supremacist, patriarchal, and militarist religious authoritarianism was preached from white evangelical pulpits and broadcast over "Christian" radio and television channels. According to that worldview, expressions of human diversity, reproductive choice autonomy, demands that racial and other social inequities be recognized and remedied, and efforts to address corporate greed were more than issues to be pondered. They were threats to "the way things used to be."

Strangely, white people in the United States who professed to follow Jesus came to view immigrants as threats rather than people to be welcomed. Those who claimed to be followers of the Palestinian Jew whose entire life was lived under Roman occupiers and whose death sentence was ordered and carried out by Roman occupiers came to champion Israeli occupation of Palestinian land. Somehow, people who professed to follow the itinerant rabbi named Jesus who rebelled against sacralized greed and disregard for the vulnerable came to champion greed and vilify vulnerable persons. Somehow, people associated with the religion of Jesus brokered so many deals with free-market capitalists, white supremacists, misogynists, and bigots that Christianity can no longer hide its complicity in imperialism, colonialism, oppressive capitalism, white supremacy, racism, sexism, homophobia, transphobia, militarism, environmental destruction, xenophobia, and global apartheid. In the minds of many people of colour, women and girls, people whose sexuality is expressed outside a heterosexual binary, people who are impoverished, indigenous people, and people who seek asylum and refuge from oppressive regimes in the world, Christianity is not a moral and ethical critique about oppressive power.

Instead, it has become such a dominant belief system for sacralizing oppressive power and providing religious cover for so much injustice that even Jesus would be mistreated, misrepresented, and murdered by it. The experiences of George Floyd, Trayvon Martin, Sandra Bland, Palestinians, immigrants, women, girls, victims from Pulse nightclub in Orlando, drone victims in Iraq and Afghanistan, people in Haiti, and survivors of domestic terror attacks where reproductive services were provided to women and girls before the US Supreme Court overturned the 1973 decision in *Roe v. Wade* by its 2022 decision in *Dobbs v. Jackson Women's Health Organization* demonstrate this point. The litany of terrors, with no end in sight at this point, do not merely fatigue the mind. They terrify the soul.

In this book, we read selected scriptural passages as parables for these situations and our times, just as the observations of Chairman Mao and Foreign Minister Coveney are in themselves a parable. This is how politicians read the signs of the times. The challenge this book attempts to confront is how Christians, standing in the tradition of the biblical prophets and of Jesus of Nazareth, and the prophets of today read and discern the signs of our own times. How do we interpret the situations contemporary politics is creating for especially the poor and oppressed, the vulnerable and excluded children of God? How do we reclaim not only our prophetic imagination but also the boldness and courage to enact it in the dismantling of what is wrong, unjust, and inhuman, as Walter Brueggemann has long since urged us to do?[13]

We talk of parables not as stories about tragedies or chaos in the observations of politicians whose politics is so flawed that their perceived wisdom drowns in the tragedies their own politics created and keeps creating. We speak of parables as Jesus told them, as subversive of the politics of these men and women of power and subversive of their ultimate intentions that in both cases, then and now, were and are so contrary to the politics of Jesus. And to be clear, for us, Jesus is not just a social but also a political revolutionary as Black liberation theologian Obery Hendricks describes him:

> To say that Jesus was a political revolutionary is to say that the message he proclaimed not only called for change in individual hearts but also demanded sweeping and comprehensive change in political, social, and economic structures in his setting in life: colonized Israel. It means that if Jesus had his way, the Roman Empire and the ruling elites among his own people either would no longer have held their positions of power, or if they did, would have had to conduct themselves very, very differently. It means that his ministry was to radically change the distribution of authority, power, goods and resources, so all people—particularly the little people, or "the least of these," as Jesus called them—might have lives free of political oppression, enforced hunger and poverty, and undue insecurity.[14]

In what follows, we take the lead of New Testament scholar William R. Herzog II, who sees the parables of Jesus as "subversive speech" coming from the mouth of Jesus as "pedagogue of the oppressed."[15] In telling these parables in the language of resistance, Jesus was subverting and undermining the narratives disseminated and enforced by the elites and the dominant classes, correcting and upending the assumptions that in turn upheld the unjust status quo. Jesus' parables questioned the situations created by the powerful, which they expected the people to accept as evidential truth. Jesus was telling these parables to the poor, oppressed, colonized, and occupied people of Galilee, teaching them how to really understand the situations they found themselves in, hence the subtitle of Herzog's brilliant study: "Jesus as Pedagogue of the Oppressed." Jesus was not just telling stories. He was decolonizing the people's minds, revolutionizing them. This is exactly what we have in mind when we ponder these selected portions of scripture as parables for our time. We read them as parables that teach us about our politics and the death-dealing calamities it creates, in contrast to the politics of God and the life-giving possibilities it creates, and that call us to prophetic faith and hope to persevere in these times of great peril.

We are eternally grateful to Rev. Dr. Jeremiah Wright and Dr. Teresa Smallwood, true and faithful prophets of our times themselves, for their willingness to grace this book with a Foreword and Preface, respectively. Our families have been lovingly indulgent in allowing us space and time not just for writing but for the inevitable back and forth in the numerous Skype sessions across the ocean as this book was planned, discussed, and written. Our publisher, in the person of Rev. John Pierce, has responded with great enthusiasm and encouragement from the start, and that in itself was already inspirational. The end product is the tireless effort of a team of skilled and patient editors. We are deeply grateful to all.

Allan Aubrey Boesak, Cape Town, South Africa

Wendell L. Griffen, Little Rock, Arkansas

Chapter 1

A Cloud the Size of a Human Hand[1]

On Manufactured Scarcity, Kairos, and the Abundance of Grace (I)

Allan Aubrey Boesak

Captured by Carmel's Tale

The story of the prophet Elijah's confrontation with the Baal prophets in 1 Kings 18 is doubtless one of the most captivating, if also one of the most frightening, in all of the Bible. Sometimes we are so fascinated by that confrontation, the challenge to the people to stop wavering—"limping on two opinions" is how Elijah, quite graphically, puts it—and the slaughter of the adherents of Baal that we, tripped up and captured by Carmel's tale, tend to miss the wider context and what I believe to be the real point. It is not the mass murder of those Baal prophets on Mount Carmel but in fact the devastating drought, already announced in chapter 17, and the tragedies of scarcity in its wake that determine the reading of this chapter. These tragedies include those unfolding in the mind and actions of Elijah, the prophet of God, whose very name is a declaration and, in this context, with tensions stretched to breaking point, a war cry: "Yahweh is my God!"

In focusing so strongly on the murder of the Baal prophets, however, we also miss the powerful relevance of this chapter as a parable for our current global political situation. I read this story as such a parable for the world we live in and the powers that control it, for the people, and for the prophet of God, seeking to confront them, challenging them, calling them all to account before the bar of God's justice and the throne of God's judgement. In the final analysis, however, it is the prophet of God who is confronted with a moment of truth, of discernment and decision, a kairos moment. For both sides, much is at stake, and for both sides, the consequences are grave.

As in Elijah's times, our world is a world in utter chaos, "shaken by deadly convulsions," as Helmut Gollwitzer, close friend and comrade of Dietrich Bonhoeffer, wrote in the years following the Second World War and the Nazis.[2] It is a world ruled by war criminals, kleptocrats and kakistocrats,[3] where W. E. B. Du Bois's politics of integrity, decency, honesty, virtue, and courage are almost nowhere to be found. Across Europe specifically, the rising tide is a racist ultra-nationalism, if not outright fascism. In the Western world in general, democracy is more and more a sham, from creeping authoritarianism to the plutocratic rule of oligarchs. The strident, and increasingly hollow, claims of exceptionalism can no longer hide the truth.[4] In Africa, democracy is like a hounded, wounded woman, constantly on the run from bloodthirsty patriarchal predators.

The desperate search for real, trustworthy, justice-seeking leadership ends with truly abysmal choices: in the UK, they fall from Boris Johnson to Liz Truss, now hastily departed after less than six weeks in office, followed by Rishi Sunak, yet another Prime Minister captured by the 1 percent. Waiting in the wings is the Labour Party's Keir Starmer, Tony Blair clone, political assassin of the progressive Jeremy Corbyn and fierce protector of the Israeli apartheid state, a person who is not by any means the better choice. In the US, it seems to be either Joe Biden or Kamala Harris. If not them, it is Donald Trump or Ron DeSantis. Abysmal. In South Africa, the white-controlled, colonialist mainstream media continue to force Cyril Ramaphosa down the people's throats despite the fact that this man is demonstrably the most incompetent, untrustworthy, corrupt, and talentless person to occupy the position of president for the last thirty years. As I write, Burkina Faso, where the presidency of Thomas Sankara in the 1980s brought such bright promise, is trying to cope with the second military coup in eight months. This is the seventh coup in five African countries in just the last few years.

It is perhaps only in Latin America, with Chile, Colombia, and Brazil taking the lead, and in the Caribbean, with the excellent leadership of Barbados Prime Minister Mia Mottley Amor, that we might be seeing some hope, even if it is only a cloud the size of a human hand. In South Africa, as I write this, our electoral system forces us into a holding pattern as we wait for the national elections in 2024 after African National Congress's elective conference has determined the chances of the country voting for a completely new direction have been severely diminished by reelecting Cyril Ramaphosa as president. We might now be faced with the infamous "lesser of two evils" scenario that has made world politics such a nightmare and democracy such a farce. Overall, though, the global scarcity of capable, liberative, justice-seeking, people-serving leadership, of the politics of decency, integrity, honesty, virtue, and courage, is of catastrophic proportions. As a result, the peoples of the world, especially the poor, marginalised, and vulnerable, are condemned to the politics of global apartheid, domination, oppression, exploitation, and dehumanization. For women, children, people of colour in general, and LGBTQI persons especially, this world has never been so hostile a place.

The issue is not only political. It is also a question of prophetic alertness, prophetic discernment, and prophetic faithfulness. The challenge this parable poses is not just for politics, and the peril it describes is not only the peril politics faces. If this story is a call for the conversion of politics, it is equally a call for the renewal of the prophetic. There is a reason why the Gospels hold nothing back about the testing of Jesus in the wilderness, after his anointing by baptism and his being claimed by God but before the beginning of his public ministry. And there is a reason why at this time of testing, after that gruelling ordeal, the angels must come to his aid. These are deadly serious moments.

There is, moreover, a reason why Jesus, too, is equally emphatic as he prepares the disciples for their mission into the world. Not only must they know that they are being sent as "sheep among wolves" (Mt 10:16, NIV), but they must also remember that "a servant [is not] above his master" (Mt 10:24, NIV). If the Tempter is so intent and persistent in entrapping Jesus into subjection to him, how shall he spare the followers of Jesus, those called to be prophets of God? "Be watchful," Jesus tells his disciples in the garden of Gethsemane as his final moments approach. "Stay awake and pray that you may not come into the time of trial" (Mt 26:41, NRSV). In other words, be alert and pay attention; stay in prayer so that you may discern, and resist, those temptations that come from being Jesus' followers. Those words have nothing to do with sleeping.

The Apostle Peter, in the letters ascribed to him, comforts, uplifts, and strengthens the church, reminding them amid their ordeals of persecution that they are a "chosen race, a royal priesthood…God's own people" (1 Pet 2:9, NRSV). That is deeply comforting and immensely empowering. Still, he also understands what risks we run in claiming those accolades for ourselves. So Peter goes on to say, "Humble yourselves therefore under the mighty hand of God…Cast all your anxiety on [God]…" (1 Pet 5:6-8). It is only then that he tells them, talking about the devil, their adversary, "Resist him, steadfast in your faith…" (5:9).

For the past five hundred years, indigenous peoples across the globe—colonized, oppressed, dispossessed, enslaved, and genocided—have experienced what it means when those titles are appropriated by white Christian invaders driven by racism, white supremacy, and capitalist greed. In our times, with the fascist Israeli apartheid state in devastating full flight and the renewed neo-colonialist onslaught from imperialist, white, fundamentalist Christianity on the Third World, with frightening arrogance reclaiming for themselves all those accolades to legitimise their theologies and their politics, it is as real as in Peter's times.

Foreseeing what was coming, Peter therefore follows this intoxicating language with an admonition: "Discipline yourselves, keep alert. Like a roaring lion your adversary the devil prowls around, looking for someone to devour" (1 Pet 5:8, NRSV). Peter is certainly talking about persecutions from without, by the Roman Empire, perpetrated upon the followers of Jesus. From history, we know that the "adversary" was real—an overwhelming, merciless political power. Those "devouring lions" were not entirely metaphorical. There was blood on the ground. We should not forget or trivialize that. While Peter is compassionate, he is also realistic. He is acutely aware of those temptations, like ravenous lions, prowling *within*. Peter knows this from experience. He knows how close the prophets of God can come to stumbling through our zeal, our self-righteousness, or our triumphalism. That rebuke from Jesus (Matt 16:23) and the crowing of that cock would never leave his mind (Matt 26:69-75).

That is why he begins chapter 5 with this: "Now as an elder myself…" (1 Pet 5:1, NRSV). Peter is not pulling rank. He speaks as one chastised by experience, by the hard lessons learned from his own misplaced zeal. Peter remembers when Jesus spoke about his coming sufferings and he Peter, overpowered by his own zeal, rebuked Jesus: "God forbid it, Lord!" (Matt 16:22, NRSV). He also remembers Jesus' angry response, "Get behind me Satan!" (16:23). That holy zeal, Peter now knows, is a potent force. Almost without our knowing it, it turns us from followers of Jesus into agents of Satan. Thus chastened, Peter says, I speak as "a witness of the sufferings of Christ" (1 Pet 5:1, NRSV)—which I, in my misguided zeal and foolishness, thought I had the power to forbid—and had to learn from my own mistakes.

Equally, though, and because God's grace is not just sufficient but abundant, Peter knows where to turn when scarcity of hope threatens faith; when scarcity of courage threatens prophetic witness; when an overflow of arrogance, abusive power, hatred, and imperial hubris threatens endurance. "But do not ignore this one fact, beloved, that with the Lord one day is like a thousand years, and a thousand years are like one day. The Lord is not slow about God's promise, as some think of slowness, but is patient with you, not wanting any to perish, but all to come to repentance" (2 Pet 3:8-9, NRSV). Keep watching for that cloud, small as a human hand.

Manufactured Scarcity

We should note, first, that this scarcity is not of "natural causes." It is manufactured. Hebrew Bible scholar Walter Brueggemann makes the point forcefully.[5] "There is no doubt," he writes, "that the contemporary world, like that ancient royal world, subscribes to a myth of scarcity." What Brueggemann means by our "contemporary world" is our world in the grip of what is now called "the 1 percent," the small but enormously rich and powerful millionaire/billionaire capitalist class and the politicians who do their bidding. The *Belhar Confession* speaks of them as those who through their greed and lust for power and domination "seek to control and harm others." Those are key words that always go together: "control" and "harm."

Note Brueggemann's wording: that world of power and privilege, then and now, *subscribes* to the *myth* of scarcity. Such scarcity is not "a given of creation." It is, rather, "an imposed power arrangement whereby some [a small minority] have too much so that, consequently, some [the vast majority] have too little." It is a myth; it need not be a reality, but the rich, powerful, and privileged classes need it to solidify their power. So they purposefully create it and present it as evident truth, in the same way that white supremacy needs the myth of Black inferiority and patriarchy needs the myth of women as "the weaker sex." Thus, the scarcity is manufactured; it is the result of economic systems and political policies deliberately designed to create scarcity for the many while securing plenty for the few.[6]

It is not that there are no decent, honest politicians with integrity and courage to be found. Looking around the world and here in South Africa, I can actually recognise them. They are not many, and they are mostly women. The reality, however, is that our political systems are *designed* to attract, accommodate, and reward the corrupt, the incompetent, and the mediocre because they will not dissent, challenge the party line, or dare to disobey those who reward them with untold riches if they do their bidding. It seems their greatest attribute is that they, in South African political parlance, can be captured. My American friends speak of their political choices as "the lesser of two evils." But that dilemma, too, is entirely manufactured.

Meanwhile, Yahweh sends Elijah to the house of a widow in Zarephath in the land of Sidon, a marginalized woman without patriarchal protection, utterly vulnerable, the poorest of the poor. There is a message in that all by itself. Elijah, with some unreasonableness it seems, presses the widow to prepare some bread for him as well as for herself and her son, even though they are on the verge of dying from hunger. Elijah nonetheless insists because, Brueggemann is arguing, "prophetic faith refuses to accept that power arrangement [of manufactured scarcity] and appeals behind it to the will and gift of the creator."[7] Equally so, our contemporary global neoliberal economic system is built on that myth of scarcity. It even *lives* by that myth of scarcity, so that "some," the so-called 1 percent, enjoy huge resources at the expense of all others who, like the widow and her small son, "can only eat and die." The myth is not just that this *is* but that this is permanent, irreversible. That there is no alternative. The narrative of the prophet Elijah and the unnamed widow of Zarephath "exposes this immobilizing myth" and invites "an embrace of an alternative that is expressed in praise and practiced as redistribution."[8] Paraphrasing Brueggemann: redistribution of wealth, land, opportunity, social goods, power, and the right to life and well-being amongst God's children on earth is an act of praise to God in heaven.

If the scarcity is manufactured, the product of policies that create and foster deliberate inequalities through deliberate exploitation, it points to deliberate politics sold, defended, and justified by deliberate propaganda. As night follows day, the politics of greed and exploitation gives rise to the politics of hunger. In this regard, then, the myth of scarcity, manufactured for the domination and exploitation of the impoverished masses and for benefit of the rich, becomes grim reality.

The scarcity is manifest everywhere and at every level. There is no real political leadership, for on the throne is Ahab, the corrupt, murderous king who has no love for God and no respect for the people he is supposed to lead. There is no real religious leadership: the court prophets, all on the payroll of the king, dominate the religious life of the people and make them "turn away from Yahweh." There is no bread, for drought always brings famine. Even the little wadi in Cherith where God sends Elijah to survive, dries up. If it were not for that widow, Elijah would not have made it.

The Triumph on Carmel

There may be some ambivalence about the number of prophets killed that fateful day. First Kings 18:19 tells of 450 Baal prophets, plus 400 prophets of Ashera, associated with Queen Jezebel, all assembled on Mount Carmel. In 18:22, Elijah mentions only the 450 prophets of Baal. However, there is no ambivalence about the slaughter itself, and that is the point here. As in any massacre, the greater numbers involved may be more shocking, but they make no substantial difference. It is the fact that human beings are slaughtered that matters. In 1985, when the South African police and army massacred more than forty people in Langa township, near Uitenhage in the Eastern Cape, the police released only twenty-seven bodies. I believed the families and the communities who insisted on the greater number. After all, it was *their* family members who were missing. They would know. Some of the media corrected me, intimating that I was exaggerating for the sake of effect and political gain. Quoting the police, they insisted that "only" twenty-seven were killed. As if the difference in numbers mattered.

Curiously, Brueggemann, in his excellent commentary, does not comment on the massacre of the 450 prophets of Baal. He remarks, "Baal is routed, and the prophets of Baal are thoroughly discredited."[9] Baal may be routed, true, but his prophets are not merely discredited, we know. They are executed, slaughtered. Brueggemann adds, "As Elijah surely would have been had things gone otherwise." One is not sure whether Brueggemann means that Elijah, too, would have been "discredited." H. H. Rowley is more direct. "Had their [the Baal prophets'] appeal to Baal been successful, it is likely that the enthusiasm for Baal would have swept away the solitary figure of Elijah."[10] After all, Jezebel was not prepared to brook any opposition at all. "That the prophets of Yahweh should resist this was but natural," comments Rowley.[11] And here, that resistance takes the form of the extreme violence of preemptive self-defence. It is almost, it seems to me, a version of the cynical play on the Golden Rule, "Do unto others before they can do it unto you." Brueggemann seems hesitant here, perhaps because he is not willing to go where the argument of Mordechai Cogan takes us:

> To brand this act as 'ugly', or to excuse it as 'necessary retribution for ordered by Elijah' as 'the new Moses on behalf of God', or even to remove it as a late element 'introduced into the story under the influence of Jehud's massacre of the devotees of Baal' would be introducing contemporary moral sensitivity foreign to the text. The slaughter at the Kishon is no different than the one over which Moses presided at Mount Sinai (cf Ex 32:26-28).... Elijah outstrips that of Phineas (Num 25:7-8) and Samuel. (I Sam 15:32-33)[12]

Cogan's thinking here goes much farther than the "man of his time" argument. He seems almost to exult in Elijah's excess. We should not be shocked by or coil in revulsion at these events *because this is what God wants*. Just as God ordered the *herem*, the wholesale slaughter, the annihilation of "all that lives," whether it was Israel's enemies in war or simply those occupants of lands they desired to conquer, as the book of Joshua describes the invasion, conquest, and occupation of Canaan. Elijah has no problem here, and presents us with no problem, because it is not Elijah at work here; it is Yahweh. The invocation of the Divine will is meant to end all argument, although it clearly does not answer every question.

Besides all this, however, I have never been convinced by the argument that "our contemporary" modern sensitivities are so much greater than that of the people spoken of in the Bible. I did not see that sensitivity at play in the brutalities of the invasions by Western, modern, "sensitive" European invaders of the lands of others, their wanton slaughter of the indigenes, their murderous greed in the theft of land and people, and their enslavement of those people. There was also the genocide of the Khoi and San in South Africa, of the Native Americans across North and South America, and of the Herero and Ovambo people in Namibia, as well as the lynching and the massacre of thousands of Africans in the United States. Not to mention Belgium's King Leopold II and his "hidden holocaust"— ten million people slaughtered in the Congo under his reign. All by "civilised," "more sensitive," baptized Christians with the Bible in one hand and the gun in the other. I see no "contemporary" moral sensitivity in the slaughter of Black people during apartheid, in their deaths on the streets of the United States at the hands of police, or in the murderous policies of the Israeli apartheid state to this day.

There is, so far as I can see, no difference between these white, civilised, Christian marauders and the "morally less sensitive" people in the time of Elijah. Dropping two atomic bombs on Japan, killing millions, when that tragedy could have been easily avoided, we now know—is that truly a sign of "our modern moral sensitivities"? Sometimes, it is argued that we modern humans have learned "the rules of war," that war can be conducted "humanely," that we have all these treaties and the Geneva Convention, as former President Barack Obama actually argued in accepting the Nobel Peace Prize.[13] But what happened to those sensitivities in the last five decades of unending wars, or in Israel and Palestine for the seventy years since the Nakba, or in Abu Graib, infamous place of the US's torture programmes initiated by George Bush but actively condoned by Barack Obama when he became president? J. A. T. Robinson's "Honest to God" that caused so much upheaval in the Christian world cannot only mean honesty towards the Bible and its many contradictions. It must also mean honesty towards ourselves, no matter how "exceptional," "modern," or "advanced" we think ourselves to be. In the history of my people, the coming of the white, Christian, imperialist colonisers represents the most devastating, apocalyptic era in our existence. What D. H. Lawrence has written about "the American soul" is true for all invaders, all colonizers, and all settler-colonialists in these "more sensitive" modern times: "The essential American soul is hard, isolate, stoic, and a killer. It has never melted."[14]

Elsewhere, I have not only invoked with approval Walter Brueggemann's argument concerning the two trajectories in the theology of the Hebrew Bible, what he calls the "royal theology" and the "prophetic theology" trajectories,[15] but also the uncovering of the "Great" and the "Little" traditions in the Bible.[16] The Great Tradition represents the thinking of the elites, the powerful and the rich in Israel, seeking legitimacy for the way in which the dominant forces in ancient Israelite society have laid claim upon the Torah. In their power, they took possession of God. In opposition to that is the Little Tradition, recalling the liberation tradition that calls upon Yahweh as the God of liberation and justice, and on God's preferential option for the poor and oppressed. That is the tradition and position of the prophets who stood up in defence of the widow, the stranger, and the orphan. It is the Little Tradition in which Jesus of Nazareth stands. To understand these two distinct voices in the scriptures is to know when to ask the vital question: which God? Whose God is here spoken of, and whose God is speaking?

I have wrestled extensively with this issue in my discussions on the role and place of Miriam, in contradistinction to Moses, in the exodus tradition.[17]

But more than that, I have been in the struggle too long, have seen too much, to afford the luxury of skipping over these shocking details. I have seen, in the 1980s, how somebody considered an enemy of the struggle or an informant for apartheid's security police was necklaced—a tyre placed around that person's neck, doused with petrol and set alight—with our youth dancing around the burning body, singing freedom songs. It is impossible for me to ignore what might now be interpreted as biblical justification of such horrific violence.

This event should, I propose, be understood within the broader framework of the scarcity of prophetic sensitivity, that is, the prophet's inability to discern the difference between the will of God and what Elijah himself, in his zeal, wanted. Nowhere does Yahweh give Elijah permission, or the instruction, to commit murder. It is also, to put it in Walter Brueggemann's unforgettable formulation, a scarcity of "prophetic imagination."[18] That happens, as we can see in the progress of Moses' inability to distinguish between his desires and God's will and in the subsequent erosion of the character of his leadership.[19] That discernment, too, is a necessary and indispensable prophetic activity. That lack of prophetic understanding and imagination, here so vividly on display in 1 Kings 18—that all-too-human, almost instinctive, vindictive bent toward retributive violence as the only solution to the problems the court prophets and Baal priests present, described by Rowley as "natural"—is what I mean by "the scarcity of prophetic sensitivity."

It is precisely that scarcity that produces the overflow of hubris, and the overflow of hubris produces the overflow of blood. For Elijah, the abundance of Yahweh's power seen in the fire from the heavens that ignites the water-drenched altar is evidently not enough. Elijah does not believe that this sign of Yahweh's power is sufficient to convince the people, to overcome the people's doubt and their "limping on two beliefs." It looms as a challenge Elijah seems to believe *he* can, and is obligated, to overcome. It is now up to him. The fire from heaven will not convince them, Elijah thinks, but my sword will. It is a scarcity of trust in the power of God and the way in which God chooses to put that power into effect.

It is almost as if the power of Yahweh has to rival the power of Elijah—hence the violence, and the horrific excess of it. The massacre of the queen's Ashera prophets/priests and Ahab's court prophets is no random act of spontaneous violence. Elijah did not "snap" as a result of some unexpected and hideous provocation. It is a calculated act, a deliberate rebuke to a God far too passive and reticent for Elijah's tastes. Elijah sees what apparently Yahweh cannot see or appreciate: a catastrophe that cannot be remedied by a nonviolent God whose signs and wonders may, if Elijah pushes really hard, convince the people but not those false prophets, and certainly not the power behind their power, King Ahab and Queen Jezebel. Elijah knows better than God that with people like Ahab and Jezebel, words, signs, and wonders—in this context the weapons of nonviolence and moral authority—have no persuasive power. Violence, however, does. As the argument goes, it is the only language the Ahabs and the Jezebels of this world can understand. To me, it seems as if Elijah, now brimming with confidence and flushed with vindication and zeal, is urging God the way he challenged the people: "Stop limping on two opinions! Now that we have shown them who the true God is, let us *really* show them *who* this God is. Let's complete the triumph!" Here, the question that arises, is, "Whose triumph is this—Yahweh's or Elijah's?"

Still, from a certain perspective, Elijah seems to have a valid point, and we have to consider it. The biblical narrator takes great pains to make clear who exactly this Ahab is. The name Ahab means "Brother of the father." Ahab's father was Omri, a king who, the story tells us, by war and bloodshed "united" a divided Israel. Tibni, the rival, "died," in other words either fell in the ensuing civil war or was assassinated, and Omri became king over all Israel. (See 1 Kgs 16.) The worst the narrator apparently can say of him are the words that become a tragic refrain about the rule of the kings of Israel, the Northern Kingdom, and of the kings of Judah, the Southern Kingdom: "Omri did evil in the eyes of [Yahweh]" (1 Kgs 16:25, NKJV). In this, he followed another king just as evil, Jeroboam, clearly an abysmal benchmark for all that was wrong in Israel's ruling classes. "He walked in all the ways of Jeroboam," is all the narrator says (16:26). No further details are necessary. The mere reference is enough. And not only did Omri do evil in the eyes of Yahweh but he did "more evil than all who were before him" (16:25, NRSV).

We should understand that when the "brother of the father"—Ahab—succeeds the father, the Bible is preparing us for a reign that will in every evil aspect mimic the reign of Omri. Even worse, for Ahab too will exceed in corruption and evildoing "all that were before him." Thus, Ahab is "the worst of all that were before him," "the brother of the father." The relationship is not just familial; it is politically genetic. When it comes to the doing of evil, alienation from Yahweh, and treatment of the people, Ahab was not just the son of Omri. He was Omri's evil twin. The despicable politics of the kings of Israel flow unhindered and unchecked from one to the other.

But we should not think that the evil the Bible is talking about is inevitable because it is in Ahab's DNA. The Bible wants to say that the evil, the corruption, the bent towards injustice and the hatred of justice is *systemic*. It has poisoned every single one of Israel's institutions; it permeates every social, political, economic, and religious structure. Ahab was born into and ascended the throne in a thoroughly, *systemically* corrupt royal rule. The generational wrongdoing brings generational injustice, which in turn causes generational suffering. It sounds like a concise history of South Africa. It is a tragedy when superlatives are the only way to describe a nation's downward spiral, and superlatives are not the same as hyperbole.

There were good reasons why, in 1960, almost a year after the Sharpeville massacre, uMkhonto we Sizwe, the African National Congress's military wing, was formed. Nelson Mandela, as accused number one in the Rivonia Trial, explained that precisely.[20] The African National Congress, Mandela testified, was formed in 1912 to defend the rights of the African people, rights that had been seriously curtailed by the South Africa Act—when South Africa became the Union of South Africa, a racist constellation built solely on white interests—and that were then being threatened by the Native Land Act. "For thirty-seven years—that is until 1949—[the ANC] adhered strictly to a constitutional struggle," Mandela said. "It put forward demands and resolutions; it sent delegations to the Government in the belief that African grievances could be settled through peaceful discussion and that Africans could advance gradually to full political rights. But White Governments remained unmoved, and the rights of Africans became less instead of becoming greater." Mandela then reached back to the words and authority of Chief Albert Luthuli:

> In the words of my leader, Chief Albert Luthuli, who became President of the ANC in 1952, and who was later awarded the Nobel Peace Prize: who will deny that thirty years of my life have been spent knocking in vain, patiently, moderately, and modestly at a closed and barred door? What have been the fruits of moderation? The past thirty years have seen the greatest number of laws restricting our rights and progress, until today we have reached a stage where we have almost no rights at all.[21]

South Africa's white, racist, violent apartheid regime, committing crimes against humanity while remaining unrepentant and recalcitrant, was for Mandela what King Ahab was for the prophet Elijah. Elijah, at Carmel, like Mandela after Sharpeville, had come to the end of words. Still, Luthuli remained steadfast, even though there were severe tensions in the ANC because of his decision to uphold nonviolence as the more excellent way.

I am still trying to see from Elijah's perspective. Keep in mind that Elijah was the one on the ground. He knew precisely what Ahab was doing because the stories were told and retold, and later they were all "written in the Book of the Annals of the Kings of Israel" (1 Kgs 14:19; 16:14; 16:20; 2 Kgs 1:18, etc., NRSV); in other words, it was common knowledge. Everyone knew. On top of all this, Ahab committed another, unforgivable transgression. "And as if it had been a light thing for him to walk in the sins of Jeroboam," writes a clearly shocked narrator, "[Ahab] took as his wife Jezebel," an apparently strong-willed, forceful personality who brought the worship of Baal and the female god Ashera even more prominently into the religious and political life of Israel (1 Kgs 16:31, NRSV).

The combination, Elijah knew, was deadly: Ahab and Jezebel, Baal and Ashera. Although in the biblical narrative the husband and wife coordination is fairly explicit, one still discovers how patriarchal readings do their best to portray Jezebel, the foreign woman, the vile villain, as the main culprit in the persecution of the prophets of Yahweh. The persecution campaign is "Jezebel's campaign against Yahwism," writes H. H. Rowley. Throughout, Rowley speaks of "Jezebel's campaign," "Jezebel's violence," "Jezebel's hatred" for the prophets of Yahweh. Rowley writes, "The queen was determined to uproot Israel's faith, to substitute Melkart for Yahweh." She was "a woman who knew how to get her way," and apparently was completely in control of the mind of the king.[22]

Rowley quotes Hebrew Bible scholar J Strachan: "Ahab's religious instincts were dull as his political instincts were keen." Still, no matter how keen his political instincts, Jezebel outplayed him: "Jezebel was just the sort of woman to carry even a strong man off his feet."[23] In this view, Ahab becomes like clay in the hands of this supremely evil woman, an innocent puppet at the mercy of this despicable puppeteer from outside of Israel.[24] Nonetheless, despite our modern male prejudices, the Bible is not unclear in this matter: Ahab, the story insists, was more evil than "all who reigned before him."

Brueggemann, correctly in my view, sees the showdown between Elijah and Ahab, between the prophet of God and the prophets of Baal, as a showdown between Yahweh and Baal, signifying something even deeper. He speaks of "a dispute between two perspectives on reality," two systems of life directly opposed to one another—rich and poor, greed and want, powerful and powerless. "There is, in the end, no middle ground."[25] Carmel foreshadows the battle between two perspectives on life in our contemporary society; between the 1 percent and the 99 percent; between neoliberalism's fabricated myth of scarcity and the Bible's celebration of God's plentiful abundance. Caught in the middle of all this, the people would be pulverized. And, as the one on the ground, Elijah would be the one to confront them both face to face. This was never going to be easy.

As 1 Kings 18 begins, we hear that Elijah is told to "present himself to Ahab," four little words behind which lurks a world of dread and terror.

Chapter 2

A Cloud the Size of a Human Hand
On Manufactured Scarcity, Kairos, and the Abundance of Grace (II)

Allan Aubrey Boesak

"Present Yourself to Ahab"

In the middle of the drought and famine, after the "many days" Elijah spent as a refugee in the widow's house in the land of Sidon, Yahweh tells Elijah to "present yourself to Ahab" (1 Kgs 18:1, NRSV). The prophet of Yahweh, "before whose face I stand" (1 Kgs 18:15, Douay-Rheims Bible), as Elijah says of himself, will now go to stand up to and face Ahab. Elijah ("Yahweh is my God") will now face Ahab, "the brother of the father" of the one "more evil than anyone before him."

For all this time, Elijah had been on the run, and God had found ways to keep him alive and his faith strong, to strengthen his sense of calling, to embolden him. The ravens that were bringing him food were an interim measure, tools for survival. But survival on one's own, isolated from a loving and supporting community, can sometimes become a rut in which the wheels of life get stuck. What Elijah truly needed was a life-giving relationship, and God knew that. "Go now to Zarephath," God says, "which belongs to Sidon, and lives there; for I have commanded a widow there to feed you" (1 Kgs 17:9, NRSV).

Note the precise location. Zarephath was a Phoenician city, exile territory. Belonging to the city-state of Sidon, the birthplace of that same Jezebel who had Elijah on her kill list, it was also enemy territory. Sidon had a second claim to fame: it was the place where the idols for the worship of Baal were manufactured through a process of smelting gold or other precious metals. That is as close to the belly of the beast as Elijah could go. It was there, in that dangerous place, birthplace of Jezebel and forming place of Baal idols, that Yahweh had prepared a widow to preserve Elijah's life. This is worthy of note, I think. In the story of Israel's liberation and struggle for authentic existence and the safeguarding of Israel's prophetic witness, there always is a woman. From Shiphrah and Puah, the courageous midwives who stood up to the pharaoh, to Jochebed and Miriam, the same Miriam who stood her ground on the riverbank and who, on the shores of the Red Sea and in the wilderness, dared to fashion such a fundamentally different model of leadership than that of Moses. From Hannah in her song to Mary in her

Magnificat, the one as revolutionary as the other, to Mary Magdalene in her bold following of Jesus, there always is a woman.

One should, of course, appreciate the superb irony of this situation, though it would be foolish to romanticise it: this is a place of extreme danger. There is drought, famine, and death all around—all the fault of Israel's king, his wife, and the ruling elites—and the one chosen by God to keep Elijah alive and from harm is a gentile woman in a foreign land. While the name of Ahab evokes the vile, death-dealing realities of abuse of power, deceit, greed, murder, and godlessness, this unnamed woman evokes life-giving realities of courage, trustworthiness, compassion, love, generosity, and godliness. While Ahab and Jezebel deal in lies and deceit, the widow recognises and speaks truth.

Elijah is the one who performs the life-giving deeds in her house, but it is *her* house, which she has opened to him and where she is keeping him alive, making it possible for him to do those life-giving deeds. If God had not needed her in order to make all this happen, God would have left Elijah at the wadi. The ravens could have served God's purposes just as well. There is a reason why Jesus, in the Lukan passage so central to liberation theology, points also to this unnamed widow. When he goes on to speak of the rejection of the true prophet of God by their own people and family, Jesus mentions Elijah and the widow of Zarephath, in whose home the prophet is not only welcomed but also finds a place of refuge and sustenance and truth (Luke 4:24-26).

And there is a reason why the crowd, a moment earlier so joyously invigorated by the liberating words of this prophet, now turn against him in anger and resentment: how dare Jesus hold up as an example of hospitality and life-giving faith, of generosity and truth telling, a gentile from an enemy nation, a woman who invokes memories of Jezebel, that most hated of women in the scriptures? She who (most deservedly, they were sure) died a more vicious death than any other enemy of God's people? How dare Jesus talk as if Yahweh is no longer *their* exclusive God, their national possession to lay sole claim upon and keep available for them alone? It is the radical inclusivity of Jesus that incenses them. So "filled with rage" were they that they "got up, drove him out of the town, and led him to the brow of the hill on which their town was built, so that they might hurl him off the cliff" (Luke 4:26, NRSV). They would rather kill him than hear the truth about God and hence about themselves.

Luke makes another point here: "all in the synagogue…," he writes (4:28). This means the elites who hated Jesus for his condemnations of their greed, wealth, and lust for power *and* the poor, oppressed, and downtrodden whom these elites despised. Apparently, when it came to ideologies of religious exclusivism, all differences were forgotten. It makes me think of the fervour with which

Black Christians in fundamentalist churches across the global South now embrace the white, exclusivist, hateful, and violent Jesus of white, American, nationalist, fascist Christianity. At that moment, oppressed and oppressor had shared limitations to God's love, mercy, and inclusive justice. Faced with this radically inclusive Jesus, all the barriers came down: rich and poor, privileged and unprivileged, abuser and abused, exploiter and exploited—they were *all* "filled with rage," and they *all* got up and drove him out. They all, *together*, wanted to throw Jesus off the cliff. All of a sudden, Jesus, who was leading the revolution against the class consciousness of Israel's ruling classes and their racial and religious exclusivist hierarchies, was faced with a classless revolt against God's radical love, radical justice, radical solidarity, radical equality, and radical inclusivity. As my American friends would say, "Go figure."

The story about the widow's extreme poverty-stricken situation, vastly exacerbated by the drought and famine—"I have…only a handful of meal in a jar, and a little oil in a jug" (17:12, NRSV)—is not a sentimental tearjerker told to evoke the reader's pity. So it concludes with the words in verse 16, "The jar of meal was not emptied, neither did the jug of oil fail.…" We should not be amazed by what can only be described as a miracle, and walk away deeply spiritually moved, while the systems of exploitation and domination that cause scarcity remain unchallenged. We should, rather, stand in awe of God's radical justice, God's radical generosity, and God's radical abundance and walk away deeply inspired and committed to the doing of justice and the undoing of injustice.

In the Bible, God's preferential option for the poor is always expressed in God's special concern for the poor, the orphan, the widow, the stranger—all of them powerless, neglected, and marginalised class in ancient Israel. In ancient Israelite society, as in our neoliberal, capitalist-controlled world, they are not only the so-called have-nots, the opposite of the haves; they are the never-will-haves. They are the downtrodden, not because they have tripped over their clumsy, ignorant selves or have been tripped up by their laziness or lack of drive but because they have been run over, held down, and trampled upon by the rich and the powerful. *The Belhar Confession* understood this and is equally direct. The poor and oppressed are not "unfortunate," or "under-privileged," or "historically disadvantaged"; they are *wronged*. They are not simply "looked down upon"; they are wilfully and systematically *oppressed*. Their situation is no accident of history; *systemic injustices* are at work here. The words the prophets speak in such outrage are so deliberate because God's outrage at injustice and God's intent upon justice are so deliberate.

We should, perhaps, before moving on, notice another important thing. Scarcity is all around, but here in this widow's house, the signs of God's abundance abound. It starts not with the abundance of flour and oil but with the abundance of her patience with and goodwill towards this man whom she does not know, yet who has the audacity to ask her for water and bread. And not only that, but to make bread for him first, before she makes anything for herself and her small son. It speaks of an amazing abundance not of female, submissive obedience but of generosity, hospitality, strength, and faith. The narrator emphasises the frightening scarcity: "I have," she says, "*nothing* baked, only a *handful* of meal in a jar, and a *little* oil in a jug; I am now gathering *a couple* of sticks…" (1 Kgs 17:12, NRSV). The diminutives in her speech underscore the threats to life scarcity brings. However, they are nullified by the faithfulness of Yahweh's abundance. The little bit of meal in that jar never runs low; the little bit of oil in that jar never runs out (17:16). She can make bread for as long as it takes, not just for the three of them but for all her household (17:15). In the midst of, in contrast to, and in defiance of the dreaded scarcity that grips the land, here is abundance.

Chapter 17, as we know it, closes with words from the widow. Dutch Hebrew Bible scholar H. A. Brongers thinks the woman is not grateful enough. He writes,

> The reaction of the woman to Eljiah's words, 'See, your son is alive again', is in her formulation somewhat disappointing. We would have expected more direct praise to the God of Israel. This does not happen, however. For the woman it is sufficient to state that the resurrection [of her son] is proof that Elijah is a man of God, and that one can, therefore, trust that the word spoken by Elijah is in fact and indeed the word of God.[1]

This woman, Brongers thinks, demeans the glory of God and the powerful presence of the prophet of God by merely stating the obvious. Accordingly, she exits the story with this cloud of scholarly dissatisfaction hanging over her head. Despite the prophet's powerful deeds in her house, she cannot bring herself to fulsome praise. She falls short.

I have a different view on this. We tend to read those words as the proper ending of chapter 17, and, mostly differently than Brongers, as the appropriate response of a deeply moved and grateful mother. However, I read those words as the beginning of chapter 18. As the time of confrontation draws near, which will prove to be the time of Elijah's greatest challenge and greatest need, not an angel nor a disembodied voice from heaven but a widow—she of the alleged deficient gratitude—speaks the words Elijah needs to hear most: "Now I know that you are a man of God, and that the word of the LORD in your mouth is truth" (1 Kgs 17:24, NRSV). We should ponder this a while. The word of Yahweh. In *your* mouth. *That* is the truth. Like Mary of Bethany who foresees the time when Jesus will need her anointing most, this widow foresees the time when Elijah, going back to "save the Israelite faith in the greatest peril it had to face between the days of Moses and the exile,"[2] will be in most need of her words of comfort and power. Mary is the one who recognises truth in Jesus and acts it out, not Judas, who has no inkling of Jesus' needs and of the gravity of the moment. And, as with Mary, this will be told by the generations "in remembrance of her" (see Mk 14:9, NRSV). She might not be named, but she will be mentioned and remembered.

So, moved by the Spirit, she speaks. Remember, Elijah, she is saying, that all the many words of those hundreds of prophets in the king's and queen's service in Samaria are not the word of God. They are not truth. Those false prophets of the court may claim truth, and they certainly will claim their words as the word of God, but their words are the lies that come from the mouth of Baal and Ashera. They might have power, but you have truth—go speak truth to power! Expose it, disrupt it, dismantle it. But equally so, go speak truth to the powerless, and empower them to see the truth, to discern the moment, and to make the right choices. Go and speak the truth that shall make your people free.

The time of preparation in exile was over; the confrontation could be postponed no longer. A murderous Ahab and an equally murderous Jezebel were on the rampage, and Elijah was the one on the ground. That confrontation would be unlike anything we could have imagined, and it would drive Elijah to deeds that would shake him to the core. Certainly deeds, by the time we reach chapter 19, that he would come to be profoundly ashamed of. His heart must have been filled with dread. After all, 18:4 tells us, "Jezebel was killing off the prophets of the LORD" (NRSV). Not just "hunting them down" but "killing them off." The brave Obadiah took his life in his hands and saved a hundred of those prophets, hiding them in the caves of Mount Carmel. But if he could save as many as one hundred, how many were actually on the run, and how many did Jezebel have killed? We seemed to be faced here with endless bloodletting. Moreover, Obadiah would tell Elijah (again reminding us that it was not Jezebel alone at fault) that the king was moving heaven and earth to find the leader of the pack, his true enemy, "the troubler of Israel" (18:17). "There is no nation or kingdom to which my lord has not sent to seek you," he said to Elijah (v. 10). Brueggemann writes, "Obadiah's whole speech is to make clear to Elijah just how bloodthirsty the king is."[3]

Taking all this into account, therefore, is it any wonder the events on Carmel unfold the way they do? And is it any wonder that Elijah might have thought that fire on a drenched altar was not enough to convince, and overcome, these ferocious and powerful enemies of God? Is it any wonder that Elijah, wearied and anxious beyond belief, took matters into his own hands, thinking that the enemies of Yahweh should not be convinced but rather obliterated? That God's will was not persuasion but annihilation? The dangers, at every level imaginable, were never more real, and Elijah knew it.

But so did the widow. Perhaps she saw, better than Elijah could, the danger to himself, the danger of that moment when the prophet of God might, in his passion *for* the truth ("I have been very zealous for the LORD," Elijah says in 19:10, NRSV), mistake his own truth for the truth of the word of God? A kairos moment not only for the people of Israel but for their rulers and for the prophets of a false god, turned upon Elijah, the true prophet of God? So the widow takes it upon herself to strengthen him for the task ahead. She lays her words of wisdom upon him: "Now I know that you are a man of God, and that the word of the LORD in your mouth is truth" (1 Kgs 17:24, NRSV).

If we read those words as the end of chapter 17, where they appear, they emphasise the widow's neediness—her need to be grateful and pay homage to a man at whose rudeness she must have wondered in the beginning but who has now turned out to be her saviour. In that case, these words become the words of a vulnerable woman without patriarchal protection humbly recognising the patriarchal protection of a very powerful man who has suddenly entered her life and changed it around. H. A. Brongers would have a point: she is not nearly grateful enough. If we read those words as the beginning of chapter 18 as I do, however, they emphasise her perspicacity, her ability to discern the moment of truth, the coming moment of Elijah's need. She understood that the peril he had to go and face was not just for the people. It was peril for himself and for his prophetic calling. That is not neediness; that is prophetic insight, prophetic power, and she uses that power to empower a man who must have been wondering how to overcome his fears and doubts in the face of such formidable foes. In their hands would be the weapons of death and destruction. Which weapons would *he* choose?

So instead of reading, "*Now* [after I have witnessed your power at work in seeing my need and coming to my aid, bringing my son back to life] I know you are a man of God," we are invited to read it this way: "Now [Elijah, I know that you might be afraid for what may lie ahead, but I have seen God's power at work through you and in you, and] I know that you are a man of God, and that the word of the LORD in your mouth is truth. [Don't doubt it! Go forth in that power!]" In doing that, she affirms Elijah's prophetic power, and that is life giving. She returns the favour of the gift of life. Go speak that truth to power, she says. Ahab may hate it, and Jezebel may refuse to hear it. Those false prophets of the court may resent every word, may discredit you, undermine you, revile you, even hurt you. Go speak that truth to the people in their confusion and powerlessness.

They need to hear it from you. *From you*! You may be one over against their hundreds, but power does not lie in numbers; it lies in truth. Know, nonetheless, the word in your mouth is the word of God. It is truth, I have seen it, and they shall know it. So she speaks, and that is called revolutionary reciprocity.

I find this utterly amazing. God is the one who calls Elijah, but this widow is the one who sustains him. God is the one who calls him, but this widow is the one who affirms him, who reminds him of who he is and that his God, not Baal, is the true, living, life-giving God. And it is only after she has spoken her words of encouragement that God speaks God's word of instruction: "Go, present yourself to Ahab" (18:1, NRSV).

Elijah goes to speak truth to Ahab and Jezebel and to confront the false prophets and the people with that truth. It will be a kairos moment for the people, but will Elijah recognise it as a kairos moment for himself?

A Kairos Turned Judgement

Reflecting the wide consensus, Brongers writes that here, on Carmel, "once and for all," it had to be made absolutely clear who Israel's God really was.[4] However, it is not as if Elijah is making an exclusivist, universal claim that Yahweh should be worshipped everywhere: in Phoenicia, Elijah left those living there to worship Melqart (the Baal god of Phoenicia), as their god. Elijah, writes Brongers, is not claiming rights for Yahweh as "*deus universalis*."[5] So even on this sensitive issue, Elijah is blameless. He shows a remarkable level of tolerance for others who do not believe in Israel's God. Here, however, in the land of Israel, there is room for no other god. This is where Elijah draws the line.

Something happened that day on Carmel, though, and it is something readers of the Bible, and not just the scholars, have been wrestling with ever since. The Baal priests were done with their futilities: the shouting, the screaming, and the pleading to Baal, a god who could not hear or respond. They, like the people earlier, were "limping" around the altar, not in indecision but in frustration, suffering the public humiliation Elijah kept heaping on them: "Cry aloud! Surely he is a god; either he is meditating, or he has wandered away, or he is on a journey, perhaps he is asleep and must be awakened" (1 Kgs 18:27, NRSV). Elijah was having fun that day. The people, caught up in the moment, must have roared with laughter. There is nothing like seeing those who used to have so much power being mocked and humiliated in public, especially when it looks like your own sins might be forgiven and that you are now on the winning side. After all, at the first words of Elijah, the people, as if they knew how this was going to turn out, shouted, "Well spoken!" (v. 24). The Baal prophets were losing their amen corner. They, not knowing when to stop and digging the hole they were in already ever deeper, shouted even louder, gashing themselves as if Baal, smelling blood, would suddenly return from his wanderings and come to their aid. By noon, they were beginning to run out of steam. The graphic, detailed description of the events is to show how thorough Elijah's triumph was that day.

Elijah was not only having fun. He must have felt enormously vindicated and empowered. Right before everyone's eyes, the tide was turning. Several commentators point out that Elijah had a habit of suddenly appearing, doing something extraordinary, and then disappearing just as abruptly. But in this passage, the people, not just his followers, the "sons of the prophet," have heard of him, and now they are seeing him in action. Elijah appears on the scene here not to comfort them in their distress—Ahab and Jezebel were still on the throne, the prophets of Baal were on the rampage, and corruption, tyranny, and murder were the order of the day—but to confront them on their faithlessness, simultaneously strengthening them enormously with his boldness and presence of power. Elijah did not come to pay homage to the king and to submit to the power of the false prophets, even though he knew, as did everyone else, how the followers of Yahweh were persecuted, hunted down, and killed by the dozens. He did not come to beg for favours. He came to fight for what was Yahweh's indisputable right: "There shall be no other gods before me." That is a religious claim with enormous political consequences, never more important than on that day, and Elijah knew it. He was eloquent; he was confident; he was fearless.

The people were in awe. In their lifetime, no one had ever spoken to them like this before, and no one had ever challenged the powerful like this before. Elijah came not to submit but to claim authority with courage and power: "I, even I only, am left a prophet of the LORD, but Baal's prophets number four hundred fifty" (1 Kgs 18:22, NRSV). What some have read as an exclamation of self-pity, I read as a bold challenge. Perhaps with the widow's empowering parting words ringing in his mind, Elijah is ready to challenge the might of Ahab. He is more than ready to challenge the hesitancy of the people. It may well be that you were intimidated by these men, he is saying to them. It may be that you are afraid to go against the king and the queen, knowing their bloodlust. It may be that you have not seen me or heard me often. Nevertheless, today you will have to choose. "If the LORD is God, follow him, but if Baal, then follow him" (v. 21). No more limping, no more vacillation, no more hesitation—choose now!

Accordingly, I suggest that we must not imagine that the cry "Well spoken!" as a response to Elijah's challenging words was something like polite applause or the vapid, mealy-mouthed "Hear! Hear!" that sycophantic parliamentarians, while checking their cell phones, mumble when their leader speaks. No, it was a full-throated bellow, picked up from person to person, reverberating in a Mexican wave from the first rows to the last. It must have been, I imagine, very much like our United Democratic Front rallies in the 1980s and like those euphoric mass meetings when Nelson Mandela was first released from prison: the *amandlas* and the *vivas* shouted out from fifty thousand throats. Rolling like thunder, the shouts and the dancing feet shook the very ground on which we marched. I remember the feeling when, before I even began to speak, while speaking, and afterward, the crowd would roar my name repeatedly, fists pumping the air, voices strong and clear, lifting us up, carrying us into the next phase of the battle. It is a heady feeling. It fills one with strength and courage, fresh every time, as if one has not known it before. Looking into the faces of the police or the army, you knew they might be holding deadly weapons, but you also knew what they knew: We can't fight this. We are losing this battle. Elijah must have felt like that on that day, looking into the faces of those four hundred fifty Baal prophets and knowing: Your days are over. And this is when a moment of triumph can become a moment of testing. When the prophet of God has to know the truth about themselves before they can speak the truth of the word of God.

"When all the people saw it…," reads 1 Kings 18:39 (NRSV). They saw the fire from heaven consuming the offering. They saw the defeat on the faces of the Baal prophets. They saw the awesome power of Yahweh. But they also, without a doubt, saw the power of the prophet of God, standing alone but in bold defiance before the Baal prophets in their hundreds. Now, Elijah's word was not just truth or truth spoken to power. It was power itself at work among them, in front of their very eyes. It was a highly emotional, heavily intoxicating moment. When they saw all this, the people fell on their faces and shouted, "The LORD indeed is God; the LORD indeed is God" (v. 39). Then, seizing the red-hot moment, Elijah ordered the people, "Seize the prophets of Baal; do not let one of them escape" (v. 40).

"With the people's help, Elijah *personally* carried out the purge of the Baal prophets," writes Mordechai Cogan.[6] The Wadi Kishon, where the actual slaughter took place, was a distance away. That means that Elijah had the Baal prophets corralled and had the people herd them down to the wadi. It was all very deliberate. Cogan quotes Gersonides' commentary at paragraph 9:1 on these events described in 1 Kings 18: "The site was chosen 'so that the blood would not pollute the land, and on this account, it was spilled into the wadi that would carry it far off.'"[7] This should give us pause. Elijah and the people actually thought that the water in the wadi would wash the blood from the ground, their hands, and their souls.

That, however, is an illusion. The land, to this day, is still being polluted, this time by the blood of the indigenous people of Palestine. Of mothers giving birth while waiting at the checkpoints. Of men and women, journalists and medical workers, of protesters in wheelchairs, deliberately targeted by snipers. Of boys and girls and babies bombed to smithereens. Of protesters run over by bulldozers demolishing Palestinian homes. In broad daylight, on worldwide television, young soldiers high-five each other at another successful hit. Even today, the Israeli apartheid state still walks in the ways of Jeroboam, Omri, and Ahab.

Day by day, moment by bloody moment, come the lessons we refuse to learn. The greatest myth about violence is not that it is controllable but that it is redemptive. The most sinful reality of violence is not that it begets violence but that it is idolatrous. The most tragic thing about violence is not that it is toxic but that it is intoxicating. The most devastating truth about violence is not its horrors but its delusions.

So we see here a double burden: one Elijah lays on himself and one he lays on the people, making them all accomplices in the slaughter. Does the awful awesomeness of this act diminish the holy awe they felt at seeing Yahweh at work in the fire from heaven? Does the power of this all-too-human act reduce or even replace the power of the divine intervention? For the prophet, this is a heavy burden to bear: the prophet's scarcity of prophetic sensitivity and abundance of hubris have become such a burden for God's people to bear, a mark on their souls that just a moment ago were cleansed from the desire to serve another god. And all of it in Yahweh's name.

If we follow Rowley's logic, that of the preemptive anticipation of violent wrath, what remains of the difference between the prophets of Baal and the prophet of God? And if we follow the logic of Cogan's take-it-or-leave-it "this is the way God's will works," that we should simply accept that this is the character of God, what precisely is the difference between Baal and Yahweh? These, I believe, might have been the questions that finally dawned on Elijah as he came down from his emotional and triumphalist high.

There may be other questions. At the end of Ahab's reign, we find 400 prophets of Yahweh at his court (1 Kgs 22:6, NRSV). Has Ahab perhaps relented, repented, turned to Yahweh at last? Not so, for this bit of good news is dampened by the fact that we learn that they were mostly false prophets who misled the king. And this was *after* the false triumph of the slaughter at Carmel. So they were still preaching falsehoods, only this time not in the name of Baal but as "prophets of Yahweh." They were certainly not among the 7,000 Yahweh reminded Elijah of to let him know that even though the fight was far from over, he was not alone.

Right until the end of the first book of Kings, the struggle between King Ahab and the true prophets of God would continue. In chapter 20, there is the dramatic scene with an unknown prophet who passes profound judgment on the king. In chapter 21, we read of Ahab's desire to dispossess Naboth of his vineyard, and of Jezebel's wicked, and successful, plans to make it happen.

In chapter 22, we meet the prophet Micaiah, who utters unforgettable words in the face of the words of the 400 court prophets and a still unrepentant Ahab whom he has to confront: "As the LORD lives, whatever the LORD says to me, that I will speak" (22:14, NRSV). Ahab dies ignominiously in 1 Kings 22 when a soldier, randomly shooting his arrow, unknowingly kills the king in his chariot, even though Ahab is in disguise. Ahab's blood pools in the bottom of the chariot. As they return to Samaria, the king's servants wash the chariots. The blood runs out, and the dogs lick it up. Ignominy, humiliation, and shame. God at work, the narrator wants to say, God at work. At the end of the book, we read, "Ahaziah son of Ahab began to reign over Israel in Samaria...." Then, in tragic inevitability, "He did what was evil in the sight of the LORD and walked in the way of his father and mother and in the way of Jeroboam..." (22:51-53, NRSV). The curse continues. The evil has not dissipated; it has multiplied. Yahweh is still not honoured. The people still suffer. So the question is, what was it all good for? Where was the solution Elijah thought the massacre on Carmel would bring?

Rowley seems to suggest some reluctance on the part of Elijah: "Often the prophet's own heart was wrung by the message he felt constrained to deliver."[8] While we know this to be true of Jeremiah (e.g., Jer 8, 9), I detect no sign of such feelings in Elijah here. Neither is any of what Elijah takes upon himself to do even vaguely suggested in the command Yahweh gives to Elijah at the beginning of 1 Kings 18. How does it happen that Elijah read so much more, and so much wrong, into those six simple words from the mouth of Yahweh: "Go, present yourself to Ahab" (v. 1)? Is this perhaps how we should understand Isaiah's fearful hesitation before the glory of the LORD of hosts in the moment of his calling: "Woe is me! I am lost, for I am a man of unclean lips, and I live among a people of unclean lips" (Isa 6:5, NRSV)? Did Isaiah, because he saw the awesome glory and power of the One who called him, better than Elijah, understand the awesome power and the awesome responsibility of the prophet of God, a person of unclean lips? The prophetic calling truly is not something to be taken lightly.

Still, God remains faithful. Amid all this frightening scarcity, God remains a God of stunning abundance. God sends a sign that the drought will be broken, that the rains will come. Even as Elijah speaks with Ahab, God lets him hear "the sound of rushing rain" (1 Kgs 18:41). Elijah returns to Carmel, not as triumphant victor but as supplicant; not to gloat and revel in an ambivalent triumph but to pray. Now, we find Elijah back on Carmel. Not in defiant pose but bowed down, with his head between his knees. Even if it takes seven times of watching for that small cloud to appear, Elijah with his head between his knees all that time, looking up only to hear from his servant whether God is listening, God's restoration of God's prophet has begun. God's generosity overcomes Ahab's scarcity of virtue, the people's scarcity of faithfulness, and Elijah's overflowing wrathfulness. Despite the continued evil reign of Ahab and Jezebel, and despite Elijah's grave transgression, God intends to keep God's promises to God's people. In God's own way, God will deal with Ahab, and in God's own way, God deals with God's prophet.

Chapter 3

A Cloud the Size of a Human Hand

On Manufactured Scarcity, Kairos, and the Abundance of Grace (III)

Allan Aubrey Boesak

Under a Solitary Broom Tree

God will restore the relationship with God's prophet. However, before this is over, that relationship will be severely tested. At Horeb, even after Yahweh has approached him with love, compassion, and sustenance, Elijah tells Yahweh that it was his "zeal for the LORD" (see 1 Kgs 19:10, 14) that had driven him that fateful day. It is clear, though, that the prophetic calling is a burden that zeal alone cannot bear. Perhaps it is not zeal but faithfulness that God desires. Elijah's reaction after the massacre is profound. Rowley explains that the battle for Yahwism was far from over, even after the triumph at Carmel: "Yahwism did not immediately gather the strength that Elijah would see. Other and more insidious perils would continue."[1]

The narrator pointedly writes that Elijah, fleeing from Jezebel's inflamed wrath after Carmel, "came and sat down under a solitary broom tree" (1 Kgs 19:4, NRSV). That "sitting down" is a gesture of utter defeat. The solitariness of the tree Elijah chooses stands like a bold exclamation mark in the life of this prophet who repeatedly speaks of his own loneliness. On Carmel, his solitary figure was a challenge to the Baal mob. Here under this solitary tree, but before the God to whom all hearts are open and before whom no secrets are hid, his loneliness is a lament, a confession of his wholly understandable weakness. I read it less as self-pity than as painful but unadorned truth: at last, he can be truthful about himself. The bravado and the defiance are no longer needed. Here, the taunting and the jokes at the expense of Baal and his prophets are no longer necessary. Elijah does not have to show endless fearlessness to show the strength of his convictions to the people. Here, before his God, there are no more pretences.

"Take away my life," he prays to God, "for I am no better than my ancestors" (19:4). He is right. His ancestor Moses was a man of relentless violence, unleashing his anger at the people at the slightest sign of dissent, always pretending that his anger was, in actual fact, the anger of his God. At every sign of dissent or rebelliousness, the wrath of God came down upon the people in acts of violence bewildering in their disproportionate ferocity. If it were not for Miriam, we would have been left to believe that in this regard, the character of Moses was a truthful reflection of the character of Yahweh.[2]

As the stories were told, Elijah's ancestors, under the leadership of Joshua, invaded the land of Canaan, ransacked and ravaged, killed in a frenzy of "holy war" zeal as many as they could, and revelled in the destruction of all life in sight. These were Elijah's ancestors, even though the authors of the book of Judges admit (in chapters 1-3) that those stories of a divinely instigated invasion and blitzkrieg through which Israel took their "promised land" were not entirely true, yet they could not let them go. They proceeded to claim that Yahweh was unhappy with their peaceful life amid the original inhabitants of Canaan and wanted now to "teach" a new generation how to make war (see Judges 3:2).

Judges also tells the terrifying story of the Levite's concubine (ch. 19) and of the unprovoked attack, fuelled by greed, on the peaceful people of a city called Laish, "quiet and unsuspecting, lacking nothing on earth, and possessing wealth" (Judges 18:7, NRSV). And Judges tells stories of horrific violence, inflicted on others, but finally, and entirely inevitably, because that is precisely how violence works, inflicted on the children of Israel themselves by themselves. The question with which the book begins, "Who shall go up first for us against the Canaanites?" (1:1), becomes, at the end, "Which of us shall go up first to battle against the Benjaminites?" (20:18). In the end, the lesson of Judges is that violence is a self-devouring beast. Elijah knows this, and he knows that God knows.

So Elijah's words are laden with truth. The widow of Zarephath will not let go. It seems that the truth the widow urged him to speak was a truth not just about Baal and his prophets or about Ahab and Jezebel. It was a truth about Elijah himself. Knowing that truth and speaking it finally now, Elijah begins to redeem himself because it was "in his mouth," about himself, the "word of the LORD." The zeal that Elijah was talking about was and still is a deadly thing, especially if it is a "zeal for the LORD." Elijah's "zeal" is a global phenomenon. White supremacy, religious nationalism, ethno-nationalism of any kind, tribalism, nationalist exceptionalism, "my country right or wrong" patriotism—this is politics driven by zeal. It is all disastrous, it is always "for the Lord," it is always predatory, and, in the end, it is always self-devouring.

The demons of violence are loath to let go of their prey. It is with Elijah as it was with the demon-possessed man from the Gospel of Mark whom we know as Legion (Mk 5:1-20). The first thing Mark draws attention to is the violence: the demoniac wrenched his chains apart, broke his shackles in pieces, was always "bruising himself" (vv. 4-5). In the Gospel, the demons are extremely reluctant to release their victim, and neither do they let go of their violence. They seek another outlet for that violence, even if it is into a herd of swine. Accordingly, because just walking away from Kishon and simply turning his back on Carmel as if nothing has happened is not a solution or absolution, Elijah now turns to violence as penance as he had turned to violence as vindication. "It is enough; now, O LORD, take away my life" (1 Kgs 19:4, NRSV).

He is not, as many have posited, contemplating suicide, I think. He could have done that himself without asking God's permission. On Carmel, he clearly knew how to handle a sword. He is asking God to execute him. As if he were still on Carmel, violence is still on Elijah's mind, and he still presumes that the mind of God is violence. Elijah wants to die, but he is knocking at the wrong door. God is not a God of death. God is a God of life whose angel tells Elijah, "Get up and eat" (v. 5). God is a God who sees a future for Elijah. His life should not end with the events on Carmel and at the Kishon, or with his wretchedness under a solitary broom tree. "Get up and eat, or the journey will be too much for you" (v. 7). You are still on a journey, God says; ahead of you is another mountain. There I shall pass by (v. 11). On that other mountain, not Carmel, I will meet you, and I, not you, shall determine the terms of our encounter. This is a parable for politicians as it is for prophets.

Not in the Wind, Not in the Earthquake, Not in the Fire

After Elijah spends the night in a cave, Yahweh asks him, "What are you doing here, Elijah?" (1 Kgs 19:9, NRSV). It is an invitation from a loving, compassionate God, wanting to seal that moment of healing. Elijah replies, "I have been very [extremely] zealous for the LORD…" (v. 10). But he has a reason for this. He explains why: the people have been unfaithful to Yahweh, forsaken the covenant, "and killed [God's] prophets with the sword." This is the first time we hear that last accusation. Always it had been Ahab and Jezebel. Now it is "the people." Is Elijah exaggerating to excuse his behaviour? Laying the blame where it does not rightfully belong? Is he, a moment ago so honest and truthful, now "walking it back"? He even forgoes mention of the main culprits in the saga. Not Ahab, not Jezebel, not their false prophets, but the people "killed your prophets with the sword" (v. 10). Or does he mean that the people killed the Baal prophets with the sword, as if he had nothing to do with any of that? We are almost too afraid to ask the question.

The prophetic calling is tinged with ambiguity. Suddenly Elijah sounds more like a politician seeking justification than a prophet of God confessing the truth. Is he actually trying to negotiate with God by blaming others for his own mistakes? Are remorse and repentance too difficult? Is confession too high a bar, even for a prophet of God? In the cave, Elijah turns what Yahweh intends to be a healing moment into a self-justifying moment.

One may think of Abraham in Genesis 18, negotiating prayerfully but passionately with Yahweh in order to spare the two cities of Sodom and Gomorrah. It is zeal at work. There, however, Abraham was negotiating, leaning heavily on God's justice and mercy and on God's faithfulness to Godself. Abraham was not doing it not for himself but for the sake of others, people he did not even know. Hence, his pleas were not based on their innocence but on God's righteousness instead. That is a different kind of zeal. Shall "the Judge of all the earth" (Gen 18:25, NRSV), Abraham asked in effect, allow the guilt of the wickedness of the many to weigh heavier on God's scales of justice and mercy than the righteousness of the few, even if there were only ten? And will the righteousness of God not outweigh them all? "Far be it from you!" Abraham boldly challenged God. Here in 1 Kings, however, Elijah is only concerned about himself. At this point, the story reads jarringly, and disappointingly, self-centred. "I alone am left, and they are seeking my life" (1 Kgs 19:10, NRSV). The difference between Abraham and Elijah is not small.

Yahweh, in an effort to save the prophet from himself, leads him to Mount Horeb where "the LORD is about to pass by" (v. 11). As Elijah had to "present" himself to Ahab, God is about to present Godself to Elijah. Yahweh is going to great lengths here. Under the broom tree, God spoke through an angel. At Horeb, Godself will appear. Outside the cave where Elijah finds refuge, waiting on God, phenomena of extreme violence shake the earth. There is a strong wind, "so strong that it was splitting mountains and breaking rocks in pieces…" (v. 11). Then came an earthquake, then a fire. The wording the narrator chooses next is deliberate and emphatic: "but the LORD was not in the wind…the LORD was not in the earthquake…the LORD was not in the fire" (vv. 11-12). Elijah's God of violence refuses to appear. Who appears instead is the God in "a sound of sheer silence" (v. 12). The repudiation of the violent zeal that destroyed like a hurricane, burned like a fire, and shook Israel like an earthquake is complete.

Verse 17 is a profound shock to the system because it is so completely out of place here, and so out of character with the God who pursues Elijah with compassion into the wilderness and refuses to let go of him. Yahweh "wakes him up," not from any nightmare but from the far more frightening darkness that is disconnectedness from God. Yahweh offers him life, does not want him to drown in the past, and speaks to him of the future. At Horeb, God presents Godself to Elijah, not in the violent phenomena that split the mountains, scorch the land, and leave gaping wounds in the earth but in the "sound of sheer silence." One would have thought this to be the turning point.

So did the question, repeated a second time, "What are you doing here, Elijah?" (v. 13) come from the lips of a God hopelessly hopeful that Elijah had come out of the dark into the light? Elijah's answer must have been as devastating to Yahweh as it is to us. He repeats, mindlessly it seems, the same mantra that he spoke after his night in the cave, *as if nothing has happened*. It is a frightening thing when even the prophet cannot hear the voice of God. The voice that speaks in verse 17 cannot be the voice of the same God we have encountered through this chapter. The God who restored Elijah's life and his calling, gave him his mantle back, so to speak, now tells Elijah that the massacre on Carmel was, after all, the right thing. It was God's will, and there is more to come because the job is not finished. "Whoever escapes from the sword of Hazael," God says, "Jehu shall kill, and whoever escapes from the sword of Jehu, Elisha shall kill" (1 Kgs 19:17, NRSV). These bloodthirsty words from a bloodthirsty God are not only out of place but out of character. Is this, after all that has happened, the true calling of the prophet of God? Is this their task in the world—killing upon killing upon killing? And to what purpose? The text does not say. Those words just sit there, in an anticipated pool of blood. This is not only Elijah's new future; it is also the future of the prophet called to succeed Elijah, poor, doomed Elisha, whose name we hear for the first time, and already it, too, is soaked in blood.

And the seven thousand? They have just been turned from the faithful remnant into the Lord's Army, into a new wave of violence. The seven thousand "have not bowed to Baal"; they have "not kissed him" (v. 18), but that counts for nothing now, for in every respect they are Baal's prophets, sent on the same killing spree as the ones instigated by Jezebel. There really is no difference at all now between the Baal prophets and Yahweh's prophets, between Ahab and Elijah, or between Baal and Yahweh. Blood fades all differences; blood, not death, is the great equalizer.

Is the voice we hear here the voice of Brueggemann's royal theology line, the voice of the establishment elites who cannot let go of their power and who desperately need God to legitimize that power and the violence necessary to uphold it? The voice that, shocked by the thought that God might be in opposition to Israel's hero, now seeks to reclaim Yahweh for themselves and their violent agenda? The voice that desperately seeks to erase any thought that Yahweh is not a God of thunder and wind, of fire and earthquake, but of sheer silence? That "sheer silence" is an understanding of power so alien that it is unthinkable, for with that power at work, all works of domination and subjugation, all those unmissable hierarchies of power and powerlessness, of ill-gained plenty and manufactured scarcity, must come to an end.

The battle between the voice of this God and the God of Hannah in 1 Samuel 2, the God who breaks the bow of the mighty but girds the weak with strength, the God who assures her that not by might shall one prevail, is on here. The God who lets "the barren [give birth] to seven" (1 Sam 2:5, NRSV), fills the hungry, and "raises up the poor from the dust" (v. 8) is the God of life and abundance, and the sheer exuberance of Hannah's song fills every sentence. Verse 6, "The LORD kills and brings to life," is not a jubilation of God's desire to kill. The battle between the God of Hannah who fills the hungry with good things but sends the rich away empty, who brings down the powerful from their thrones, and who proclaims that might is right continues throughout the scriptures. Yahweh is not like President Obama, taking pleasure and pride in his "Tuesday morning kill list."[3] It means that the strong, the vengeful, and the genociders of this world, despite their power, do *not* have life and death in their hands. That power belongs to Yahweh, the God of life.

But there is a stubbornness that clings with grim lethality to this part of the story. Apparently, it holds for Elijah. Twice more he kills. Twice more he calls fire from heaven to consume the soldiers King Ahaziah has sent after him (2 Kgs 1:9-12). But this time, as with Moses, Elijah lets his God do the killing. Nonetheless, the senselessness that always accompanies killing not only prevails; it mounts. It is King Ahaziah who sins, but it is his soldiers, who had nothing to do with his transgressions and who, on pain of death, must carry out the king's orders, whom Yahweh consumes with fire.

More than Elijah Is Here

Besides this utterly confounding, out-of-place-and-context statement that just hangs there, going nowhere except as preemptive justification for Jehu's reign of terror (see 2 Kgs 9), it seems to me that Elisha, once he receives Elijah's mantle, does something remarkable, and it is the beginning of a transformation. The first acts of Elisha's prophetic life are not the miracles he performs in 2 Kings 2:19-25. As the fiery chariot takes Elijah away from him, Elisha runs after it, shouting, "Father, father! The chariots of Israel chariots and its horsemen!" (2 Kgs 2:12, NRSV). I have always understood that to be a moment of singular clarity. This, and not the miracle stories, is Elisha's entry into his prophetic calling. Here Elisha confirms, and shouts out, that the "weapons" of Israel are not horses and chariots, swords and armies—in other words, instruments of threat, violence, war, and destruction—but solely the power of the prophetic word. Elisha shouts it out in defiance of that repeated "shall kill, shall kill, shall kill." Elisha's cry is that this is what Elijah should represent. This is how Elijah should be remembered, not by that utterly shameful, bloody episode on Carmel.

It might have been Elisha's fondest wish and fervent prayer, but this one single moment of light is not allowed to last. It makes me think of the media and their barrage of constant propaganda on behalf of the elites, incessantly trumpeting the rightness of the dominant narrative which favours the powerful in society. Noam Chomsky and Edward Herman called it "manufactured consent."[4] Just in the last two decades or so, we have been bombarded with lies, deceit, and manufactured "evidence" about Iraq, Saddam Hussein, and weapons of mass destruction, with chemical attacks on his own people by Asad in Syria. Yet there was a moment when *The New York Times* in the US and *The Guardian* in the UK, no longer able to uphold the fiction, had to admit to the lies told by George Bush and Tony Blair. And now, scarcely a decade later, Western media are back, as confident as ever, with the highly implausible story that Russia had, against all logic and political sense, blown up its own pipeline in the Baltic Sea to leave Europe, and especially Germany, without the regular flow of gas they need to stay alive.[5] And they persist with the story, even though no one less than President Biden himself had openly declared that the US was willing and ready to eliminate the Nord Stream 2 pipeline. That moment of sober reflection and honesty is gone, not allowed to last long enough to turn a change of narrative into a change of heart. Something like that seems to be happening here.

And was there an "Isaiah moment" for Elijah as well? As Elijah gets ready to be taken from Elisha, Elisha asks for "a double share" of his spirit (2 Kgs 2:9, NRSV). Elijah does not grant his wish but responds, "You have asked a hard thing" (v. 10). It might be granted to you, or it might not. Elisha did inherit Elijah's mantle, but of the "double share" of Elijah's spirit there is no further word. Does this mean that Elijah now better understands the heavy burden of the prophetic calling but also realizes how the fierceness of his own zeal had tainted the spirit of his prophetic calling? Was it *that* spirit of zeal and wilfulness and violence that he was now so hesitant to bequeath to Elisha? Can it be that the violent zeal of his own spirit had crowded out the Spirit of Yahweh, even momentarily but long enough to let loose the vengeful spirit of Carmel? That Elijah, at the very end, did not want his successor to inherit such a heavy burden?

So, at the same moment that Elisha performs his first miracle, the first act of violence occurs. The young men who mock Elisha are cursed by the prophet. Two bears come out of the woods and maul the young men (v. 24). Whether they die as a result, we are not told. Perhaps not, but it is curious that this event occurs immediately after Elisha's first miracle where he purifies the water supply of the city, so that "from now on neither death nor miscarriage shall come from it" (v. 21). The prophet who was supposed to continue the killing spree brings life instead, and even though his curse seems to work, it is not certain whether it also causes death. But here, too, the narrator, seeing that the contradiction seems too much to bear, leaves it unexplained.

At first, Elisha's works of wonder seem to parallel those of Elijah. For the rest, though, his deeds are his own, and they, in the end many more than Elijah had wrought, are persistent affirmations of life, including for Naaman the Aramean. This also includes the army of the Arameans that Elijah's God delivers into the hands of the king of Israel. Upon the bloodthirsty eagerness of the king to slaughter them all while he has them at his mercy, Elisha says, "Set food and water before them…and let them go to their master" (2 Kgs 6:22, NRSV). This is a triumph of the diplomacy of nonviolence, refuting the savage desires for death and destruction. It is all life giving. Can this be a correction of that depressing, death-inviting prophecy about the life and work of this prophet? I think so, as it is a correction of Elijah's misguided zeal. And if this is so, is this kairos moment also turned into a moment of redemption for Elijah?

When Moses and Elijah later appeared with Jesus on the mountain at the transfiguration (see Matthew 17), it was not so that Jesus could be legitimised by those two reminders of Israel's glory in the eyes of disciples who were, even as late as at Jesus' ascension, still expecting the restoration of the kingdom of Israel. It was so that they, Moses and Elijah, could be legitimised by Jesus. It was, as Paul Lehmann correctly saw, not only the moment of the transfiguration of Jesus. It was the transfiguration of politics.[6] The violent, zealous politics of Moses and Elijah would be transformed by the truly revolutionary politics of Jesus. Now, there was a real possibility that the politics of abundance that was of Jesus could become the politics of his followers. The drought has been broken, the myth of scarcity has been overcome by the abundance of life and light. Even though Jesus himself never made this claim, I think it perfectly legitimate, as I read this passage, to come to the theological conclusion that in Jesus, we see someone greater than Elijah. To paraphrase Jesus on Jonah, "More than Elijah is here."

Chapter 4

Calling Zacchaeus

On Repentance, Reparations, and Black Theology (I)

Wendell Griffen

In her preface to *The 1619 Project*, journalist Nikole Hannah-Jones observes that historian and journalist Lerone Bennett Jr. documented that African people had lived "on the land that in 1776 would form the United States" since 1619, when a ship named the *White Lion* arrived at Jamestown, Virginia, a year before the *Mayflower* arrived. Black Americans were enslaved, kidnapped, transported, sold, whipped, raped, castrated, terrorized, and abused in other ways from 1619 through the next 246 years. Their descendants have received nothing to repay, repair, or otherwise account for the legion of wrongs they suffered. That is a colossal moral, ethical, social, political, economic, and humanitarian issue. Yet it is one about which theologians have seldom commented.

I have been a follower of the religion of Jesus since my parents and other Black elders introduced me to it during my childhood. My faith, like that of my Black parents, elders, and ancestors, was forged by the religion of Jesus taught and preached from the Bible, set to music in Negro Spirituals and gospel songs, and pondered in Black congregations.

I turned away from Eurocentric Christianity almost forty years ago when I dropped out of seminary extension studies sponsored by Midwestern Baptist Theological Seminary. The prospect of being credentialed by the religious system that gave moral, ecclesial, and ethical approval to invasion of indigenous societies, land theft, genocide, chattel slavery, imperialism, white supremacy, militarism, wealth privilege, patriarchy, sexism, bigotry, terrorism of LGBTQI persons, techno-centrism, and xenophobia was intellectually, morally, and ethically disgusting to me. Instead, my theological perspective is bottomed on how the religion of Jesus has been interpreted by Negro Spirituals and gospel songs.

My theological luminaries are Howard Thurman, James H. Cone, and South African liberation theologian Allan Boesak. My ethics is inspired by Henry Highland Garnett, Sojourner Truth, Frederick Douglass, Nat Turner, W. E. B. Du Bois, Martin Luther King Jr., Malcolm X, Katie Cannon, Emilie Townes, Kelly Brown Douglas, and Cornel West. My pastoral theology is guided by writings from Peter Paris and the examples of Jeremiah A. Wright Jr., J. Alfred Smith, and Amos Brown. My hermeneutics and homiletics are built on the writings by Walter Brueggemann, Walter Rauschenbusch, William Sloan Coffin, and William Augustus Jones, and on the work of Gardner Taylor, Samuel DeWitt Proctor, and Henry and Ella Mitchell. These people rescued my faith in the religion of Jesus from Eurocentric Christianity with its devotion to personal, commercial, social, and geopolitical empire. I mention their names to emphasize that my exposure to their work and ministries happened outside any seminary context.

I.

In scripture, "righteous" and "righteousness" are words about honesty, truth, and justice. So, when Jesus pronounced a blessing on people who "hunger and thirst for righteousness" in Matthew 5:6 (NRSV), he was commending people who have a passion for honesty, truth, and justice. He was not commending people who cheat, steal, lie, and misuse power to oppress others.

The encounter between Jesus and the chief revenue commissioner of Jericho named Zacchaeus recorded in Luke 19 clearly makes this point. People remember Luke's account of that encounter for different reasons. Some are impressed by the fact that Zacchaeus wanted to see Jesus so much that he—a wealthy man—went to the trouble (and humility) of climbing a tree. Allan Boesak has written that Zacchaeus was so despised that being in a tree was probably the one place he felt safe:

> It was not just because he was a man of small stature. The people knew him. He knew he would not be welcomed by them. Why would anyone give up their place in the crowd, and their chance to see Jesus, for someone like him? Amongst the crowd, the hostility would have been palpable and perhaps physical. That tree was the safest place for him. It is also a symbol of his isolation. Amongst the poor and oppressed, those extorted by men like Zacchaeus every day of their lives, but expectant and hopeful that day, Zacchaeus would not have been made to feel welcome.[1]

Some people point to the fact that Jesus addressed Zacchaeus by name, invited himself to dine with Zacchaeus, and was welcomed into the home of this rich fellow. How did Jesus know Zacchaeus? The narrative is silent on those points. We also don't know what Jesus and Zacchaeus ate or how long the meal lasted.

But we know Jesus and Zacchaeus talked long enough and deeply enough for Zacchaeus to reconsider how he became so wealthy. Zacchaeus promised to refund four times the value of any of his wealth obtained through fraud—meaning through dishonest means. And Zacchaeus promised to give half of his possessions to the poor. He committed to transfer half of his wealth to impoverished people. The result of the encounter between Jesus and Zacchaeus was that the rich man voluntarily pledged to divest himself of half of his wealth and redistribute it to people who were poor.

Zacchaeus wasn't talking about making a charitable donation to the Salvation Army. He wasn't talking about setting up a Zacchaeus Foundation for the study of poverty. He was talking about giving away half of what he owned so that he and his poor neighbors would know income security. The pledge to give half his wealth to the poor demonstrates what Bryan Stevenson (founder of the Equal Justice Institute) has said about poverty. According to Stevenson, the opposite of poverty is not wealth; the opposite of poverty is justice.

Justice always is about the fair use and distribution of power and resources. A society where some people are extraordinarily wealthy while others are poor is unjust because resources—including but not limited to money and other possessions—are unfairly withheld by the wealthy few and not redistributed for the numerous poor. It is unjust for wealthy people to have much more than they need while poor people suffer because they do not have what they need. It is unjust for wealthy people to use their extraordinary wealth to enrich themselves rather than redistribute wealth to benefit their impoverished neighbors. It is unjust for wealthy people to control land and refuse to share with poor people who need housing.

But that was not all. Zacchaeus also pledged to refund four times the value of anything he obtained by dishonest means. In doing so, Zacchaeus demonstrated another truth: Wealth obtained through injustice can never be justly retained; instead, it produces damage that must be repaired and wrong that must be remedied. Zacchaeus admitted that some of his wealth—including the comfortable lifestyle and the lavish hospitality he could extend to Jesus—was based on dishonest gain. To hold on to that wealth was to persist in dishonesty. To trade that wealth for more wealth amounted to earning a profit on dishonesty. When Zacchaeus pledged to pay back four times the value of anything he had obtained through fraudulent (meaning dishonest) means, he was pledging to make reparations! Both the pledge to divest and the pledge to make reparations resulted from the deliberate encounter Jesus had with Zacchaeus.

Jesus did not go to Jericho on a whim. Jesus did not invite himself to dine with Zacchaeus for personal privilege. Jesus did not invite himself to dine with Zacchaeus to be featured in the society section of the *Jericho News*. Jesus went to Jericho and invited himself to dine with Zacchaeus—the chief revenue commissioner in the prosperous Jericho region—because Jesus was hungry and thirsty for justice!

Jesus shows that hunger and thirst for justice requires us to challenge the ways that wealthy people have come to control so much. What unjust conduct, policies, and practices are in place that produced the land holdings of a few and the homelessness of so many? What unjust labor practices result in so many people working so hard and remaining in poverty while a few people live in luxury without lifting a finger? What labor was stolen? What land was obtained through oppressive methods? What water rights are held because people were cheated or because wealthy people preyed on the vulnerability of their less fortunate neighbors? How much should be returned because it should never have been taken? How much should be restored?

What Zacchaeus said about restoring four times what he had obtained through dishonest means was based on principles of restitution and reparation. Consider these passages (NRSV, my italics):

> When someone steals an ox or a sheep and slaughters it or sells it, the thief shall pay five oxen for an ox and four sheep for a sheep. *The thief shall make full restitution or, if unable to do so, shall be sold for the theft.* (Exodus 22:1, 3)

> ...or anything else about which you have sworn falsely, you shall repay the principal amount and add one-fifth to it. *You shall pay it to its owner when you recognize your guilt.* (Leviticus 6:5)

> Speak to the Israelites: When a man or a woman wrongs another, breaking faith with the LORD, that person incurs guilt and shall confess the sin that has been committed. *The person shall make full restitution for the wrong, adding one-fifth to it and giving it to the one who was wronged.* (Numbers 5:6-7)

We are finally witnessing people wrestling with racial injustice in ways they have not done before. However, Zacchaeus shows that, like people in a desert, they need help. They need prophetic people to show up and challenge them like Jesus did.

Jesus, the itinerant preacher from Galilee, showed up in Jericho to confront the chief revenue commissioner about being unjustly wealthy. Jesus showed up to confront Zacchaeus about having twice as much as he needed to have aplenty. Jesus showed up to confront Zacchaeus about being wealthy through dishonest gain. Jesus showed up to challenge Zacchaeus to take on a life of economic repentance that involved downsizing, restitution, and wealth redistribution.

This shows that people who are hungry and thirsty for righteousness, like Jesus, must confront the holders of unjust wealth. In obedience to the example of Jesus, we must challenge people like Zacchaeus to divest themselves of wealth obtained through dishonest means. That includes challenging them to understand that holding on to unjustly obtained wealth is a sign of moral and ethical depravity, not financial health. In other words, people who hunger and thirst for righteousness will challenge people like Zacchaeus with the imperatives of restitution and reparation for racial injustice.

That requires admitting that the wealth of our society was built on racial injustice. Racial injustice is the original sin of this society and is embedded in its moral, ethical, religious, commercial, political, and social DNA. It also requires that prophetic people preach—whether they are clergy or not—about the debt created by that injustice. Relief and rescue from the moral desert of reparations will not come without the kind of prophetic intervention and interaction Jesus had with Zacchaeus. It is up to prophetic people to recognize this truth and live into it.

II.

First, we should understand the difference between "restitution" and "reparation." Restitution refers to an *obligation owed by a person or party to repay a debt owed or repair a wrong inflicted on another person or party*. Reparation refers to an *obligation owed by a society or government to repay a debt owed or repair a wrong inflicted on persons or parties*. At the heart of both ideas—restitution and reparation—is a sense that wrongful conduct has caused harm, loss, injury, or suffering to another person or party (restitution) or to a group of people (reparation).

Why has no reparation been made to Black people for slavery and the racial injustice that continues from it? One reason is explained in Isaiah 59:1-10 (NRSV):

> See, the LORD's hand is not too short to save, nor his ear too dull to hear. Rather, your iniquities have been barriers between you and your God, and your sins have hidden his face from you so that he does not hear. For your hands are defiled with blood, and your fingers with iniquity; your lips have spoken lies, your tongue mutters wickedness. No one brings suit justly, no one goes to law honestly; they rely on empty pleas, they speak lies, conceiving mischief and begetting iniquity. They hatch adders' eggs, and weave the spider's web; whoever eats their eggs dies,

and the crushed egg hatches out a viper. Their webs cannot serve as clothing; they cannot cover themselves with what they make. Their works are works of iniquity, and deeds of violence are in their hands. Their feet run to evil, and they rush to shed innocent blood; their thoughts are thoughts of iniquity, desolation and destruction are in their highways. The way of peace they do not know, and there is no justice in their paths. Their roads they have made crooked; no one who walks in them knows peace. Therefore justice is far from us, and righteousness does not reach us; we wait for light, and lo! there is darkness; and for brightness, but we walk in gloom. We grope like the blind along a wall, groping like those who have no eyes; we stumble at noon as in the twilight, among the vigorous as though we were dead.

White supremacy—the actual theology followed by this society—has shamelessly condoned and justified the greed, robbery, violence, deceit, and other injustices associated with slavery and racialized oppression of Black people since its inception.

When European colonizers cheated, lied, and robbed the indigenous people in this land of their land, water, and wages, white supremacy sacralized the operation. European governments set up colonial governments that licensed land theft, cheating, and the murder of indigenous people. People who called themselves followers of Jesus condoned it and supported it. Then the colonizers kidnapped Africans. They set up shipping companies to transport and trade enslaved Africans. Insurance companies and banks financed the whole operation. Slavery of Black people was continued openly in this society for 246 years. People who called themselves followers of Jesus condoned it and supported it.

The cover story in the June 28, 2020, issue of *The New York Times* magazine is titled "What Is Owed" and is written by Nikole Hannah-Jones. She began the story with these words: "If true justice and equality are ever to be achieved in the United States, the country must take seriously what it owes black Americans." With that introductory statement, Hannah-Jones argued that this nation must move beyond slogans and undertake deep conversation about reparations for Black Americans and added this truth: "A truly great country does not ignore or excuse its sins. It confronts them and then works to make them right."

One job of religion is to challenge society to confront its sins and work to do right by people who have been wronged. However, most religious people have shown no interest in engaging in conversations about reparations. For example, the Southern Baptist Convention (SBC) was founded in 1845. During its 150th anniversary meeting in Atlanta, Georgia, in 1995—twenty-five years ago at the time of this writing—Southern Baptist messengers adopted an eloquent resolution admitting that slavery played a role in the formation of the SBC. The resolution admits that Southern Baptists "defended the right to own slaves, and either participated in, supported, or acquiesced in the particularly inhumane nature of American slavery." The resolution also laments that racism and "historic acts of evil such as slavery from which we continue to reap a bitter harvest...[have] separated us from our African-American brothers and sisters" and resolves to apologize "to all African-Americans for condoning and/or perpetuating individual and systemic racism in our lifetime...."[2]

Yet that 1995 resolution was conspicuously and suspiciously silent about healing the damage, injury, and harm African Americans suffered from 246 years of chattel slavery, another century of legalized segregation, and continued systemic practices and policies in every aspect of American society that are the legacy of that wicked history. The 1995 resolution did not contain a word about reparations to people whose ancestors were enslaved, dehumanized, defrauded, terrorized, and marginalized and who continue to suffer from that blatant violation of divine love, truth, and justice.

Baylor University, the largest Baptist institution of higher education in the world, was also organized, founded, and funded in 1845—175 years ago—by white men who owned enslaved persons. Baylor is home to the George Truett Theological Seminary. But when the Baylor Board of Regents issued a unanimous resolution admitting its slaveholder sponsorship and purporting to apologize for it, the resolution did not mention anything about reparations.[3]

Greed and robbery are root causes of racism and racial injustice. Slaveholder religion did not create the greed, robbery, and racism. Slaveholder religion, including religion practiced by white people who called themselves followers of Jesus, was developed to justify kidnapping, robbery, rape, torture, lynching, terrorism, human trafficking, and the other evils associated with slavery.

We will never have a serious conversation about racial justice in this society until we talk about reparation for the moral, ethical, political, and monetary debt this society owes descendants of African people who were enslaved, robbed, raped, cheated, terrorized, kept illiterate, and dehumanized. But we will not have that conversation about reparation until and unless prophetic people insist on it.

The second reason reparations have never been paid to the descendants of enslaved Black people is that we who are Black have been timid about demanding reparations. We have been timid in the face of white privilege. We have been timid in the face of terrorism. We have talked about desegregating schools, restaurants, hotels, theatres, and other establishments. We have talked about voting rights.

But we have not talked, boycotted, protested, demonstrated, or otherwise made demands for reparation. Religious and fraternal organizations have not made reparations a subject at local, state, and national meetings. In the same way that we criticize white religious leaders for failing and refusing to address reparations, we must also admit that Black and Brown religious leaders also have been derelict.

In his book titled *The Debt: What America Owes to Blacks*, Randall Robinson makes this point so clearly—albeit with language that some people will find unseemly—that I will not try to sanitize his words.

> The issue here is not whether we [Black people] can, or will win reparations. The issue is whether we will fight for reparations, because we have decided for ourselves that they are our due....
>
> Let me try to drive the point home here: through keloids of suffering, through coarse veils of damaged self-belief, lost direction, misplaced compass, shit-faced resignation, racial transmutation, black people worked long, hard, killing days, years, centuries—and they were never *paid*. The value of their labor went into others' pockets—plantation owners, northern entrepreneurs, state treasuries, the United States government.
>
> Where was the money?
>
> Where *is* the money?
>
> There is a debt here.
>
> ...Jews have asked this question of countries and banks and corporations and collectors and any who had been discovered at the end of the slimy line holding in secret places the gold, the art, the money that was the rightful property of European Jews before the Nazi terror. Jews have demanded what was their due and received a fair measure of it.
>
> Clearly, how blacks respond to the challenge surrounding the simple demand for restitution [reparations] will say a lot more about us *and do a lot more for us* than the demand itself would suggest. We would show ourselves to be responding as any normal people would to victimization were we to assert in our demands for restitution that, for 246 years and with the complicity of the United States government, hundreds of millions of black people endured unimaginable cruelties—kidnapping, sale as livestock, deaths in the millions during terror-filled sea voyages, backbreaking toil, beatings, rapes, castrations, maimings, murders. We would begin a healing of

our psyches were the most public case made that whole peoples lost religions, languages, customs, histories, cultures, children, mothers, fathers…. And they were never made whole. And never compensated. Not one red cent.[4]

That is what makes the encounter of Jesus with Zacchaeus so powerful. Jesus did not shirk his moral and ethical duty to confront Zacchaeus about his greed. Jesus was not afraid to call Zacchaeus out. Jesus refused to pass through Jericho without meeting Zacchaeus, confronting Zacchaeus, and calling on him to make restitution for anything he had obtained by dishonest means.

Jesus refused to practice a religion that turned a blind eye to robbery. What about us?

Jesus refused to practice a religion that condoned wage theft. What about us?

Jesus refused to back down. What about us?

What are followers of Jesus doing to confront this society about the unpaid and constantly mounting debt owed to the descendants of people whose lives and labor and culture and language and ancestry and religion were robbed?

What are the descendants of those robbed workers doing in God's name to make this society face its moral and ethical duty to make reparations for 246 years of stolen labor, another 100 years of legalized segregation, and the ongoing harms and losses associated with racial injustice?

Chapter 5

Calling Zacchaeus

On Repentance, Reparations, and Black Theology (II)

Wendell Griffen

In the summer of 2020, I preached about reparations to Black people for harms, losses, and injuries caused by this society intentionally, persistently, and openly because of 246 years of legalized chattel slavery, another 100 years of legalized segregation, and ongoing violations of God's love and justice from effects of that injustice. Beginning with Luke's account about the encounter between Jesus and Zacchaeus, the rich chief revenue commissioner of Jericho, I emphasized that the divine imperative that we love God with our whole being and love one another as neighbors requires that this society make reparation for the harms, losses, and injuries inflicted by this society upon Black people. And I argued that followers of Jesus have a moral and ethical duty to lead the call for reparations.

I.

One sermon in that series pondered reparations by looking at Mark's account about the encounter between an unnamed wealthy man and Jesus that is found in the Gospels of Matthew (Mt 19:16-30) and Luke (Lk 18:18-30). People have termed this the story of "Jesus and the rich young ruler." However, one of the early Christian theologians (Origen of Alexandria) recorded in his commentary on Matthew that two rich men approached Jesus as he traveled.

The lesson has several remarkable features. The passage states that a man of wealth and influence (a ruler) approached Jesus, humbly knelt before him, and addressed him as "Good Teacher" before asking, "What must I do to inherit eternal life?" The man did not appear discouraged when Jesus rejected his flattery. When Jesus reminded him about the obligation to honor God in interpersonal relationships ("You shall not murder. You shall not commit adultery. You shall not steal. You shall not bear false witness. You shall not defraud. Honor your father and mother," Mk 10:19, NRSV), the young man declared that he had faithfully kept those requirements from his youth.

Then Mark 10:21 reads, "Jesus, looking at him, loved him and said, 'You lack one thing; go, sell what you own, and give the money to the poor, and you will have treasure in heaven; then come, follow me." Before that comment, the man seemed serious about being identified with Jesus. But when he heard that direction from Jesus, "he was shocked and went away grieving, for he had many possessions" (10:22).

At that point, Jesus remarked to his disciples, "How hard it will be for those who have wealth to enter the kingdom of God" (10:23). The disciples were perplexed (the J. B. Phillips translation reads *staggered*), so Jesus repeated the point and drove it home with a proverb: "It is easier for a camel to go through the eye of a needle than for someone who is rich to enter the kingdom of God" (v. 25).

Jesus told the young ruler to "go, sell what you own, and give the money to the poor...then come, follow me" (v. 21). Jesus did not welcome the man and "disciple him" to use his wealth to "sow" into his ministry. Origen of Alexandria wrote in his *Commentary on Matthew* that Jesus said to the perplexed rich man, "How can you say 'I have fulfilled the Law and the Prophets' when it is written in the Law: 'You shall love your neighbor as yourself'; and many of your brothers, sons of Abraham, are covered with filth, dying of hunger, and your house is full of many good things, none of which goes out to them?" What does this have to do with reparation and following Jesus?

Jesus refused to allow flattery to blind him to the dramatic inequality between the rich ruler and the rest of society. He directed the man to "push back" from his wealth, to divest himself of it and become one of the common people. Jesus directed this man to share his wealth with impoverished people and follow him as a commoner. Instead, the man preferred to hold on to his possessions.

Like the rich young ruler, white Baptists who founded the Southern Baptist Convention were enthusiastic about "eternal life" and preaching the gospel of Jesus. But they refused to give up owning enslaved Africans. They refused to pay Africans for their work. They refused to treat Africans as neighbors. To justify their greed, wage theft, human trafficking, kidnapping, rape, and the other violations of love and justice associated with chattel slavery, "rich rulers" in this society established the Southern Baptist Convention in 1845. That was also the year that slaveholding, Bible-quoting, and Bible-preaching white Baptists who claimed to follow Jesus established Baylor University, the oldest and largest continually operating Baptist institution of higher education in the world.

Less than twenty years later, slaveholding, Bible-quoting, and hymn-singing white Baptists were at the forefront of what would become the deadliest war ever fought by the United States, and the last war waged on US soil, because they, like the rich young ruler, would not "push back" from slaveholder religion, slaveholder economics, and slaveholder social relationships.

Let us be clear. Like the "rich ruler" who approached Jesus and called him "Good Teacher," church folks stole the lives, labor, and livelihood of millions of their siblings for centuries.

Like the "rich ruler," church folks were saddened about the thought of pushing back from that stolen wealth.

Like the "rich ruler," church folks have tried to associate themselves with Jesus without redressing the poverty, sickness, and other results of systemic racism, slavery, and ongoing discrimination.

Sadly, people who call themselves followers of Jesus court favor from "rich ruler" types to the point that congregations would rather not do what Jesus did and tell people who trust in wealth to divest and share with those who are poor. Unlike Jesus, who taught that it is hard for people who trust in wealth "to enter the kingdom of God," people who claim to follow Jesus in this nation do not tell wealthy people to "push back," divest their wealth, redistribute its value to those who are poor, and live in solidarity with those who are not affluent.

On April 16, 1862, President Abraham Lincoln signed into law the District of Columbia Compensated Emancipation Act, a law that called for $1 million in reparations to be paid for emancipated Africans who had been enslaved in the District of Columbia—but the money was to go to the white people who enslaved them, worked them without pay, and kept the proceeds from their work. I do not know how many slaveowners received "reparations" from the District of Columbia Compensated Emancipation Act of 1862. I have no information that any of the emancipated Africans received a penny. The District of Columbia Emancipation Act included up to $100,000 to resettle formerly enslaved persons, but the resettlement was to be in Haiti and Liberia, not in the United States.

Then, as now, church people with "rich ruler" religion weren't told to "push back" from the stolen wealth this nation and its institutions garnered from enslaved persons. Instead of following the example of Jesus, who confronted the unnamed "rich ruler" and later confronted the rich tax collector named Zacchaeus, church people who claim they follow Jesus refuse to challenge "rich ruler" religionists who do not "push back." Perhaps that is why church folks are not "stepping up" about reparations. Perhaps we have people with "rich ruler" religion that pretends to follow Jesus while trusting wealth—even when the wealth has been obtained and is being held because of theft, not thrift. And perhaps "rich ruler religion" explains why the religion of Jesus is associated with concern for the wealthy rather than concern for the poor.

"Rich ruler religion"—religion that does not push back from unjustly obtained and held wealth—should not be associated with Jesus. And unless followers of Jesus confront "rich ruler religion," "rich rulers" like the unnamed man in this passage and like Zacchaeus will never become people who embrace the divine imperative of reparations for the stolen lives, stolen labor, and fraud that continue to haunt our society.

II

I contend that the love and justice of God require that followers of Jesus join the demands for reparations for Black children of God who descended from enslaved Africans. The law of Moses, writings of the Hebrew prophets, and teachings of Jesus—especially the narrative in the Gospel of Luke about the encounter Jesus had with Zacchaeus, the chief revenue commissioner of Jericho—support the demand for racial reparations. I now must stress three things.

First, we must remember that reparation is a moral, ethical, and social *requirement from God*. Unpaid debts, unrepaired injuries, and unrequited harms and losses separate people from God and each other. That reality requires that we understand reparation for racial injustice to be a theological imperative.

Wealth, privilege, and status based on violence, theft, deceit, hate, hypocrisy, and fear are never based on justice and peace. When wealth, privilege, and status are grabbed by those means, the people who grab it must always depend on and resort to more violence, deceit, hate, hypocrisy, and fear to hold on to it. The biblical lesson about Cain and Abel in Genesis 3 and the lesson about Moses and the burning bush in Exodus 3 prove this point.

When Cain murdered Abel, he did not escape God. When the Egyptians enslaved and oppressed Hebrew workers, they did not escape God. In both instances, the biblical message is that God witnessed the violence. God witnessed the theft of life and labor. God witnessed the willful disregard for God and others. And God confronted Cain and the Egyptian empire (through Moses) about that willful defiance of divine sovereignty, love, and justice.

Martin Luther King Jr. famously said that the moral arc of the universe sweeps wide yet always bends towards justice. Justice requires that wrongs we inflict on others be made right. Justice requires that debts be repaid. Justice requires reparation. Because the universe "bends towards justice," the universe bends toward reparation whether people like it or not. And until reparation is made, the relationship between wrongdoers and their victims is skewed, unbalanced, and untrue. Until reparation is made, wrongdoers must constantly fear vengeance from victims who have been robbed, brutalized, deceived, and otherwise wronged. Until reparation is made, that fear drives wrongdoers to defend their wrongful privilege, status, and wealth by force. Violence begets more violence.

The moral and ethical history of what we today call policing and law enforcement towards indigenous people in this society, African Americans, and Latino children of God is rooted in centuries of sacralized and legalized violence perpetrated by white children of God against people of color and the stolen wealth obtained and distributed on racial grounds across generations. White violence, theft, deceit, hate, and hypocrisy against people of color produced the racial inequities that ravage our society and account for white privilege. White people sanction the use of violence by law enforcement to protect property more than Black, Brown, and Red lives because white wealth is bottomed on violence against Black, Brown, and Red children of God.

The messages that God confronted Cain about murdering Abel and sent Moses to confront the Egyptian empire about enslaving and oppressing Hebrew immigrants teach that wrongdoers cannot escape divine scrutiny. And those messages teach that God knows the truth wrongdoers try to deny. God knows the debt owed for taking lives. God knows the debt owed by stealing labor and land. God knows and requires that the debts be repaid, the wrongs be remedied, and the injuries be healed. Reparation is a moral, ethical, and social imperative from God, not an elective. Those who deny that truth defy the sovereignty and justice of God.

People whose greed drives them to lust after and violently grab wealth, privilege, and status must use violence to hold on to it. In a moral universe, that means they must somehow manufacture explanations to justify that violence. Greed and lust are not morally justifiable explanations for premeditated and otherwise indefensible violence. Hence, throughout history and in every society, humans have tried to justify premeditated and indefensible violence by claiming that religion, law, manifest destiny, science (including education), and commerce uphold it. Racism and white supremacy are perversions used to justify the greed and lust of perverted religion, perverted law, perverted science, perverted history, and perverted public policy.

We should remember these things whenever we confront racial inequities and white supremacy. Religion, law, commerce, science, and every other institution have been perverted and corrupted by greed and lust for power, wealth, and status. Perverted religion, science, law, and other institutions operate to maintain and expand racism and white supremacy across generations, across cultures, and across political players.

Perverted religion, science, law, and other institutions are the principalities and powers of spiritual darkness in high places (see Eph 6:12) that followers of Jesus have wrestled against in every era and place. In the context of racial justice (both in the US and across the world), perverted religion, law, education, science, politics, and economics have always been used to justify greed and covetousness for the lives, land, and other resources of people from Africa, Asia, America, and

Australia and continue to be religiously blessed and sanctioned. This not only gives wrongdoers a false sense of merit. It also tempts oppressed people to question the goodness and justice of God.

Secondly, when we speak of reparation being a requirement, we should also emphasize that it is morally, ethically, and socially required. This means there must be financial reparation, legal reparation, political reparation, educational reparation, cultural reparation, and religious, medical, and emotional reparation for the harm, loss, and trauma inflicted across 400 years on Africans who were enslaved and on their descendants. Remember that financial, legal, political, educational, cultural, religious, scientific, medical, and mental health institutions were complicit in and enabled the harm, loss, and trauma African Americans suffer. They must also repair the damage, harm, and loss associated with their premeditated and indefensible violations of divine love and justice.

But societal institutions will not meet, let alone fulfill, the moral, ethical, and public imperative for reparation without prophetic leadership. Notice that I said *prophetic* rather than *religious* leadership. Religious institutions and their leaders are so corrupted by idolatry to greed and empire that most pastors, religious educators, and religious bodies are morally, ethically, and institutionally compromised by white supremacy and racism. This is what Robert P. Jones meant when he wrote that white Christians are Cain and have been "white too long."[1]

We need look no further than Al Mohler and the trustees of Southern Baptist Theological Seminary and the president and regents of Baylor University to see that leaders of white religious institutions have served greed, covetousness, white supremacy, racism, and empire too long to speak prophetically about racism and white supremacy, let alone provide prophetic leadership about reparation for the harm, loss, and debt associated with it.[2] When it comes to racial injustice, most white religious leaders (including pastors, religious educators, and denominational leaders) are "blind guides." They should not be followed.

III

The so-called parable of the prodigal son (Lk 15:11-32) and the passage involving Jesus and Zacchaeus (Lk 19:1-10) highlight that reparation is resisted and that prophetic efforts toward reparation are resented. In both passages, religious people who suffered from systemic wrongs perpetrated by the "tax collectors and sinners" "grumbled" because Jesus socialized with them. So, my third point of emphasis is that we remember that Jesus did not dismiss those "sinners" as moral monsters beyond the reach and power of prophetic influence.

It is easy to criticize white people for being opposed to reparations, and we should do so. But it is somewhat disingenuous to criticize white people for opposing reparations by terming them moral monsters. Moral monsters should not be expected to tolerate demands for reparations, let alone consider themselves morally, ethically, and socially obligated to meet such demands. It is self-contradictory—if not unfair—to denounce people as inhuman and then blame them for not responding humanely to moral and ethical demands for justice.

Jesus illustrated in the parable of the gracious father (or prodigal son) and his encounter with Zacchaeus that God delights in restoring broken relationships. That was the point Jesus stressed in the lessons about the widow who swept her house to find one lost coin and the shepherd who left ninety-nine sheep to find one lost sheep and the father who welcomed a wayward son back with a feast and party.

God is obsessed with oneness. In the divine economy, all things add up to equal one. All things are part of the one. God is one wonderful Creator over all creation, one wonderful progenitor over all beings, and one who does not rest while anything violates the relationship of oneness between God and everything and everyone else. Jesus summed up this idea in Luke 19:10 in these words: "For the Son of Man came to seek out and to save the lost."

We should remember that reparation is about repairing a broken relationship. Something has happened to damage a relationship. In the Prodigal Son parable, a son broke ties with his family of origin. In the lesson about Jesus and Zacchaeus, the Jericho revenue commissioner had become the tool used by Roman colonizers to exact taxes from the indigenous Palestinians of Judea. What chance did Zacchaeus have to come to his moral and ethical senses about reparations for the unjust wealth he gained from dishonest tax collecting if Jesus had not invited himself to dinner? What chance did the people who had been victimized by Zacchaeus have to get reparations if Jesus had joined the grumbling church folks who snubbed Zacchaeus? And what chance did Jesus have to prophetically challenge Zacchaeus unless Jesus met Zacchaeus where Zacchaeus was both comfortable yet also vulnerable—in the house Zacchaeus occupied because of unjust tax collecting? Jesus did not treat Zacchaeus and other tax collectors as moral monsters beyond redemption. Instead, he included Matthew, a tax collector, among his first followers.

Reparation can be demanded from privileged people only by people willing to make the demand. However, we will not demand reparation so long as we think privileged people are moral monsters, incapable of realizing their wrongful conduct and making amends for it. Grumbling about privileged people will not present them with a moral and ethical demand for reparation. This does prevent criticizing people who hold on to white privilege. Nor does it prevent us from denouncing white-privileged people who refuse to support reparation demands.

We should criticize and denounce white-privileged people who pretend to be innocent or ignorant concerning racial inequities long suffered by Blacks and other people of color.

In Luke 15:1-2, we read that religious critics of Jesus "were grumbling" because Jesus socialized with "tax collectors and sinners..." (NRSV). In the parable involving the generous father who welcomed a wayward son, the elder brother grumbled and refused to join the feast and celebration the joyful father hosted for his returned son (Lk 15:25-30). And in Luke 19:7 we read that people "began to grumble and said, 'He has gone to be the guest of one who is a sinner'" as they saw Jesus go have dinner with Zacchaeus.

Are prophetic people guilty of "grumbling" about the notion that the same love and justice of God that upholds the demand that reparations be paid to descendants of formerly enslaved persons also commands us to obey the example of Jesus regarding white people who enjoy undeserved privilege and the fruit of generations of societally approved oppression?

Are we guilty of writing them off as moral monsters?

Are we the folks God must beg to rejoice when privileged people come to themselves and become agents of justice rather than hoarders of privilege?

Are we following the example of Jesus or of the "church folks" who grumbled about him socializing with "tax collectors and sinners"?

We do not have a transcript of what Jesus and Zacchaeus talked about when Zacchaeus hosted Jesus for dinner at his house. But judging from the pledge Zacchaeus made about giving half his wealth to the poor and restoring four times the value of anything he had obtained dishonestly, it is fair to surmise that Jesus didn't spend the day talking with Zacchaeus about sports. Jesus talked with Zacchaeus about justice, love, and the reason Zacchaeus was scorned and considered an outcast by the Palestinian community. Jesus talked with Zacchaeus about the "great chasm" that existed between his affluence and privilege and the oppression and suffering experienced by other Palestinian Jews.

Jesus went to dinner with Zacchaeus as a prophet, not to obtain a personal favor or advantage. From that moral and ethical vantage point, Jesus pressed Zacchaeus to "come to himself," to use the words in the parable of the gracious father (or prodigal son). And like the father in that parable who restored the wayward son, and the shepherd who found the lost sheep, and the widow who found the lost coin, Jesus pursued Zacchaeus in the spirit of seeking community.

But the grumbling "church folks" behaved like the pouting elder brother in the parable of the gracious father. They grumbled as Jesus dined with tax collectors like Matthew and Zacchaeus. They grumbled about Jesus. They grumbled about Zacchaeus. Their grumbling did not induce Zacchaeus to pledge to give half his wealth to the poor and restore four times what he had unjustly taken.

We do not know if people who are "lost" because of their idolatry to white supremacy and privilege will follow the example of Zacchaeus or not in any given instance. What Jesus teaches in these passages, however, is that we who live according to the love and justice of God have no excuse for treating them as if they are moral monsters and beyond redemption. They are children of God as we are. God wants them to be in right relationship with God, with people of color, and with themselves.

The "Son of Man" came to seek and to save those who are "lost" due to idolatry to white supremacy, racism, and white privilege. Followers of Jesus have no excuse for failing to follow his prophetic example. We have no excuse for behaving as if we cannot or should not behave towards white privileged people the way Jesus did with Zacchaeus. And we certainly have no reason to believe privileged people are going to behave as Zacchaeus did when we treat them as if they are moral monsters.

We should be encouraged by the biblical lessons about how God confronted Cain about murdering Abel, how God directed Moses to go to Egypt and lead the liberation of Hebrew immigrants from bondage, how the gracious father welcomed a wayward son in Luke 15, and how Jesus went out of his way to schedule a prophetic confrontation and dinner invitation with an oppressive Palestinian tax collector named Zacchaeus. Taken together, these lessons teach us that God works on behalf of oppressed people. God works to confront oppressors like Cain and Zacchaeus. God treats them as moral beings, not monsters. And with God, they are not beyond redemption, restoration, and reclamation.

With God, reparation is not only possible but also required. With God, the lost can be found. The wayward can return. And the wicked can be confronted.

God believes in reparation. Do we? God believes that prophetic people can make a reparatory difference by confronting privileged oppressors. Do we? God believes that suffering people can be reconciled with people like Zacchaeus when people like Zacchaeus engage in reparations. Do we believe? Do we believe God can do through us what God did through Jesus with Zacchaeus? Do we believe in God that much?

If so, we should follow the example of Jesus with Zacchaeus. We should make a prophetic demand for reparation to privileged people like Zacchaeus. Like Jesus, we should make reparations part of the conversation and then watch what God does with our faithfulness to the example of Jesus.

But if we don't believe in God that much, we should stop calling ourselves followers of the Jesus who deliberately stopped in Jericho, invited himself to dine with Zacchaeus, and stayed until Zacchaeus came to himself and resolved to make restitution for his wrongfully obtained and enjoyed wealth. If we are against reparations, then we are against Jesus and Zacchaeus no matter what we call ourselves.

Chapter 6

Grapes, Thorns, Figs, and Thistles

On the "Hateful Faithful"

Wendell Griffen

"You can't handle the truth!" People familiar with the 1992 motion picture *A Few Good Men* recall that angry retort shouted by Colonel Nathan Jessup (played by actor Jack Nicholson) in response to the "I want the truth!" cross-examination demand from Lieutenant Daniel Kaffee (played by Tom Cruise) during the movie's dramatic finale. Whether you can handle it or not, I'm going to share some hard truth. Buckle up.

In 2016, Donald John Trump was elected President of the United States as the candidate of the Republican Party after receiving overwhelming support from a voting bloc known as "conservative evangelical Christians." Although those voters have claimed for decades that they stand for "family values," they campaigned and voted for Trump knowing his serial marital history (three marriages) and abuse of women (misogyny). They did so weeks after Trump bragged that his maleness, wealth, and celebrity enabled and entitled him to sexually assault and verbally abuse women.

Some people have been astounded that Trump, whose adult history is characterized by open disdain for service to anyone or anything other than himself and who has shown no outward interest in faith and obedience to any religious belief, has been embraced by US voters who claim to be "conservative evangelical Christians." They may wonder why those voters supported Trump after he pardoned former Arizona sheriff Joe Arpaio, who was convicted of criminal contempt of court when he violated a court order to stop racially profiling Latinos.

Why didn't "conservative evangelical Christian" support for Trump drop after he called Haiti and nations in Africa "shithole countries"? (This widely reported racist slur was made during a January 2018 White House meeting with a bipartisan Congressional delegation meeting at the White House.)

Why didn't Trump's support decline from people who previously viewed Bill Clinton unfit to remain in office after Trump's personal attorney, Michael Cohen, revealed that Trump paid him to hide news of Trump's tryst with a former erotic film actress named Stormy Daniels? Why didn't their support fall after Trump's administration insulted people in Puerto Rico after Hurricane Maria in 2017?

Why did "evangelical Christian conservatives" continue supporting Trump after he publicly called white supremacists "nice people" when their Unite the Right event in Charlottesville, Virginia, led to the death of Heather Heyer? Why do people who claim to be "conservative evangelical Christians" and revere Jesus support Donald Trump when his administration separated thousands of children from their parents at the US southern border, failed to adequately track where refugee children had been taken, and refused the children decent housing, sanitation, and loving care? Why do 77 percent of white evangelical Protestants approve of Trump's job performance (according to a recent poll from the Public Religion Research Institute), including half who strongly approve?

The answer to these questions is as clear as it is unpleasant. Trump enjoys good standing with "conservative evangelical Christians" *because* his racism and white supremacy, patriarchy and sexism (including discrimination against women and girls, homophobia, and transphobia), fear and bigotry towards immigrants (xenophobia), and support for Zionist nationalism (regarding the Palestinian-Israeli conflict in the Middle East) fit their notion of "religious liberty" and American empire.

In 1948, South Carolina Governor Strom Thurmond and southern Democrats known as "Dixiecrats" bolted from the Democratic National Convention because they opposed policies of racial integration promoted by Hubert Humphrey of Minnesota and President Harry Truman (who issued an executive order to desegregate the US armed services). In 1954, the US Supreme Court outlawed racial segregation in public education in the landmark *Brown v. Board of Education* decision. White evangelical Protestants—"conservative evangelical Christians"— sided with Strom Thurmond and the segregationists against desegregation. In doing so, they followed the tradition of their predecessors who supported slavery, opposed Reconstruction-era policies to remedy the effects of slavery, and gave open support to the Ku Klux Klan and other domestic terrorist groups.

After 1964 (the year Congress enacted and President Lyndon Johnson signed the Civil Rights Act that officially outlawed racial segregation and reversed the 1896 US Supreme Court decision in *Plessy v. Ferguson*), white voters in the states of the former Confederacy who called themselves "evangelical Christian conservatives" began identifying in growing numbers with the Republican Party. Those voters objected to desegregation and increased participation by Black and other non-white voters in elections. They opposed efforts to shape public policy in more inclusive and equitable ways.

The presidential campaigns of Barry Goldwater (1964), Richard Nixon (1968 and 1972), Ronald Reagan (1980 and 1984), George H. W. Bush (1988), George W. Bush (2000 and 2004), and Donald Trump (2016) were built on overt and subtle appeals to the fears, prejudices, perceived grievances, and other views of "conservative evangelical Christians." Those predominantly white and Protestant voters in the US South and Midwest have become more politically active about whether women are entitled to decide to have abortions without governmental interference. They have opposed protecting voting rights of persons of color. They have objected to governmental regulation and protection of the air, soil, water, and communities from toxins. They oppose federal, state, and local regulation of firearms in the United States while blindly cheering US military interventions around the world. And white evangelical Christian conservatives have refused to recognize, let alone protect, the humanity and rights of people who are lesbian, gay, bisexual, transgender, queer, and intersex (LBGTQI) to marry, work, parent, and exercise other aspects of freedom without discrimination by the government.

It is a mistake to disregard or understate the role of white supremacy and white religious nationalism in Donald Trump's 2016 campaign. White supremacists and religious nationalists fumed, bristled, and schemed for eight years during the Barack Obama presidency. They were mortified when Obama, a Black man whose middle name was Hussein, defeated John McCain, a white decorated veteran of the Vietnam War, son and grandson of veterans, and recognized national security and defense hawk. They were shocked again when Obama's signature first-term initiative, access to affordable health care, became law thanks to the strong and shrewd legislative maneuvering of Nancy Pelosi, the first woman to serve as Speaker of the House of Representatives, a wife, mother, and grandmother who is a devout Catholic and proponent of reproductive freedom for women.

When Obama was able to nominate and secure confirmation of two pro-choice women on the Supreme Court (Justices Elena Kagan and Sonia Sotomayor, the latter of whom is also the first person of Latino ancestry to join the Court), the bastion of white supremacy, patriarchy, and religious nationalism suffered yet another shock. These things happened before the sudden death of Justice Antonin Scalia in February 2015.

Scalia was the Court's leading conservative. He led the fight to criticize the landmark decision in *Roe v. Wade* that recognized the right of women to choose whether to have abortions. Scalia also opposed efforts to protect LGBTQI persons from discrimination, opposed civil rights legislation to protect voting rights of groups historically discriminated against on account of color, and authored a Supreme Court decision that limited the power of state and local governments to regulate handguns. So "conservative evangelical Christians" smugly cheered when

Senator Mitch McConnell of Kentucky, the Senate Majority Leader, refused to allow the Senate to hold confirmation hearings and vote on whether to confirm Judge Merrick Garland, Obama's nominee to succeed Scalia.

The hard truth is that "conservative evangelical Christians"—whom I term "the Hateful Faithful"—are the dominant force behind Trump's xenophobic, racist, and otherwise questionable policies. The Hateful Faithful fiercely support Trump because they crave the power of his office to achieve their imperialistic and authoritarian aims. In that sense, Donald Trump's presidency fulfills dangers Cornel West identified in a book titled *Democracy Matters: Winning the Fight against Imperialism*.[1] Writing during the first term of President George W. Bush, West predicted our current situation:

> Just as demagogic and antidemocratic fundamentalisms have gained far too much prominence in both Israel and the Islamic world, so too has a fundamentalist strain of Christianity gained far too much power in our political system, and in the hearts of minds of citizens. This Christian fundamentalism is exercising an undue influence over our government policies, both in the Middle East crisis and in the domestic sphere, and is violating fundamental principles enshrined in the Constitution; it is also providing support and "cover" for the imperialist aims of empire. The three dogmas that are leading to the imperial devouring of democracy in America—free market fundamentalism, aggressive militarism, and escalating authoritarianism—are often justified by the religious rhetoric of this Christian fundamentalism. And perhaps most ironically—and sadly—this fundamentalism is subverting the most profound, seminal teachings of Christianity, those being that we should live with humility, love our neighbors, and do unto others as we would have them do unto us.... The battle for the soul of American democracy is, in large part, a battle for the soul of American Christianity, because the dominant forms of Christian fundamentalism are a threat to the tolerance and openness necessary for sustaining any democracy.
>
> ...The basic distinction between Constantinian Christianity and prophetic Christianity is crucial for the future of American democracy. America is undeniably a highly religious country, and the dominant religion by far is Christianity, and much of American Christianity is a form of Constantinian Christianity. In American Christendom, the fundamental battle between

democracy and empire is echoed in the struggle between this Constantinian Christianity and prophetic Christianity.[2]

As West correctly observed, "Constantinian Christianity has always been at odds with the prophetic legacy of Jesus Christ.... The corruption of a faith fundamentally based on tolerance and compassion by the strong arm of imperial authoritarianism invested Christianity with an insidious schizophrenia with which it has been battling ever since."

In the United States, the schizophrenia West identified allowed what he termed "strains of Constantinianism" to be "woven into the fabric of America's Christian identity from the start." And West added this observation:

> Most American Constantinian Christians are unaware of their imperialistic identity because they do not see the parallel between the Roman empire that put Jesus to death and the American empire they celebrate. As long as they can worship freely and pursue the American dream, they see the American government as a force for good and American imperialism as a desirable force for spreading that good. They proudly profess their allegiance to the flag and the cross not realizing that just as the cross was a bloody indictment of the Roman empire, it is a powerful critique of the American empire, and they fail to acknowledge that the cozy relation between their Christian leaders and imperial American rulers may mirror the intimate ties between the religious leaders and imperial Roman rulers who crucified their Savior.[3]

Although I heartily recommend *Democracy Matters* (and especially chapter 5, which is titled "The Crisis of Christian Identity in America") to anyone interested in a thorough analysis of people I call the "Hateful Faithful," I respectfully disagree with Cornel West on one issue. The elections of Ronald Reagan, George H. W. Bush, George W. Bush, and Donald Trump conclusively prove that American Constantinian Christians are quite aware of their imperialistic identity. After all, Trump's campaign slogan—"Make America Great Again"—is an explicit adoration of empire.

We need not quibble about whether Franklin Graham, Jerry Falwell Jr., Robert Jeffress, Mike Huckabee, and other nationally known Constantinian Christians "see the parallel between the Roman empire that put Jesus to death and the American empire they celebrate." That does not mean they are "unaware of their imperialistic identity." Instead, Constantinian Christians reject the prophetic identity of Jesus. As Cornel West observed, "Constantinian Christians fail to appreciate their violation of Christian love and justice because Constantinian Christianity in America places such a strong emphasis on personal conversion, individual piety, and philanthropic service and has lost its fervor for the suspicion of worldly authorities and for doing justice in the service of the most vulnerable among us, which are central to the faith."[4]

I contend that the Hateful Faithful are heretics because Constantinian Christianity is now (and has always been) heretical to the gospel of Jesus. At best, Hateful Faithful claims of allegiance to Jesus are ill conceived. At worst, their claims of allegiance to Jesus are fraudulent. Any claim that Jesus is the center of one's faith and living by people who condone bigotry against immigrants, racism, sexism, murder of political enemies, denial of access to healthcare services to people who are needy, and mistreatment of vulnerable persons is beyond unpersuasive. Such a claim of allegiance to Jesus amounts to moral and ethical nonsense.

So count me among the people who do not consider the Hateful Faithful to be followers of Jesus. I do not believe people who cheered the murder of Iranian General Qassim Suleimani are followers of Jesus because nothing in the teachings of Jesus supports murdering enemies. There is no "Blessed are the assassins" clause in the Beatitudes (see Matthew 5:1-12). I do not believe people who support policies that forcibly separate asylum-seeking parents from their children and that create and operate concentration camps where the children have been denied loving care, basic hygiene, and comfortable shelter are followers of Jesus because Jesus taught (at the end of Matthew 25) that how one treats immigrants shows whether one knows the Son of God.

The hard truth is that the hateful are faithful, but not to Jesus. Like Constantine, they have hijacked the gospel of Jesus and are fraudulently using Christian identity as a disguise for white supremacy, patriarchy, bigotry and discrimination, authoritarianism, greed, militarism, and lust for empire. Donald Trump is their Savior, not Jesus. That is why I agree with what Cornel West wrote in *Democracy Matters* near the end of his analysis about the crisis of Christian identity in America:

> To see the Gospel of Jesus Christ bastardized by imperial Christians and pulverized by Constantinian believers and then exploited by nihilistic elites of the American empire makes my blood boil.... I do not want to be numbered among those who sold their souls for a mess of pottage—who surrendered their democratic Christian identity for a comfortable place at the table of the American empire while, like Lazarus, the least of

> these cried out and I was too intoxicated with worldly power and might to hear, beckon, and heed their cries.[5]

I do not want to be numbered among the Hateful Faithful. Neither does Jesus, judging from what he declared near the end of the Sermon on the Mount:

> Beware of false prophets, who come to you in sheep's clothing but inwardly are ravenous wolves. You will know them by their fruits. Are grapes gathered from thorns or figs from thistles? In the same way, every good tree bears good fruit, but the bad tree bears bad fruit. A good tree cannot bear bad fruit, nor can a bad tree bear good fruit. Every tree that does not bear good fruit is cut down and thrown into the fire. Thus you will know them by their fruits. Not everyone who says to me, "Lord, Lord," will enter the kingdom of heaven, but only the one who does the will of my Father in heaven. On that day many will say to me, "Lord, Lord, did we not prophesy in your name, and cast out demons in your name, and do many deeds of power in your name?" Then I will declare to them, "I never knew you; go away from me, you evildoers." (Matthew 7:15-23, NRSV)

Chapter 7

Wolves, Shepherds, and Hirelings

On the Power of Combative Love (John 1:29-34; 10:1-5, 7-14)

Allan Aubrey Boesak

"In the Beginning Was the Word"

I must admit that I have not always understood that Prologue to the Gospel of John, and if I'm honest, I would have to say that in many ways, much of it still mystifies me. New Testament scholars have written whole books just on the Prologue to the Gospel of John. Still, this incredibly beautifully written first chapter, like the whole Gospel, is not so hard to understand if one thinks about it. So let's think about it together.

Unlike the apostle Paul, a learned man who in his letters to the churches was using the most sophisticated and difficult Greek, John wrote his Gospel in what is known as Koine Greek, the simplest form of Greek, the Greek of the common people—everyday street Greek, so to speak. If one reads the New Testament in its original Greek, that makes the Gospel of John the easiest book to read in the whole New Testament. John opens with those ethereal phrases, I think, because he cannot get over the mystery of what he is writing, the stunning beauty of it, the amazing truth of the things the Spirit is revealing to him.

> In the beginning was the Word, and the Word was with God, and the Word was God. He was in the beginning with God. All things came into being through him, and without him not one thing came into being. What has come into being in him was life, and the life was the light of all people. The light shines in the darkness, and the darkness did not overcome it. (John 1:1-5, NRSV)

We are all gripped by the beauty of these words and inspired by the lofty prose, but what does it mean, really?

In his mind, John's audience is not philosophers and teachers and doctors of law, the learned classes of his time—all men, by the way. It is the ordinary people, the ones excluded from learning in those times, the women, the slaves, the peasants, the working classes who, excluded from Roman society or reduced to non-persons, found refuge, respect, love, and dignity in the church. Despised and oppressed on earth, they are nonetheless uplifted by *this One*, this Word become flesh, and through him connected with God and the beginning of all things. That is immensely empowering. They are empowered to be different than what Roman society decided for them to be. Plunged into the darkness of imperial oppression, they have come to know the Light that shines in the darkness and is not overcome by it. Rome may have designated them for all forms of death, but the One they follow is life. This is not mere poetry. These are conscientizing, liberating words that provoke agency.

In an earlier publication, I tried to make sense of the issues presented to us in the first chapters of the Gospel of John.[1] Immediately following the Prologue, John gets down to business and deals with the undisguised enmity Jesus faces from the powers that be, Rome and the Jerusalem elites. Jesus hears disturbing rumours of animosity towards him from some Pharisees; they are angry that he is making and baptizing more disciples than John the Baptist (4:1-2). In chapter 1, the hostility towards John comes from "priests" and "Levites" representing the temple. The hostility toward Jesus, in chapter 4, comes from the Pharisees, part of the intellectual elite. The consolidation of the onslaught from the powerful and privileged political establishment in Jerusalem against this new movement has begun. For the moment, it is on two fronts, but after the Baptist's death, the focus will be on Jesus alone. Their concern, more like angry frustration, about Jesus' growing following is not because they are so protective of the Baptist and his ministry. "John, of course, had not *yet* been thrown into prison," the author reminds us (3:24, NRSV), though that is already the plan. They are concerned because they are perturbed that the prophetic work John had started seems to be taken over by Jesus and that Jesus' support amongst the "little people" is growing. To them, that is cause for great alarm.

Not only was John baptizing and "people kept coming" (3:23), but now Jesus was "making and baptizing more disciples" (4:1) than even John. Clearly, matters were getting out of hand. The fact that John goes to the trouble to explain that it was in fact not Jesus but his disciples who were baptizing people (4:2) shows that the powerful are in no mood for technicalities: the plan is in place, it is Jesus they want, and it is Jesus they will get, no matter what. Such a seemingly innocuous aside opens a world of malicious intent. The empire is at work and John is intent on exposing it. As was the case with the Canaanite woman in Matthew 15, Jesus withdraws from the conflict—the time for that final confrontation was not yet— leaves Judea, and returns to Galilee.

The confrontations with the established order take place very early in John's Gospel. They not only set the scene for what is coming but open the curtain on the nature of Jesus' ministry. In chapter 1 (vv. 26-34, NRSV), John the Baptist, in intense argument with the priests and Levites sent from Jerusalem, points to Jesus as the one chosen by God. It does not matter who I am, he says; what matters is who Jesus is. It is not about me or Elijah—that is all distraction. It is about another one. That one is "among you"; his presence is not hidden, and it will not be suppressed. He is "coming after me"; he will not only continue this work but will raise it to deeper intensity and greater heights, for "he ranks ahead of me." His authority, his power, will be greater than mine. I, even though I stir the hearts of the people and cause discomfort and anger in the hearts of the powerful, am "not worthy to untie the thong of his sandal." Whatever I do, what he will do will be greater, more radical, more powerful.

This is no less than the announcement of a revolution, and all of this will be seen so that Jesus "might be revealed to Israel" (John 1:31, NRSV). His purpose will be clear, unequivocal, and revolutionary, and the people will recognize it as such. They will see what God really has in mind for Israel, and it will not be what is on the agenda of the rich, the powerful, and the privileged. Whatever powers you think I have, John the Baptist insists, his will be greater, for he will be baptized by the Holy Spirit "descending from heaven like a dove," and "it remained on him," and he himself will baptize "with the Holy Spirit" (vv. 32-33). Twice John says, "I myself did not know him" (vv. 31, 33), but be assured that he who is among you already will be known by all—the great and the small, the rich and the poor, the oppressed and their oppressors, for "this is the Son of God" (v. 34). And because this is of God, and Jesus is the Son of God, there is no power on earth that can buy him, deny him, or defy him. What happens here is quite remarkable: in 1:29-35, John the author allows John the Baptist to bring the lofty words of John 1:1-18 down to earth so that ordinary folk, those whose "flesh" Jesus had taken on, can understand. This is what it means when "the Word becomes flesh." John the Baptist "breaks it down" and "makes it real." This is the declaration of the revolutionary, combative love Jesus brings and to which John testifies.

So even if John begins in almost heavenly language, he hopes the whole church will understand: this is not just poetry meant to soothe the mind and make the church feel good. It is combative love to stir the soul, to straighten the knees, to move the feet. Love for God, love for justice, love for the people. That is a different kind of power.

Secondly, though, John helps us by connecting the heavenly with the earthly, the divine with the human, the mystical with reality. So in John 1:6 he says, "There was a man sent from God, whose name was John" (NRSV). *Now* we understand. John will also introduce us to the man Jesus, a man of flesh and blood, from occupied Galilee in occupied Palestine. This is not heaven; this is earth, the wilderness. This is not philosophical musing; this is harsh reality. John the evangelist introduces Jesus through John the Baptist. The man from heaven clothed in the language of divine robes is introduced to us by the man wearing clothes made from camel hair. The heavenly language of John the evangelist must always be translated into the fiery language of John the Baptist. Standing in awe of the mystery, we embrace the prophetic. Our souls tremble before God, so our knees do not tremble before the powers of this world.

In this way, the lofty words about Jesus, "The Word became flesh" (v. 14) are connected to the words, "There was a man sent from God, whose name was John" (v. 6). "The Word" came from God, but John the Baptist was also "sent from God." The prophet of God is connected to the Son of God. Unlike Luke in his Gospel, John does not connect Jesus to John because they were family, cousins. Family connection is not a validation here. John makes the connection because they were both "sent from God." For that reason, prophets of God in our world, in these times, should not be concerned about familial connections or heritage or lineage. Our connection is with the truth that we, like Jesus and John the Baptist, are all sent from God. That is our validation. That is our authority. That is also our vindication.

"We Have Found the Messiah!"

There is another striking thing about these first chapters of John's Gospel, and it all centres on the words "testimony" and "testify." First, John testifies about himself, and he does it without obfuscation or evasion. He is not to be intimidated by the hostile interrogations of the Jerusalem elites. "I am the voice of one crying out in the wilderness," he says (John 1:23, NRSV). In other words, I am the prophet sent from God. I am the one in the wilderness where my people have been banished and are suffering abuse, neglect, and impoverishment. Oppression, exploitation, humiliation, exclusion from meaningful life—that is the wilderness! But I am also the one who is called to tell our people that it is time to stop the moaning, the groaning, and the self-victimising; it is time to get to work, to restore, to reclaim: "Make straight the way of the Lord!" (v. 23). "Every tree that is not planted by my Father shall be rooted up!" (Matt 15:13). The time for prophetic engagement has come.

Then John testifies about Jesus, "the one greater than I." This greater one is the Lamb of God who will take away the sins of the world (v. 29)—Jesus, the one on whom the Spirit of God descended and on whom the Spirit remains (v. 32). What John has in mind is what we read in Luke 4:16-18. But perhaps John also has in mind what seems to have always been on his mind, especially through those difficult days when his ministry was threatened because some people hated so much what he was saying, when his very life was forfeit because they feared him so much. On his mind in those dark days, full of fear and wracked with doubt, would be the question he finally poses to Jesus: "Are you the one who is to come, or shall we look for another?" (Matt 11:3, ESV).

In those days, not the days of Herod Archelaus sitting on the throne but the days of John the Baptist in the prison cell he would not leave alive, Jesus, the one sent from God, would say to the one sent from God, "Go and tell John what you hear and see: the blind receive their sight, the lame walk, those with a skin disease are cleansed, the deaf hear, the dead are raised, and the poor have good news brought to them. And blessed is anyone who takes no offense at me" (Matt 11:4-6, NRSV). I say "*not* the days of Herod Archelaus but the days of John the Baptist" because here Jesus declares that the movement of history is ultimately not determined by the power of the powerful but by the power of the powerless. What John heard was this: Herod may be able to take your life, but it is not in his power to stop the work of God in the world. The days of Herod will come to an end, but the reign of God is not only unstoppable; it will have no end.

John's testimony is followed by the testimony of the newly recruited disciples, Andrew, Simon Peter, Philip, and Nathanael: "We have found the Messiah!" (see John 1:41, 45). Everyone testifies about Jesus except Jesus himself. The first time Jesus testifies about himself is in John 4, in his amazing conversation with the Samaritan woman at the well, our sister from Sychar. It is a conversation about traditions, theology, and politics—a conversation that makes clear in how much esteem Jesus held women in general and the woman at the well in particular. The first time in John's Gospel when Jesus acknowledges that he is indeed the Messiah, the anointed one of God, is to a woman. That conversation of equals is yet another demonstration of radical inclusion that brings sustained hope and healing, first to women but then to all of us.[2]

But here is the thing. Jesus does testify about himself, but not in words. His testimony about himself, how he sees himself, how he sees his ministry, and how he understands his calling by God and his mission set by God as he is sent from God *is all in what he does*. Let others say about me what they will, he says; I will show them who I am by what I do. So instead of letting Jesus speak to testify about himself, John tells us about the wedding in Cana, where Jesus turns water into wine (John 2:1-11).

This wedding is in Cana, in Galilee, the land of the poor, the oppressed, and the occupied. The guests are village people from a peasant community where everyone knows everyone. This is not a "by invitation only" affair. Everyone comes, invited or not. This RSVP thing is not for us. The "everyone" mentioned in John 3:16 comes down to earth, narrowed down to "everyone" in the village. The inclusivity is taken for granted. Unlike the feasts of the rich where the food is always plentiful and the wine always flows, at this wedding, in a community where a wedding is a village affair and one cannot cater for everyone who comes to celebrate, the wine runs out. There is no cellar with enough reserves for the overflow of guests. Jesus turns water into wine, and the point, in my view, is not only the miracle (the Gospel hardly spends time on the miracle itself), even though this is a sign of Jesus' "glory" (John 2:11, NRSV).

More to the point is his presence at the feast of the poor, sharing with them his gifts and his power and his blessings. Running out of wine, which is essential to the joy of the festivities, is a disaster, and the groom and bride's honour is at stake. *Them*, he will not disappoint. For *them*, he will turn water into wine so the feast can go on. Why should a lack of resources spoil their celebration of this very special day? Why should an uninterrupted, joyful, plentiful feast be the exclusive privilege of the rich? At the much-publicized weddings of the wealthy, the famous, and the glamorous, there is never a problem of running out of wine or food or worldwide attention. So the turning of water into wine is once again, like the multiplication of bread for the multitudes as we have seen in the other Gospels, a sign of the abundance of God's reign and a scathing critique of the skewed socio-economic realities that are reflected even on this level. This Messiah, whom Simon and Andrew had found, was to be like none other. In God's economy, there is always abundance.

This is followed by the "cleansing of the temple" with an outraged Jesus "making" the whip himself, driving all the animals out, then turning to the people doing business there and "pouring out," scattering, the money of the money changers onto the floor before overturning their tables (John 2:13-22, NRSV). This is not, as some scholars argue, "a temper tantrum" Jesus throws. It is a revolutionary act of resistance, showing God's outrage at the fact that God's house of prayer and worship should be turned into a "den of thieves" (v. 13, NLT). This is the text Steve Biko turns to when he speaks of Jesus as "a fighting God."[3] This early, John establishes Jesus' solidarity with the poor and downtrodden; this early, he reveals the revolutionary nature of Jesus' mission.

After the extraordinary and life-changing conversation with the sister from Sychar, Jesus' testimony about himself is all actions: the healing of the official's son; the healing on the Sabbath, and the feeding of the five thousand, all showing God's overturning of an economy of scarcity for the poor amidst the abundance of the rich. Finally, just before we get to our text in John 10, Jesus heals the man born blind. Jesus embodies the holiness of God in the streets with the poor, the blind, the hungry. He brings healing by offering them the power to see, to fill their hunger, to rise up and walk, to have meaningful life, to have hope again.

This is how we should understand those beloved words, "For God so loved the world…" (John 3:16). It is combatant, revolutionary love that turns the world upside down.

"Here Is the Lamb of God…"

We should, however, also understand them in yet another way: "Here is the Lamb of God who takes away the sin of the world." John the Baptist says this twice, on two separate occasions (John 1:29, 36). For years, following traditional exegesis, I took this in a "spiritual" sense and preached it as if it were a "revival" text. I now think the Baptist refers to "the world" John spoke of in 3:16. You, John is saying, you religious elites with your power of naming and framing and shaming, have declared the world—outside of your borders of sanctity, control, and manipulation—unholy, defiled, filled with sinners. Those you have designated "sinners" are the poor and the downtrodden; the oppressed and the weak; the sick, the lame, and the blind; the ones made landless, voiceless, and hopeless through your greed and exploitation. You created a world filled with those you detest and look down on: tax collectors, prostitutes, fatherless and abandoned children, marginalized women without patriarchal protection, married women useful for childbearing and for serving men but unworthy of dignity and respect. The world of Galileans, who "lived in darkness" and from whom could come nothing good, and Samaritans, "bleeders from birth" whom you despise; the world of deplorables and expendables.[4]

"The world" is Jesus' world of the poor and the oppressed people in occupied Galilee and occupied Palestine. It is the world of unspeakable violence, unceasing humiliations, never-ending enslavement. It is the world of Roman imperial rule and dominion, of the most brutal suppression of any sign of revolt and resistance, of unchecked, unbridled abuse of power. It is the world where the leaders of the people in Jerusalem, instead of standing up for the people, have made deals with the Roman occupier for their own benefit, amassing huge wealth, protecting their own privileges. It is a world where the rich are getting richer by the day, and the poor are worth less than a pair of sandals.

It is *that* world "this one" is coming to save, for he understands the heart of God (John 3:16), and he is "the Lamb of God." He will "take away" that which you have declared their "sin," making the victims of your exclusivist lust for power and control responsible for the plight you have caused, for their stigmatization and their pain, for the guilt they feel because they do not meet your criteria for acceptability. This Jesus, Lamb of God, will be the saviour of "whosoever" believes in him. The radical inclusivity of God's embrace reflects the radical inclusivity of God's radical liberation. That is hope fulfilled and healing sustained. That is love revolutionised.

And just to be clear: the hope I am speaking of is not the sentimental, head-in-the-clouds optimism politicians are so eager to talk about and many of us are so eager to believe. That is not hope. It is a sentimentalising, paralysing blindness to the realities of the world that keeps us from raising either our voices in anger or our fists in struggle. I embrace rather the African Church Father Augustine's understanding of hope. Hope, Augustine says, is a mother with two beautiful daughters. The one is named Anger and the other Courage—anger about what is happening around us, at what is being done to us and especially to others who are weaker and more vulnerable than ourselves, and the courage to rise up, stand in the breach, and do something about it. That is the hope that activates and empowers. That is the hope that sustains us because it brings healing.

Our world today is not so much different from Jesus' world. German theologian Helmut Gollwitzer speaks of the world in the times of Nazi Germany as a world "in deadly convulsions."[5] It is a hostile world, a world in the grip of evil, quite specifically the world of Adolf Hitler, of the Nazis, of challenge and risk of persecution, of the ultimate limits of betrayal, horror, and death.

Our world today reflects that world, and it is, as the Accra Confession of the World Communion of Reformed Churches states, a "scandalous world," a world "fallen among thieves." But here's the thing: this world is only "scandalous" if seen through the eyes of those who suffer. For the fearmongers and warmongers, for those who profiteer from every kind of human misery—from war to pandemics to floods and droughts and tornadoes—for the billionaires whose fortunes grew by $10.3 trillion through their manipulation of COVID-19 over just the first year, it is a wonderful world.

It's a wonderful world for those who at this very moment, with one eye on the television following the war and the other on their bank accounts, rejoice in the war in Ukraine because they make billions from selling the weapons that kill millions, those who wish that the war would go on and on. Those who profit from a war in Ukraine that should never have happened, that could have been stopped before it began if politicians were not so corrupt, egotistic, and greedy, if these leaders would only keep their promises of peace and have the courage to talk rather than gloat in their pathetic *machismo*—for those people it's a wonderful world right now. That is why we are called, said Dietrich Bonhoeffer, to look at reality and history from below—through the eyes of the victims of violence and greed, of exploitation and exclusion. If we do that, we are looking through the eyes of Jesus.

This world—with its hostility; its vast and deadly inequalities; its predilections for injustice, domination, and exploitation; its hunger for power for power's own sake; its calculated, carefully cultivated cynicism that is the first and last line of defence against those who fight for justice and the humanisation of the world—seems to have conquered the minds of most. It is in this world that people of faith are called to give witness. The witness I am speaking of is "witness" in its original sense, *marturia*, that is, to stand up and stand for what is truthful and right; to stand in the breach for the weak, the vulnerable, the marginalised, and the excluded. To stand where God stands, with the poor, the oppressed, and the wronged, and to be ready to suffer for what is just, and decent, and humanizing.

We are not called to hide from the world. We are called to witness to the world. We are not called live with our eyes closed or turned heavenward; to act as if the world, with all its ugliness and pain and unnecessary death, does not exist. Faith is not opium. Jesus is not a holy high that provides eternal bliss. When we say Jesus, we say justice; when we say justice, we say Jesus; and the more we say justice, the more we have to say Jesus, because without his love, grace, and mercy we will not have the strength to fight for the justice the Lord demands.

Jesus came, John the Baptist testifies of him, to "take away the sins of *the world*." Jesus came not to conceal, to hide, or to cover up but to reveal, to expose, to take away the sins of the world. What sins? The sin of acting as if God is not a God of indivisible, radical love; indivisible, radical justice; indivisible, radical solidarity; indivisible, radical inclusivity. The sin of not wanting to believe that love and compassion and justice will save you but that your wealth and power and status will. Those sins! The sin of believing that violence is redemptive and is the first and last thing we should turn to when confronted with problems. The sin of believing that the only business of the church is the saving of souls and that it in no way has anything to do with saving the world. Those sins! The sin of believing that self interest can replace self-sacrifice; that neutrality can replace solidarity; that we can love God without loving our neighbour; and that sentimentalism and sycophancy are substitutes for love and justice. Those sins! That is why we do not live with our heads in the clouds.

Jesus came into this world and was not content with the state of the world and of God's people. He came not to placate the powerful or pacify the powerless. He came to revolutionize the world, and that is why we, his followers, are not content to live in an unjust world, not content with oppression and exclusion and exploitation. Jesus came to revolutionize the world and to teach us that while we are keeping our feet firmly planted on the earth, our minds are on "the things above" (Col 3:2, NASB), the things that make for peace. That is why, writes Dietrich Bonhoeffer, we will be "all the more stubborn and purposeful in protesting here on earth."⁶ "Stubborn"—we are not giving up, no matter how hard the struggle, no matter how cynical or vicious the response. Our protest is "purposeful"—it is not a form of begging.

Jesus does not testify much about himself in those first chapters of John's Gospel. He does, however, have some things to say about John the Baptist. It is because John the Baptist was not afraid to bear witness to God's love, justice, mercy, and judgement that Jesus spoke so highly of him. John the Baptist, Jesus testifies, was "a burning and shining lamp, and you were willing to rejoice for a while in his light" (John 5:35, NRSV). That is a powerful testimony to the truthfulness, faithfulness, and boldness of a prophet of God. And it comes from the mouth of Jesus. But it raises questions: Can Jesus say that about us? Or is it only that we are happy to "shine for a while in the light" of other prophets, religious or secular, whom we think are more faithful, more truthful, more courageous than we are? Does "for a while" mean only until it becomes too uncomfortable, too risky, too sacrificial?

"I Am the Good Shepherd"

Jesus came to save the world because he is the good shepherd. Ten or twenty years ago, this world was scandalous enough. Now, in 2022, it has become infinitely worse. What we have come to call "global apartheid" has tightened its grip on our world in general and around the throats of the poor and vulnerable in particular. By 2018, the world's 2,153 billionaires had more wealth than the 4.6 billion people who make up 60 percent of the world's population, says the Oxfam 2020 Report, "Dignity Not Destitution."⁷ Global inequality is not just growing; it is "shockingly entrenched" and "out of control."

That is why followers of this Jesus do not live with our heads in the clouds. We walk this earth with eyes wide open, and we see, understand, interpret, and judge this world through the eyes of those who suffer. Then, and only then, do we give witness. Through those eyes, this world is scandalous not just because it is, in traditional Reformed formulation, "fallen." It is scandalous because it has fallen "among thieves." The poor and the oppressed know that this scandalous world did not just happen. The world God created has been invaded, overtaken—stolen. The oppressed peoples of this world, the destitute and the excluded, the despised and left behind, the have-nots and the never-will-haves know the reality of evil and the power of evil human agency. They know, as Jesus knew, those who "come only to steal and kill and destroy" (Jn 10:10, NRSV). They know Jesus is not dramatic, cleverly using hyperbole to catch attention. They have seen those thieves come from their faraway lands. They know what it means to be invaded, set upon, and enslaved. To have their lands, their bodies, their children stolen, all of them sold on auction blocks. Their dignity, stories, hopes, aspirations, dreams, and future—*stolen*! They saw their cultures destroyed, their religions denigrated and cast aside; they saw genocide and massacres and ethnic cleansing, and they buried their loved ones in graves dug in land no longer theirs. They know Jesus spoke not one word of a lie. Jesus knew the truth because he saw the truth through the eyes of those who suffer, those still being robbed, still being killed, and still being destroyed as we speak. The theft is of a grandiosity that continues to stun the mind.

Our people are in deep need of healing. We have been deeply traumatised by the ravages of imperialism, colonialism, and apartheid. We have been overrun, genocided, massacred, and scattered across barren lands, away from the lands our ancestors called home. Fifty years ago, our people had no love or respect for the apartheid regime. We were traumatised by their oppression, their exploitation, their callousness, and their hatred. Black people felt, wrote Steve Biko, like "stepchildren of a God whose presence they cannot feel."[8] We were robbed of our humanity and our dignity. We were ruled by wolves who robbed and killed and destroyed. We were enslaved under the brutal rule of a pharaoh whose racist arrogance knew no bounds. We were traumatised. Now, fifty years later, we find ourselves facing yet another pharaoh, but this time a pharaoh who looks like us. That is a trauma of a different kind.

Fifty years ago, we were robbed by the people who came here to steal our land, destroy our communities, erase our religions, kill the dreams of our children and the hopes of our elders. But we did not invite them—they invaded us. We did not vote for them—they ruled without our consent. We did not love them or trust them because they were power-hungry racists, acquisitive, greedy white supremacists who cared not a whit for our people or our humanity. They were our rulers, not our leaders.

Fifty years later, we are ruled by leaders we have elected because we loved them. But this is what Dr. Barney Pityana has to say of them: "We have become an aggressively filthy, selfish, individualistic and greedy society that cares only for itself and its own."[9] Their corruption screams to the heavens. They steal not only from every single state entity, the treasure that belongs to the people—over R100 billion from Eskom alone, we have heard—but also from Sassa, the agency responsible for paying out the pensions of our elderly and the grants meant for our babies. It is a trauma of a different kind.

Gender-based violence was a pandemic long before the COVID pandemic. South African men raped seventy-year-old grandmothers as easily as two-year-old babies. Unemployment has never been so high, and youth unemployment is at 50 percent levels for urban areas and over 70 percent levels in rural areas. Our people are suffering from undeserved generational impoverishment, while whites enjoy—undeserved—generational wealth built on the backs of disempowered, disenfranchised indigenous people. This while the systems of corruption create new millionaires every second week, and the president brags about buying a buffalo for R19 million. It's a trauma of a different kind.

In 1960, we had the Sharpeville massacre. In 2012, we saw the Marikana massacre. The bodies on the ground and at the foot of those hillocks were still Black, but this time, the orders to shoot to kill came from those we had elected and trusted. The hands that held the guns that shot the bullets were Black hands. The political cover-up was thought out in Black minds, in the minds of those we thought loved us. It is a trauma of a different kind.

Our people are wounded. We have been ravaged by wolves who have come to steal, kill, and destroy. We have been scattered into places where there is no possibility of life. We have been deceived and misled by hirelings who pretended to be shepherds but either got bribed by the wolves to sell us out to be devoured or ran away, abandoning us to the ravages of exploitative and destructive systems, betraying the trust we have put in them. We are in deep need of healing, as we are in need of a revolutionized society. And that is why we are reading the story of the Good Shepherd.

Wolves and Hirelings

Jesus talks like this because, far better than our theologians and preachers with their otherworldly theology but this-worldly agendas, Jesus knew what oppression in this world is and what liberation from oppression in this world means.

The Gospel of John speaks of the followers of Jesus as "sheep" in the same way the prophet Ezekiel does. In contrast to some biblical scholars who reject the term, it is not a humiliating, disempowering term, the expression of a petty, jealous God who intends to keep us small, hopelessly dependent, and bereft of all agency and intelligent initiative. It is not the contemptuous way some politicians or the always all-wise pundits sometimes speak of the voting public, calling them "sheep" who cannot think for themselves and can be propagandized into voting against their own, best self-interests, so awed by power they dare not utter a word of protest.

In the Bible, from Ezekiel 34 to John 10, "the sheep of God's pasture" is an expression of justice-seeking, protective, engaging, empowering, and combatant love for those on whose behalf God intervenes because their lives are precious in God's sight. In Ezekiel, God swears that Godself will "seek out" and "rescue" them out of the hands of those who have "scattered" them and robbed them of sustenance, denied them existence. This is a God outraged by injustice, selfishness, and greed. The words, "Ah, you shepherds of Israel…!" (Ezek 34:2, NRSV) are not an expression of grief only. It is grief riddled with disgust. They are an expression of divine anger, of outraged love. What follows those words is a devastating indictment filling full ten verses, culminating in the utterly fearsome judgement, "Thus says the Lord GOD, I am against the shepherds" (v. 10). Over against the rage stands the love.

Yahweh is keeping the two firmly together because God's outrage at injustice is always inseparable from God's love for justice: "I will rescue…I will feed them…I will bring them out…I will seek out the lost…I will make them lie down…I will bind up the injured…I will strengthen the weak" (Ezek 34:11-16, NRSV). But because this love is not sentimental nothingness, kowtowing to earthly powers, bending the knee to inflated egos, or endorsing pietistic sophistries, Yahweh shall not only feed them with "rich pasture" (v. 14), taking care of the body. Yahweh promises, "I shall feed them *with justice*" (v. 16), taking care of the politics. Because this love is a combatant love, Yahweh vows, "I shall judge between sheep and sheep" (v. 17). And because this love is a revolutionary love that changes everything, Yahweh declares, "I myself shall be the shepherd of my sheep" (v. 15).

This is what is playing in Jesus' mind when he speaks of sheep and when he says, "I am the good shepherd…. And I lay down my life for the sheep" (John 10:14-15, NRSV). Then there are the thieves (wolves) who come to steal and kill and destroy (v. 10). Jesus also talks about the false shepherds, the "hired hands," he calls them (vv. 12-13). Those who are called to be shepherds but run away when the wolves come because they are afraid, or they have been bribed, or they long for position and power; they crave those privileges they believe only the wolf can give them as reward for their obeisance.

The Bible calls the leaders of the people shepherds of the flock. Of the false shepherds, and the hired hands who become their accomplices, God says in Ezekiel 34:

> You eat the fat; you clothe yourselves with the wool; you slaughter the fatted calves, but you do not feed the sheep. You have not strengthened the weak; you have not healed the sick; you have not bound up the injured; you have not brought back the strays; you have not sought the lost, but with force and harshness you have ruled them. So they were scattered because there was no shepherd, and scattered they became food for all the wild animals. …therefore, you shepherds, hear the word of the LORD: Thus says the Lord GOD: I am against the shepherds; and I will demand my sheep at their hand, and put a stop to their feeding the sheep;

no longer shall the shepherds feed themselves. I will rescue my
sheep from their mouths, so that they may not be food for them.
(Ezek 34:3-5, 9-10, NRSV)

This is a parable for wolves who come to steal, kill, and destroy, for wolves in sheep's clothing, and for hirelings with one eye on the hills and the other on the money.

But our text is so powerful and empowering because it not only names those who "come to steal and kill and destroy" (John 10:10, NRSV). It also uplifts the One who came "that they may have life." The poor and oppressed know that this is not some accidental, poetic juxtaposition. Jesus is the very opposite of the thieves and killers. *They* come to steal, destroy, and kill. Jesus comes to give abundant life. Jesus speaks, and stands, *in opposition* to the destroyers of life. Here speaks the incarnation of God on earth, amongst God's people: the incarnation of God's justice, of God's revolt against evil and injustice, against destruction and death. Jesus' speech is enacted revolt. He is in rebellion against those who steal dignity and life. Jesus rebels against those who have come to steal the glory of God to claim for themselves in their idolatries of supremacy and power.

They come, Jesus knows, and as John Calvin has correctly perceived, not only to rob the poor and oppressed but also to rob God of God's rights. God has rights, writes Calvin.[10] I think he means God's right to be the God of justice, liberation, and peace. God's right to be the God of the poor, the protector of the widow, the orphan and the stranger, the defender of the defenceless. God's right to keep in God's care the dignity of those created in God's image. In standing up and standing in for the despised, the wretched of the earth, Jesus is standing up for God.

Jesus is neither a stranger nor a hireling. His sheep are his own. The thieves know that Jesus is the one standing between them and their prey. His sheep know his voice and feel protected and comforted. Jesus is not the hired hand who flees when danger comes. Jesus is the gate the thieves must break down to get to the people. Jesus is the Good Shepherd the empire must kill first in order to get to the flock. And the empire does kill him, but he "takes up his life again" (see John 10:17) because he is Lord. His resurrection is God's rebellion against the powers that steal, kill, and destroy.

Jesus is the Good Shepherd. So the texts says repeatedly. In John 10:27 and 28, Jesus says, "My sheep hear my voice. I know them, and they follow me." Notice how the intimacy grows. "I give them eternal life, and they will never perish." This is followed by the assurance of protection by a powerful, compassionate, and loving hand: "No one will snatch them out of my hand." Combative love.

Combative, Revolutionary Love

Notice also how the love moves to take centre stage. Jesus has laid down his life for the sheep, but he has indeed "taken it up again" (see John 10:17). And it is this Good Shepherd, the risen Lord, who now, at the end of John's Gospel, appears to the disciples on the shores of the Sea of Galilee where he speaks to Peter. Some say this portion is an added piece, that John's Gospel actually has its natural ending at 20:31. But for some reason John, perhaps later, or someone else even later, thought chapter 21 was important enough to add.

And I can understand why. Some say it is because the Western church was already moving in the direction our Roman Catholic siblings find so important: the primary position of the pope. I think, though, we should consider some other reasons as well. First, this "added piece" begins with the reminder of the abundance that Jesus always brings. The disciples, discouraged after trying all night and having caught no fish, let the nets down upon Jesus' word (John 21:3-6). The number of fish they catch is so large the boat almost sinks. John's Gospel begins with the abundance of wine at a peasant village wedding feast. It ends with the abundance at a resurrection feast. The abundant life Jesus brings is unstoppable.

Second, the emphasis is not only on Peter (see John 21:15-19). Just two verses on, after the conversation with Peter, there is another conversation with "the disciple whom Jesus loved" (v. 20, NRSV). Jesus speaks of abundant life to him as well. That is not a discussion on eschatology. That is an immediately present love in this life and the next.

I want to plead for some room to consider yet a third point. Jesus engages Peter so personally and insistently because Jesus knows that Peter, despite his overconfidence, does not truly understand what it means to follow Jesus. His stubborn and at times almost aggressive misunderstanding of Jesus' mission, life, and death, as the Gospels tell us, and his hesitant embrace of the radical inclusivity of Jesus' ministry, as Luke tells us in Acts, are perhaps signs of this. A sign is perhaps also what we are told in the extra-canonical Gospel of Philip. Peter could not stand the fact that Jesus apparently was so close to Mary Magdalene and that she, a woman, understood the mind of Jesus better than he did. There, his words speak volumes: "Is it possible that the Lord spoke of secrets with a woman, of which we [men] knew nothing?" In the Gospel of Thomas, Peter is said to be emphatic in his proposal that Mary Magdalene should be excluded from the circle of disciples. Perhaps Jesus understood how much Peter still had to learn.

Again, the emphasis is not on Peter. It is about love. And again, Jesus' love is not an empty, sentimental love that justifies wrongdoing, covers up the lie, and consequently, as Paul would teach us, cannot possibly rejoice in the truth. This is the love of the Good Shepherd. It is combative, revolutionary, revolutionizing love. That is why the love spoken of here in John 21 should not ever be dislodged from the context of the Good Shepherd, the robbers, killers, and destroyers, the wolves and the hirelings of John 10.

This is the love that stands in for the despised, the denigrated, and the excluded and stands up against the powerful and the doers, justifiers, and profiteers of evil, the love that makes us choose for the wounded Other, even if it means risking all we have. That is the love Jesus offers, the love that assures us, even in dire circumstances, that "no one will snatch them from my hand" (John 10:28, NRSV). So when Steve Biko says that Black Theology sees Jesus as "a fighting God," he is absolutely right.

And Jesus not only speaks to Peter. Jesus tells the other, unnamed disciple that he shall live "until I come" (John 21:23, NRSV). That is the abundance of life Jesus talked about earlier. Still John is not finished. The abundance of Jesus' love, his always-present presence, the indestructible memory of him, his ever-flowing grace and mercy, and his justice-affirming power are so overwhelming that all the books in the world cannot contain it (see v. 25).

No, it is not about the supremacy or power of the pope; it is about the supremacy and power of love. The love that cares, the love that has compassion, the love that hates injustice, the love that fights for justice, the loves that rescues, saves, redeems. It is not about position or status or privilege; it is about caring and compassion. It is what makes us holy, what sets us apart from the wolves; it is what sets us apart from the hired hands.

The Place of Anointing

In John 10:40, the writer tells us a crucial thing. Jesus, John writes, "went away again across the Jordan" (NRSV). To where? "To the place where John had been baptizing earlier." It could very well read, "To the place where John had baptized him." John adds, "and he remained there."

Jesus went back to where he was set apart, where he first received the call, where the heavens opened, no, were "torn apart," Mark insists (Mark 1:10, NRSV), for his anointing. Jesus went back and remained there, to feel the water again, to see the Spirit like a dove again, to see the heavens open and to hear that Voice again: "You are my Son, the Beloved" (Mark 1:11). He needed that for the task that lay ahead. He would need that as he worked and ministered and healed. As he stood up for the poor and the oppressed against the powers in Rome. When they called him Satan and Beelzebul. When they hunted him and hounded him so that he had no place to lay down his head. When they accused him falsely, arrested him, mocked him, flogged him, and dragged him before the high priest and the governor. As those he loved most deserted him, betrayed him, sold him for thirty pieces of silver. As they placed the cross upon him, let him carry it up that hill. And Jesus would need God's reminder again as they nailed him to the cross and kept him there until he would shout out loud, "My God, my God why hast thou forsaken me?" (Matt 27:46, KJV).

Jesus went back to the place of his anointing, so that being broken and wounded and forsaken, he could heal the broken and wounded and forsaken. Jesus went there not only to remain for a while but more so that *what he first found there could remain with him*!

So in a very special way, this parable becomes one for those who are not wolves or hirelings: if you feel tired, that the road is too long and the mountain too steep, if it all becomes too much—go back to the place of your anointing!

When you are in the storm and there is no hiding place—go back to the place of your anointing!

When your own heart is too broken to heal the broken heart of another and yet you must because you are a pastor—go back to the place of your anointing!

When you are in need of prayer but your words are stuck to the roof of your mouth or feel like sand between your teeth—go back to the place of your anointing!

When those you depend on desert you; when those you trust betray you; when those you love turn their backs on you, when they make you feel like a motherless child—go back to the place of your anointing!

Go to that river. Go stand in that water again. Feel the wings of the Holy Spirit dove against your face again; see the heavens open again, hear that voice again: "This is my Beloved Child, in whom I am much pleased."

Let that remain with you.

Chapter 8

Shiphrah, Puah, Rahab, and the Magi

On Epiphany, Empire, and Prophetic Resistance

Wendell Griffen

Followers of Jesus observe the Epiphany of Our Lord each year on January 6, twelve days after Christmas Day. It symbolizes the visit of the Gentile magi to the boy Jesus in Bethlehem. And the Epiphany teaches how devotion to Jesus caused the magi to disregard instructions from King Herod to return to Jerusalem and inform Herod where they had found Jesus.

One seldom hears or reads sermons that address the relationship between devotion to the incarnate presence of God and disobedience to the calls of empire. That is odd. Throughout the Bible, there are accounts of people engaging in civil disobedience against imperial edicts because of their devotion to God.

Consider the account about the Hebrew midwives named Shiphrah and Puah that is chronicled in Exodus 1. In that passage, the ruler of an unjust empire tries to recruit the midwives who attend pregnant Hebrew women in a wicked scheme of population control. The Egyptians are concerned that the birth rate among the immigrant Hebrew population will eventually cause Egyptians to become a minority. Based on fear that the growing Hebrew population is a national security threat, the Egyptian ruler orders the midwives to kill newborn male Hebrew babies so a racist society can continue its oppressive ways.

According to the Exodus narrative, the midwives disobeyed the imperial command because they revered God. They did not openly declare that they would defy the genocidal order. Instead, they falsely asserted that the infants were already born before they could kill them during the delivery process. Their subterfuge protected the future of the Hebrew people. Moses lived and became the liberating figure we encounter in the Hebrew Testament because Shiphrah and Puah revered God and refused to murder newborn Hebrew boys.

Between the account about Shiphrah and Puah we find in Exodus 1 and the narrative in Matthew 2 about the visit of the magi to Jesus in Bethlehem are numerous other accounts about devout people who disobeyed imperial demands. In Exodus 2 we read that Jochebed, the mother of Moses, hid him for three months after his birth, and his sister Miriam intervened and persuaded the daughter of Pharaoh to allow the child to be nursed by a Hebrew woman (the baby's own mother, Jochebed). Jochebed cared for the boy until he was weaned and then took him to Pharaoh's daughter, who named him Moses and raised him as her own son (Exod 2:1-10). This early scriptural narrative shows that civil disobedience—including subterfuge related to it—is a moral and ethical value that transcends cultural, class, ethnic, and religious categories.

Narratives about civil disobedience to imperial authority are not rare in scripture. Moses murdered an Egyptian who physically abused a Hebrew resident, attempted to hide the evidence of his crime, and eventually became a fugitive from the Egyptian pharaoh (Exod 2:11-15). Years later, the Exodus narrative reports that what Shiphrah, Puah, Jochebed, and Miriam began as acts of individual civil disobedience became a frontal challenge to imperial power when Moses and Aaron, sons of Amram and Jochebed and brothers of Miriam, demanded that the Egyptian empire release the Hebrew population to leave Egypt as free people (Exod 6:26-27). The Hebrew canon later details how Rahab, a sex worker living in Jericho, defied the imperial authority of that city by hiding Hebrew spies (Josh 2:1-21; 6:15-17, 22-23).

The early chapters of Daniel present the same message. Daniel 1 contains the account of how Daniel, Hananiah, Mishael, and Azariah refused to follow the royal meal plan prescribed for them by their Babylonian captors. In Daniel 3, we read how Hananiah/Shadrach, Mishael/Meshach, and Azariah/Abednego defied imperial orders by their refusal to worship a golden statue. When we read at chapter 6 about Daniel's deliverance from a den of lions for disobeying a royal edict that banned prayer to any deity other than the ruler of Babylon, we are reading about civil disobedience by a person who was outnumbered, marginalized, and vulnerable but who defied imperial authority and threats because of reverence for God.

The confrontation we read about in Amos 7:10-17 between Amos of Tekoa and Amaziah who was priest at Bethel and the exchange we read at Jeremiah 20:1-6 between Jeremiah and the priest Pashhur present the same issue but with a different twist. Unlike the other narratives mentioned, the confrontations in these passages involved people who were followers of God. However, Amos and Jeremiah challenged social inequities in their respective societies on religious grounds while Amaziah and Pashhur treated the prophets as enemies of the state.

These biblical narratives make two key points. The first point is that people can experience a revelation or insight that corresponds to the wider meaning of an epiphany. The second and more important point is that such events can inspire people to disobey imperial power on moral and ethical grounds. That is what the magi did by choosing not to return to Jerusalem and inform Herod of where they found Jesus. Given the way these points are repeated in scripture, it is remarkable how much emphasis is given to the admonition from Paul found in Romans 13:1-7 about obedience to civil authority. Why is that message emphasized while other passages about disobedience to imperial commands are ignored?

The disregard of the many messages that affirm civil disobedience on moral and ethical grounds is not inadvertent. Preachers and religious educators who embrace Christian nationalism do not negligently do so because the accounts of Shiphrah, Puah, Jochebed, Miriam, Rahab, Jeremiah, Amos, Daniel, Mishael, Hananiah, Azariah, and the magi we read about in Matthew's Gospel are missing from their Bibles. Instead, the embrace of Christian nationalism is calculated, deliberate, intentional, and purposeful. Unfortunately, preaching and praxis often do not attempt to critique empire, let alone instruct faithful people to disobey or defy imperial exercises in oppression. Instead, scripture has been misconstrued—or even worse, perverted—to defend notions of tribal, national, ethnic, political, economic, religious, racial, patriarchal, and heterosexual hegemony and power in service to empire.

That conduct fails to recognize a point succinctly stated by Palestinian Christian scholar Mitri Raheb (president of Dar al-Kalima University College in Bethlehem, president of the Synod of the Evangelical Lutheran Church in Jordan and the Holy Land, and senior pastor of the Evangelical Lutheran Christmas Church in Bethlehem, Palestine): "[T]he entire Bible, both Old and New Testaments, struggles to find a faithful response to various and recurring empires. I understand *sacred history* to be one response to the *secular* histories of brutal empires."[1]

Faithful exposition of scripture requires showing how people across the biblical eras recognized and responded to what Raheb calls "various and recurring empires." Their responses must be judged according to the love and justice imperatives of God that run through scripture culminating in the gospel of Jesus. At that point, exposition involves identifying principles that are applicable to current situations involving power dynamics and human interactions. Unless this critical process is undertaken, biblical exposition will fail to confront people about how lust for power and empire leads to personal and group conduct that dishonors God and harms self and others.

Preachers and Empire

Billy Graham was the most recognized preacher in the world during his lifetime. His role in the growth of the Christian evangelical movement during the second half of the twentieth century is not disputed. Yet Graham did not address the issue of empire across his many years of public ministry. The following account by Samuel DeWitt Proctor, a Black theologian who worked with Bill Moyer and Sargent Shriver to advance President Lyndon Johnson's war on poverty initiatives, provides an example. The account is found in Proctor's memoir, *The Substance of Things Hoped For*, as follows:

> One day Bill Moyers called from the White House and asked me to leave fast, go to the airport, and fly to Charlotte, North Carolina, with Billy Graham. We were helping a lot of poor mountain people near where he lived, and we wanted to get his support.
>
> All through the flight down we talked church, religion, and social change. When we reached his mountaintop home, we had a delicious lunch and more conversation. It all settled down to a stalemate: Dr. Graham felt that his business was to preach the gospel and change the hearts of individuals. Changed persons would then change society.
>
> I countered with the teachings of Jesus in chapter 25 of Matthew's gospel, in which he admonished that at the day of judgment we would all be separated into sheep and goats. One got to be a sheep by feeding the hungry, giving water to the thirsty and clothing to the naked, visiting those in prison and taking in the stranger. The sheep entered into the Master's joy. Goats did not do such things and were consigned to a burning hell.
>
> Reverend Graham smiled and said that I was making Jesus a "liberal." It was odd, though, that while he officially avoided political involvement, he often boasted of advising several presidents.[2]

Billy Graham is correctly remembered for his "Crusades" across the United States and throughout the world and for his preaching about human sin, divine grace, and eternal life. However, he refused to apply the gospel of Jesus to elimination of societal inequities and imperial aggression.

In chapter 2 of his 2021 book, *Decolonizing Christianity: Becoming Badass Believers*,[3] Miguel De La Torre exposed the root of Graham's disregard for the love and justice imperatives Jesus proclaimed. De La Torre observed that proponents of the Social Gospel had told the nation and business leaders that capitalist greed caused the 1929 economic collapse that produced the Great Depression. When President Franklin Roosevelt used "religious jargon to sell his New Deal, which was picked up by liberal ministers throughout the nation and preached from their pulpits," business leaders were inspired during the 1940 National Association of Manufacturers (NAM) conference by Rev. James W. Fifield, who preached against the sins of the New Deal and that salvation could be found through free enterprise and deregulation.

According to Fifield, business leaders were not responsible for the Great Depression but were saviors. Miquel De La Torre then adds the following historical perspective.

> During his talk, Fifield—nicknamed "The Apostle to Millionaires"—suggested clergy would be the key to regaining the upper hand in the capitalist struggle against Roosevelt's liberal policies and dictatorial tendencies. This watershed moment made Christianity and capitalism soulmates in white America's imagination under the phrase "under God," which they then set out to popularize. Moving forward, the United States would henceforth be known as a Christian nation.
>
> J. Howard Pew, president of Sun Oil, along with his brother Joseph N., despised Roosevelt and their former business competitor John D. Rockefeller, whose brand of ecumenism, interdenominationalism, and internationalist Protestantism that prioritized science and reform, was leading the nation, they believed, toward secularism. Committed to Christian libertarianism, they became patrons of Fifield's work by the mid-1940s, outsourcing the task of persuading citizens to embrace capitalist ideology to the church. Later, they would back an obscure tent-revivalist preacher and fiercely pro-capitalist named Billy Graham. Called by Pew, not God, Graham railed against all liberal social programs—the New Deal, the Fair Deal, the New Frontier, and the Great Society—during his crusades. Social ills such as racism would not be remedied by government, Graham preached. Their solution could be manifested only with the second coming of Christ.[4]

De La Torre writes that Graham and other white Christian nationalist "visionaries" "cemented a nationalist Christianity that merged the state with the growing power of a group of wealthy white male capitalists who were steadfastly opposed to the Social Gospel" and whose goal "was the Christianization of government, business, education, media, family, entertainment, and religion through the creation of a quasi-democratic theocracy."[5]

The result of their efforts to achieve that goal is shown by the events of the final decades of the twentieth century.

> The 1950s until the start of the new millennium was the golden age of white Christianity within the United States. The tentacles of nationalist Christianity spread and flourished under the tutelage of Billy Graham, Abraham Vereide, and Doug Coe—avatars for white capitalist men. These early religious superstars were called to strengthen a quasi-religious ideology that ensured the profit, power, and privilege of the few. With the Nixon administration of the early 1970s, a move away from Eisenhower's civil religion was in full force. Nixon, with Billy Graham's support, used Christian nationalism to divide rather than unite people by branding antagonists to his war in Vietnam or his administration as foes to Christian values. The cultural wars that would consume the 1980s, bringing about national discord still being felt today, found their footing when Nixon and Graham separated the faithful (those committed to their cause) from the ungodly, secular unfaithful. Basically, white conservative Christians began to flex their political muscles to ensure the phrase "under God" referred only to them.[6]

The present state of the United States and the world is the result of the unholy union between the free-market fundamentalism and Christian nationalism mentioned by Miguel De La Torre and the "giant triplets" of racism, materialism, and militarism that Martin Luther King Jr. denounced as heresies to divine imperatives of love and justice.

A year to the day before he was assassinated, King, a Black Baptist pastor, defined the war in Vietnam as a civil rights issue on April 4, 1967, in an address titled "Beyond Vietnam: A Time to Break Silence" to a meeting of Clergy and Laity Concerned about Vietnam at Riverside Church in New York City. In doing so, King called for what he termed "a radical revolution of values" in the following words:

> The war in Vietnam is but a symptom of a far deeper malady within the American spirit.... I am convinced that if we are to get on the right side of the world revolution, we as a nation must undergo a radical revolution of values. We must rapidly begin the shift from a "thing-oriented" society to a "person-oriented" society. When machines and computers, profit motives and

property rights are considered more important than people, the giant triplets of racism, materialism, and militarism are incapable of being conquered.

A true revolution of values will soon cause us to question the fairness and justice of many of our past and present policies. On the one hand we are called to play the good Samaritan on life's roadside; but that will be only an initial act. One day we must come to see that the whole Jericho Road must be transformed so that men and women will not be constantly beaten and robbed as they make their journey on life's highway…. A nation that continues year after year to spend more money on military defense than on programs of social uplift is approaching spiritual death.

America, the richest and most powerful nation in the world, can well lead the way in this revolution of values. There is nothing, except a tragic death wish, to prevent us from reordering our priorities….[7]

Public reaction to King's message was swift and hostile. Several editorial writers attacked him for connecting Vietnam to the civil rights movement. The *New York Times* issued an editorial claiming that King had damaged the peace movement as well as the civil rights movement. *Life* magazine assailed the speech as "demagogic slander that sounded like a script for Radio Hanoi." The *Pittsburgh Courier*, an African American publication, charged King with "tragically misleading" Black people. And at the White House, President Lyndon Johnson was quoted as saying, "What is that goddamned nigger preacher doing to me? We gave him the Civil Rights Act of 1964, we gave him the Voting Rights Act of 1965, we gave him the War on Poverty. What more does he want?"[8]

King was assassinated in Memphis, Tennessee, exactly one year after he delivered the speech written by Vincent Harding, a Black historian and trusted friend. Harding always believed the speech was the reason King was murdered. "It was precisely one year to the day after this speech that that bullet which had been chasing him for a long time finally caught up with him," Harding said in a 2010 interview. "And I am convinced that that bullet had something to do with that speech. And over the years, that's been quite a struggle for me."[9]

Nine years after his death, King was posthumously awarded the Presidential Medal of Freedom by another Baptist from Georgia, President Jimmy Carter. Carter, a white Baptist Sunday school teacher, was committed to racial justice, gender equality, human rights, justice for Palestinians, environmental protection, and worker justice. His personal and political history was clearly different from that of his 1980 rival, former California governor Ronald Reagan.

However, Jerry Falwell, Pat Robertson, Bill Bright (founder of Campus Crusade for Christ), and James Robison (mentor to Mike Huckabee who later became governor of Arkansas and candidate for the Republican Party presidential nomination in 2008 and 2016), and other white Christian nationalists looked past Reagan's ecumenicalism and marital history in 1980 to lead white Christians to elect Reagan in 1980 and 1984. They embraced Reagan because his support for free-market capitalism, abortion, affirmative action, welfare, and Cold War militarism agreed with their sense of empire, including patriarchy, white supremacy, and religious nationalism. Somehow, leading figures of white Christianity chose devotion to imperial and capitalist power over the gospel of Jesus.

Meanwhile, a federal holiday was established to commemorate Martin Luther King Jr.'s birthday. His statue has been placed in Washington, DC. Numerous cities and towns have renamed major traffic arteries for him in the United States, and he is revered throughout the world as one of the most prophetic souls of the twentieth century, if not the modern era. When President Barack Obama took the oath of office to begin his second term, he placed his hand on a Bible that belonged to King and alluded to him during his inaugural address.

Yet the veneration of King has not included any significant or serious effort by US policymakers, social commentators, and moral leaders—including clergy, laity, associations, denominations, and educational institutions—to embrace the "radical revolution of values" King called for in "A Time to Break Silence." The "giant triplets" of racism, militarism, and materialism have not been confronted. The US currently devotes more of its budget to national defense and homeland security than to educating children, fighting disease, feeding the hungry, and alleviating poverty.

Recent Failures in Expository Discernment

We may never learn the true financial cost of the tragic military misadventure known as the war in Iraq. As the tenth anniversary of the war in Iraq approached, Reuters reported on a study by a team of academicians that tallied the cost of the war at $1.7 trillion, a figure that did not include $490 billion owed to Iraqi war veterans for disability benefits. The study projected that expenses related to the war in Iraq could grow to more than $6 trillion over the next four decades.[10]

The US invaded Afghanistan after Al Qaeda terrorist followers of Osama bin Laden commandeered and crash-bombed four commercial airliners on September 11, 2001, killing 2,977 and wounding more than 6,000 people in New York City, Washington, DC, and Pennsylvania. When intelligence assessments traced the terrorists to Afghanistan, Congress authorized President George W. Bush to use military force. The "war on terror" began in Afghanistan because that was where Osama bin Laden lived. Bin Laden was finally found in Pakistan and killed in 2011, ten years after the Taliban regime that governed Afghanistan was defeated by US forces at the end of 2001.

For the next twenty years, Taliban fighters matched wits and tactics while waging guerilla warfare against a multi-national military force led by the United States that was better equipped, had more personnel, and was better financed. Two thousand, four hundred forty-eight (2,448) US service members died. Tens of thousands more were injured. The United States has spent more than $2.26 trillion—including more than $500 billion for interest—for the military effort in Afghanistan and neighboring Pakistan since 2001.[11]

The war in Afghanistan reminds us that those who do not learn from past mistakes are likely to repeat them. Years ago, scholar Akhilesh Pillalamarri wrote that Afghanistan has long been known as the graveyard of empires.[12] Nevertheless, the United States repeated the respective mistakes of the British and Soviet empires in the nineteenth and twentieth centuries by invading and trying to occupy the country. In doing so, US political and military leaders disregarded other truths. Despite US outrage about the 9/11 terrorist attacks and determination to seek revenge on Osama bin Laden and the Al Qaeda network that operated from Afghanistan, foreign troops and weapons would never outlast Afghan mores, customs, history, ancestral warrior pride, and centuries of refusal to be ruled by foreign invaders, especially when the invaders propped up corrupt and incompetent indigenous rulers and Afghan military personnel who would not fight for the future of their society even with overwhelming military, logistical, and diplomatic advantages. A combination of bloodlust, Western hubris, white supremacy and racism, conservative Christian nationalist imperialism, and capitalist greed to enrich people who profited from selling weapons and war materiel were also contributing factors to the decision to wage the longest war in US history.

For those reasons, it was not enough to invade Afghanistan in 2001. It was not enough to chase bin Laden from Afghanistan. It was not enough to displace the Taliban from political power twenty years ago. It was not enough to eventually find and kill bin Laden in 2011. It was not enough to capture, kill, torture, and hold his lieutenants indefinitely in Guantanamo and other sites around the world—but never in the United States.

No matter how many troops were deployed, how many drone missions were flown, and how many US military personnel were killed and wounded, bloodlust, cultural incompetence, disregard for military and political history, hubris, white supremacy and racism, Christian national imperialism, capitalist greed, and national pride transformed the 2001 invasion of Afghanistan into a twenty-year fiasco that bedeviled the presidencies of George W. Bush, Barack Obama, Donald Trump, and Joe Biden. History will not be kind to the political and military leaders who counseled the nation to commit itself to that misadventure. And history will not be kind to religious leaders in the United States who cheered and counseled the nation to go along with it. Religious leaders—people skilled in biblical exposition—did not warn the nation about the moral and mortal dangers of bloodlust. Religious leaders blessed the bloodlust while they offered pastoral support to grieving families and to people maimed and scarred by the physical, emotional, social, and spiritual wounds of warfare.

Religious leaders cannot blame the Central Intelligence Agency, State Department, Pentagon, and political parties for failure to discern and denounce the patriarchy, misogyny, and militarism that drove so-called Christian evangelical conservatives to champion war in Afghanistan a decade after bin Laden was killed. Meanwhile, the same Christian evangelical conservatives railed against the Taliban and other Muslim extremists. Prophetic discernment should have led more clergy in the United States to know and declare that these forces were merely different sides of the same hateful faith coin.

The failure of prophetic discernment and activity concerning the war in Afghanistan did not honor the lessons about Shiphrah, Puah, Jochebed, Miriam, and Rahab. It did not honor the messages proclaimed by Amos, Daniel, and the other Hebrew prophets, including Jesus. It did not honor the tradition of prophetic men and women who condemned bloodlust in later centuries. It did not honor the tradition of prophetic people who challenged the imperialist aims of the Crusades.

That failure also disregarded the example of clergy who challenged the war in Vietnam three decades before 2001. Over the course of twenty years, religious leaders in the United States did not challenge public thinking about the war in Afghanistan the way Clergy and Laity Concerned about Vietnam challenged the public fifty years ago. Religious leaders refused to follow the prophetic examples of William Sloan Coffin, Martin Luther King Jr., Father Theodore Hesburgh, and Rabbi Abraham Joshua Heschel in calling on political, military, and opinion leaders to ponder the tragic mistakes that were being made in Afghanistan.

Instead, Billy Graham, Jerry Falwell, Pat Robertson, Tony Perkins, Phyllis Schlafly, Richard Land, Robert Jeffress, Paige Patterson, James Dobson, and Franklin Graham were considered by journalists, including religious writers, as exemplars of strong religious leadership. Meanwhile, the same journalists—including religious writers—dismissed Jeremiah Wright Jr., Jim Wallis, and Congresswoman Barbara Lee of Oakland, California (and Allen Temple Baptist

Church), who cast the only vote in the US House of Representatives against the Authorization of Military Force in Afghanistan that set the stage for what became known as the Forever War. To make matters worse, US religious leaders and congregations courted Hillary Clinton, Barack Obama, and other politicians and distanced themselves from Wright, Wallis, and Lee.

Billy Graham and other "good" evangelical preachers refused to support desegregation efforts, including King's work in Birmingham, Alabama, that led to his historic "Letter from Birmingham City Jail." They did not join King and other prophetic people in calling for the United States to end its military adventure in Southeast Asia. They did not oppose the racist apartheid regime in South Africa. And they denounced Jimmy Carter after he declared that the Israeli regime's conduct amounts to apartheid in Palestine.[13]

Palestinians whose homes and lands have been and are being seized, whose olive groves have been damaged, and who are being driven from their land by Zionist settlers supported by the US-financed Israeli government and the US-financed and US-armed Israeli Defense Ministry are like Naboth, the commoner in Jezreel whose vineyard was coveted by King Ahab so he could convert it to a vegetable garden (see 1 Kings 21). In the same way that Naboth was falsely accused and executed as a pretext for what amounted to a land grab, Palestinians are being murdered, tortured, detained without trial, and subjected to countless indignities every day. Their experience is like that suffered by the Indigenous Black population of South Africa during the apartheid era in that nation and like that of the Indigenous people of this nation.

US support for the apartheid regime in South Africa did not change until prophetic people, including people of faith and those who disavowed religious affiliation, engaged in years of sustained advocacy, civil disobedience, and demands for boycott, disinvestment, and sanctions against the apartheid regime. Prophetic people, including some religious bodies, pulled their investments from corporations that did business in South Africa. For those people, experiencing the presence of God's grace and truth meant more than pietism. It meant becoming allies with God in obedience to divine imperatives of love and justice to change the world.

US policy surrounding Israeli West Bank settlements reminds us how gentrification of urban neighborhoods and similar displacement efforts by land speculators and commercial real estate developers force people from their homes and neighborhoods by "urban renewal," zoning changes, and other dispossession schemes like what happened to Indigenous people and Naboth. "Good evangelical Christians" who support and are complicit in Zionist racism concerning illegal Jewish settlements in the West Bank are part of a long and bitter history of white evangelical tolerance for, if not endorsement of, injustice. The usual sponsors of legislation to suppress, censor, and punish prophetic opposition to Zionist racism in Palestine through laws that punish supporters of the Boycott, Divestment, and Sanctions (BDS) movement against Israel and Israeli settlement business entities are "good" white evangelical Christians whose understanding of following Jesus is bottomed on the type of pietism preached and practiced by Billy Graham, Bill Bright, James Robison, Mike Huckabee, and other Christian nationalists.

At the same time US leaders—including religious leaders—are venerating King's memory, they have ignored or rejected his call for the United States to use its wealth and prestige to lead the world in a radical revolution of values that rejects war as the preferred means of resolving differences. Former President Barack Obama could not have been guided by the vision of the Baptist preacher whose Bible he used for his second inauguration. Although Obama could not persuade US officials and global allies to embrace a military response to Syria the way George W. Bush did concerning Iraq, US militarism continues to cast an ominous cloud over the world and hinder efforts to address glaring problems at home.

Jonathan Tran's 2012 lecture about the war policies of the Obama administration reminds us that Obama articulated what Tran termed "a theology of war."[14] It is more than sadly ironic that the first African American to hold the office of President of the United States oversaw a policy of killing American citizens by using armed drones. The militarism King criticized was also clear in the virulent response by Obama and other US leaders to the disclosures by Edward Snowden that the US engaged in wholesale spying on American citizens and others throughout the world—including the leaders of nations considered its allies.

Decades after King was murdered by a gunman, on December 14, 2012, the nation suffered the massacre of twenty children and six adult staff members of Sandy Hook Elementary School in New Town, Connecticut, by a shooter who had already killed his mother and later killed himself. The militarism that drives US global policy seems to have turned on our own children. The response to the Sandy Hook massacre was not, however, to confront the giant of militarism. Firearm manufacturers and the National Rifle Association (NRA), their lobbyist, like defense contractors and their lobbyists, now hold more influence than ever before.

Sadly, devotion to corporate profit-making continues to hamstring efforts to make our society and the world safe. Thus, militarism has joined forces with materialism so much that American schools look and feel more like fortresses than places where children are nurtured to learn, work, and play together. We somehow are blind to the stark moral and ethical contradiction of singing "Let

There Be Peace on Earth" while arming schoolteachers and cheering people who openly brandish handguns.

The moral and ethical disconnect between the rhetoric used to venerate King and the persistence of entrenched racism in American life continues to afflict us. Policymakers refuse to acknowledge the plain truth that the "law and order" and "war on drugs" mantra used by every US president since Lyndon Johnson produced the mass incarceration of millions of people who are disproportionately persons of color. Thanks to the not always covert racism of "law and order" and "war on drugs" enthusiasts, more Black people are politically and socially disenfranchised in the United States now than were enslaved in 1850, ten years before the Civil War began, a fact Professor Michelle Alexander forcefully presented in her 2010 book titled *The New Jim Crow: Mass Incarceration in the Age of Colorblindness*.[15]

Oppressive law enforcement policies that gave rise to civil unrest during Dr. King's lifetime still operate against people who are Black and Brown. Years after President Obama and Attorney General Eric Holder became the first Black individuals to hold their respective offices, the terrorism of racial profiling remained as prevalent as when Dr. King was assassinated, if not more so.

Insensitivity to the insidious racism that poisoned the United States when King was killed has not changed. Trayvon Martin,[16] Oscar Grant,[17] and Amadou Diallo,[18] like Martin Luther King Jr., were Black men shot to death by people who claimed the moral and legal right to take their lives. The racism and militarism King deplored in 1967 were major factors in causing the August 9, 2014, death of Michael Brown Jr., an eighteen-year-old unarmed Black teenager shot to death by Darren Wilson, formerly of the Ferguson, Missouri, Police Department.[19] That racism and militarism also accounted for the killing of Eric Garner, who was choked to death on July 23, 2014, by Daniel Pantaleo while other New York Police Department officers pressed their knees on Garner's torso despite his repeated statement "I can't breathe!"[20]

The world has since then suffered the trauma of George Floyd's murder by former Minneapolis Police Officer Derek Chauvin, who pressed his full kneeling weight against Floyd's head and neck as the helpless man died, pleading for his mother while other officers stood by and failed to intervene.[21] Nor will the world forget how Elijah McClain died at the hands of Aurora, Colorado, police.[22] Plainly, the United States has not become more informed about or responsive to racial injustice since King died. We have simply militarized the injustice in brazen ways. We have not confronted or corralled the giant triplets of militarism, materialism, and racism. Rather, we have added sexism (including homophobia and transphobia), classism, and techno-centrism to the mix. The triplets are sextuplets now.

Judgment on Expository Misfeasance about Empire

There is a strange silence from pulpits about social inequities. Following the example set by Billy Graham and other white Christian nationalist preachers whom Miguel De La Torre termed "avatars for white capitalist men," many pastors and preachers appear unable to understand and declare that people who revere God also live to challenge and dismantle oppressive power as liberators, healers, and prophets. The reasons for avoiding prophetic critique of empire vary from concern about losing favor with congregants to fear of persecution. However, there has never been a time when prophetic critique of and resistance to empire occurred without risk. Shiphrah and Puah, Rahab, Elijah, Amos, Daniel, John the Baptist, and Jesus faced the same risks.

Many religious leaders refuse to engage in prophetic exposition and ministry because they prefer pietistic popularity and abhor prophetic perseverance. In the same way that Amaziah opposed the prophetic presence and exposition of Amos, preachers steeped in the tradition that produced James Fifield, Billy Graham, Jerry Falwell, James Robison, and Robert Jeffress equate love of empire with love for God.

In his "Letter from Birmingham City Jail," Martin Luther King Jr. wrote that he had "been so greatly disappointed with the white church and its leadership" and added,

> In the midst of blatant injustices...I have watched white churches stand on the sideline and merely mouth pious irrelevancies and sanctimonious trivialities. In the midst of a mighty struggle to rid our nation of racial and economic injustice, I have heard so many ministers say, "Those are social issues with which the gospel has no real concern," and I have watched so many churches commit themselves to a completely otherworldly religion which made a strange distinction between body and soul, the sacred and the secular. So here we are moving toward the exit of the twentieth century with a religious community largely adjusted to the status quo, standing as a taillight behind other community agencies rather than a headlight leading men to higher levels of justice....
>
> The contemporary church is often a weak, ineffectual voice with an uncertain sound. It is so often the arch-supporter of the status quo. Far from being disturbed by the presence of the church, the power structure of the average community is

consoled by the church's silent and often vocal sanction of things as they are.

But the judgment of God is upon the church as never before. If the church of today does not recapture the sacrificial spirit of the early church, it will lose its authentic ring, forfeit the loyalty of millions, and be dismissed as an irrelevant social club with no meaning for the twentieth century. I am meeting young people every day whose disappointment with the church has risen to outright disgust.[23]

Proof of the "outright disgust" that people have with what King termed "the church of today" is more apparent now than in 1963 when King's letter was addressed to religious leaders in racially segregated Birmingham, Alabama. In his 2021 book, *Christians against Christianity: How Right-Wing Evangelicals Are Destroying Our Nation and Our Faith*, Obery Hendricks Jr., former president of Payne Theological Seminary and a renown biblical scholar, wrote,

> [I]t is such a curious thing, perhaps blasphemy even, that today so many Christians seem to define themselves not by those they love, but by those for whom they have *no* love: Muslims, gays, immigrants, women who seek to exercise full sovereignty over their own bodies, and those who seek succor and asylum in our land from deadening poverty and the threat of deadly violence in their own. These Christians cry bitter tears for the unjust execution of Jesus two thousand years ago, but have few tears for the injustice visited daily upon those among us for whom Jesus expressed great love: the desperately poor, the sick and vulnerable, the refugees struggling to find a better life for the babies at their breasts....
>
> Like the character Stamp Paid in Toni Morrison's classic novel *Beloved* after he witnessed malevolence he could not comprehend, I, too, asked the heavens: "What kind of people are these?" ...The answer should be obvious to anyone who has paid attention to current events: it is the result of successful shilling for Trump [former President Donald Trump] by a cadre of influential evangelical leaders who seem to have decided that the teachings of Jesus can be ignored when those teachings get in the way of their quest to dominate American society.[24]

On January 6, 2021, the date of the Epiphany of Jesus Christ, white nationalists stormed the US Capitol. They threatened lives and vandalized the Capitol. When some of them reached the chamber of the US Senate, they offered a prayer of thanksgiving in the name of Jesus after openly waving the campaign flag of defeated President Donald Trump. On the date of the Epiphany, right-wing people who professed to follow Jesus tried to overthrow the government of the United States.

Obery Hendricks has identified the problem. The divine imperatives of love and justice have been rejected by "a cadre of influential evangelical leaders who have decided that the teachings of Jesus can be ignored…" because they are bent on empire. That is not merely shameful. It is heresy.

Chapter 9

"Only Don't Go Too Far Away"

On the Perils of Negotiating with Pharaoh (Exodus 8:28)

Allan Aubrey Boesak

Four Little Words

How do four little words become twelve whole chapters? Yahweh speaks them first to Moses in Exodus 3 and the people cross the Red Sea in chapter 14, feeling free and safe enough to rejoice in their liberation from slavery only in chapter 15. I am talking about that well-known cry, "Let my people go!" that has become so ingrained, and so sacred, in the history of oppressed Black people holding on to their faith in their struggles for freedom, justice, and dignity from the times of the first invasions and slavery until today. They are at the heart of Black Liberation Theology from its earliest beginnings. They are in our spirituals, our sorrow songs, and our struggle songs—sung by choirs and ensembles of every kind, by our most celebrated artists from Paul Robeson to Mahalia Jackson to Benjamin Dube and Spirit of Praise to the wonderfully jazzified version by Louis Armstrong. They became the title of our own Albert Luthuli's autobiography and of Henrietta Buckmaster's wonderful story of the Underground Railroad, both about our struggles for freedom. They touch our hearts every time. Four little words that inspired millions over millennia; that empowered disempowered people, made them rise up in resistance to every kind of tyranny; words that made every pharaoh, ancient and modern, quake in those boots they tried to keep on the neck of their victims. This is what Yahweh, in the tradition presented to us in Exodus 3 onwards, commanded Moses to demand from Pharaoh.[1]

Whether Moses heard those words as "Bring my people out," "I will rescue them," "I will deliver them," "I will redeem them," or "I will bring out," as we find them scattered throughout that part of the exodus story in various Bible translations. They first came as an unwavering, divinely resolute declaration from the mouth of the God who called him. And they all meant the same. The power in those words from the Liberator-God was to become power in the mouth of Moses as Yahweh sent him forth: "Go and tell Pharaoh: Let my people go!" That is the essence of Moses' calling. That is the heart of what Yahweh wanted him to convey to Pharaoh. That is the authority with which Moses was charged to confront

Pharaoh. All of God's radical, indivisible love for God's people, God's radical, indivisible solidarity with God's people, God's radical, indivisible commitment to justice, and God's radical, irreversible determination to liberate God's people from Egypt's enslavement are summed up in those four little words.

In this light too, I understand the meaning of the burning bush. That fire is not some divine magic trick to dramatize a special moment. It is the fire burning in the heart of God, made visible for Moses to see and understand. Here the burning bush is God's burning desire for justice and freedom for God's people; it is God's unrelenting hope that we, God's children, will join God in God's struggle for our freedom and dignity *as* God's children. It is also God's burning outrage against oppression and enslavement. It is a fire not even the power of the pharaoh can extinguish. The reason why the bush is not consumed is because God's desire for justice will not ever burn out. It is out of that fire that the voice comes: "Let my people go!"

And because this Liberator-God misses nothing—"I have *observed*...I have *heard*...I *know*..."—it is not just their physical freedom God is concerned about. Yahweh knows what oppressed people everywhere would discover: there would be no freedom unless it starts with the liberation of the mind. Hence, we read not just of Israel's physical suffering but also of their mental bondage. The "cruelty" of Egypt included the misery of their "broken spirit" so that they did not, *could* not, believe Moses when he first brought them the message that their God was intent on their freedom from slavery (Exod 6:9). With this in mind, a painful little detail, mentioned as a matter of course in Exodus 5:15-16, becomes important.

> Then the Israelite supervisors came to Pharaoh and cried, "Why do you treat your servants like this? No straw is given to your servants, yet they say to us, 'Make bricks!' Look how your servants are beaten! You are unjust to your own people." (NRSV)

Notice the words "the Israelite supervisors." The "taskmasters" were Egyptian. Under them but over the Hebrew slaves were "Israelite supervisors." Use their own to abuse their own—it's a device slave masters throughout the centuries have refined and perfected. Notice further the words "your servants." Not once, but thrice. The submission to their enslaved state is without reservation. And it gets worse, for notice especially the complete giveaway in verse 16: "You are unjust to your own people." Absorb this for a moment. They are Israelites, they are Pharaoh's slaves, yet they call themselves his "own people." Total confusion about their sociopolitical reality brings total confusion about their identity. They are going to Pharaoh not as Israelites but as the lowest echelon of the ruling class, slaves with special privileges. In shock, they complain to Pharaoh that he is unjust, not to all the slaves but to *them*. How confused must one be to expect justice in a system fundamentally, irredeemably, intrinsically unjust? They think themselves in an exalted position just because Pharaoh has made them "supervisors" over their own enslaved kith and kin. Pharaoh makes them his junior partners in the oppression of their own people, and they believe they therefore "belong" to him. So beguiled are they by this pharaonic deception that they are shocked to rediscover that in Pharaoh's eyes, they are, after all, still no more than slaves.

To please Pharaoh, they abuse their own. Punishment and humiliation of one's own people should always be even harsher to show how loyal one is to the slave master. We know this from experience. When, in 1985, Black Police Captain Gregory Rockman saw the brutality with which the Black police in Mitchell's Plain waded into the protesting Black students, he described the police as "a pack of wild dogs." Under direct orders of the white officer in command of the Riot Squad that took over Mitchell's Plain that day, they had to show the white man just how loyal they could be. Perhaps the closest, and most recent, example of this is the killing of twenty-nine-year-old Tyre Nichols by five Black police officers in Memphis, Tennessee. The killing was apparently brutal and deliberate, so much so that from the local District Attorney to President Biden pleas for calm had gone out to the community. The five officers are facing murder charges as I write this. The killing is shocking for many reasons, the most important perhaps because the police officers were also Black. But it is unsurprising and is illustrative of the point I am trying to make.

This is their life, though. Pretending not to be a slave, revelling in borrowed power to keep their own people enslaved, abused by Egyptian overseers, reminding them that they are and will remain, after all, no more than slaves, and then reacting with shock and indignation—just how deep does the internalization of that slave mentality go?

Of course, there is the argument that collaborating with the slave master offers one a better chance of survival. That may be true for a while. In certain situations, survival is not an unworthy goal. But what if survival becomes not merely the only goal but the permanent frame of mind? Then the pertinent question becomes survival as what? As a slave with perks? What does survival mean if your slave status is not ever really changed, if your "privileges," such as they are, can be revoked at the slightest whim? Does one ever survive in isolation from one's community, in the deepest sense alienated from oneself, simultaneously feared, despised, and shunned by those whose yoke one shares? How does one survive outside the circles of solidarity and the shared longings and struggles for freedom? Can the occasional, patronizing, and grudging pat on the head from the slave master ever replace the embrace of love? Especially if that pat on the head is the reward for the harm one has done to one's own? Is it not then that survival becomes the ultimate goal, completely erasing and replacing all desires for and dreams of freedom? It is a terrible and tragic logic, but it works every time.

Moreover, we now see why, from the beginning, Yahweh is so insistent: "I will send you to Pharaoh to bring *my people*, the Israelites, out of Egypt" (Exod 3:10, NRSV). Yahweh says this for the first time in chapter 3. But these precious words, claiming the Hebrews as God's own people, emphatically not the pharaoh's enslaved chattel, will come again and again (6:7; 7:16; 8:1; 8:20, 21, 22, 23; 9:1, 13, 17; 10:3). Moses must know this, the people must understand this, the supervisors must be reminded, the pharaoh shall hear and admit: "These are my people," says the Lord. Your claim on them is not just without validity; it is hereby completely and utterly nullified. This is not an affirmation of a narrow, racial, nationalistic and religious exclusivity. This is God's radical, inclusive, and preferential claim on the lives, dignity, worthiness and future of God's oppressed and despised children, everywhere, at any time.

All of this encapsulated in four little words.

Black enslaved and oppressed people have always understood this, and I find it useful to recall the words of nineteenth century Presbyterian minister from the United States, Henry Highland Garnet, and they are, almost all by themselves, a parable of struggle.[2] First is his insistence that there can be no negotiation about one's freedom with slave owners or any other oppressor: "…[G]o to your lordly enslavers and tell them plainly, that you *are determined to be free*.… Tell them in language *which they cannot misunderstand*, of the exceeding sinfulness of slavery, and of a future judgment, and of the righteous retributions of an indignant God. Inform them that all you desire is FREEDOM, and that nothing else will suffice." All of this, Garnet would have understood, is captured in those four little words that he, as a Black preacher to enslaved people, must have preached on many times.

What every oppressor, then and now, must understand is that the oppressed are determined to be free. They must be told in language that cannot be misunderstood that God is a God of justice and freedom and judgment and that freedom is what is desired: there is no substitute. The demand is for freedom not as defined by the oppressor—a "freedom" that requires the permission of and the limitations set by the oppressor. This is a lesson that post-1994 Black South Africans and post-2008 Black Americans have been learning through painful experience. The words "nothing else will suffice" are a reminder that appeals to "gradualism," tinkering with "reforms" or adjustments to the system of oppression, will not be acceptable; that the endurance of the oppressed is not to be confused with endless patience or with acceptance of a calendar for freedom set by slave owners. Slavery is evil, and as such it cannot be reformed or modified; it can only be irrevocably eradicated.

Second, though, here Garnet raises another truth we have always known but constantly have to be reminded of, even though Frederick Douglass, Martin Luther King Jr., Albert Luthuli, Malcolm X, and Nelson Mandela never tired of telling us so. Power is never willingly given up by the oppressor. It has to be wrested from their hands by the oppressed. Freedom is never handed to the oppressed on a silver platter; it is the gift of struggle and sacrifice. Hence Yahweh's repeated warnings of Pharaoh's "hardened heart," meaning that the people must prepare for the fact that their slave masters would not let them go without Yahweh's "outstretched arm" and "mighty acts of judgment" (Ex. 6:6, NRSV). Seven times in chapter 6, Yahweh assures Moses that this is a battle Yahweh will fight for them. Seven times Moses hears "*I* will."

That does not mean the people will not be drawn into this conflict between Yahweh, the God of their liberation, and Pharaoh, the god of their enslavement. The moment Pharaoh hears of Yahweh's intentions to set them free, they will suffer, even more unjustly and undeservedly than before. They will be punished simply for expressing their longings for freedom. Chapter 5's detailed description of the "bricks without straw" episodes, the intensification of physical punishment, the repeated accusations and psychological abuse from Pharaoh—"You are lazy! Lazy!"—as excuse for more punishment all make the point.

Neither does it mean that they will be mere passive spectators, exempt from the struggle for their freedom. They are required to get up, gather their families, pack their things, take their livestock, demand reparations from the Egyptians ("plunder" is the word Yahweh uses), and go. Face whatever the pharaoh throws at them, but *go!* As I pointed out in *Children of the Waters of Meribah*, if the women, Shiphrah and Puah and later Miriam, needed no cajoling and prodding, as Moses clearly did, to understand their people's need for liberation and their calling in that struggle for liberation, why could the elders of Israel not see the kairos moment created for them by Yahweh? The women had no direct encounter with God; for them there was no burning bush, no promise of a land of milk and honey. They needed no reminder that Yahweh had seen, heard, and knew their sufferings. They did not need some divine argument about what was right, what served justice, and how the righteous should respond to injustice and oppression. Why was all this so hard for the men of Israel?[3]

It seems that no matter at which point of history we find ourselves, Frederick Douglass's wisdom remains with hammer blows to our collective conscience:

> If there is no struggle, there is no progress. Those who profess to favor freedom and yet deprecate agitation are men who want crops without plowing up the ground; they want rain without thunder and lightning. They want the ocean without the awful roar of its many waters. The struggle may be a moral one, or it may be a physical one, and it may be both moral and physical, but it must be a struggle. Power concedes nothing without a demand. It never did and it never will. …The limits of tyrants are prescribed by the endurance of those whom they oppress.[4]

Did the assembly of elders, the men of Israel—unlike the women who risked the wrath of Pharaoh and put their lives on the line for the sake of their people—want crops without ploughing up the ground; rain without thunder and lightning; the ocean without the roar of its many waters? Is that why they "did not listen" even as Moses relayed to them Yahweh's intentions for their freedom in seven different ways (see Ex. 6:1-13)?

Perhaps there is still another lesson to be learned here. The more we refuse to listen and to accept the challenges of freedom, the more we enslave ourselves. The more we deny our right to freedom, the more we alienate ourselves from our noblest selves. The longer we stay with Pharaoh, the more we suffer with Pharaoh. Is that the reason why in six out of the ten plagues the children of Israel are no exception? The only explicit exceptions are plagues 4, 5, 7, and of course 10. There is no consensus on this point among scholars, and much fierce debate, but still this begs the question: why are the only explicitly mentioned exceptions the water turned to blood, the diseased livestock, the thunder and hail, and the death of the firstborn sons? The longer we stay with Pharaoh…

Even so, the question we asked at the beginning still needs an answer: how do four little words become so many thousands of words? I think it is due to the power and the intoxication of negotiation. Negotiations are a testing of what is called "the balance of powers." They are also a testing of will. They become necessary when those in power realize that they cannot cling to power exclusively any longer. They have to give in to those demanding power but, if they can help it, not to the extent that the fundamentals of the systems and structures that have guaranteed their own power are undermined. So they negotiate, looking for weaknesses in their adversaries that they can exploit and turn to their advantage while parading their own as strengths. Their greatest weakness is already in their need for negotiations. Their strength is in pretending and in convincing the adversary that this weakness is political wisdom, even magnanimity.

Those with power test the depth of their challengers' desire for change—not just the parameters or the paradigms but the fundamentals. It is a game of skill. It is a matter of understanding the nature of the terrain of contestation way beyond the negotiating table. The ones with power proclaim that "in the end" we all "want the same thing." However, for them, "the same thing" actually means "the same old thing"; fundamentally, nothing changes. Negotiations are a fight for the right to define: who defines freedom or dignity, democracy or justice? What constitutes transformation and change, and who sets the pace for those?

Do the adversaries understand the meaning and workings of power? Would they be satisfied with just a *taste of power*, of the same kind of power that oppressed and deprived them for so long—power just enough to satisfy and reward the few with promises, lavish but mostly empty, for the masses? The taste of power: the symbols and rituals of political power while economic power and control remain in the hands you shake across the table. Or do they seek power as M. M. Thomas of India described it, "as the new sense of dignity and historical mission" embraced by all the people? Power as "the bearer of dignity and for significant and responsible participation in society and social history"?[5]

Of course, *something* has to be given away, but the crucial question is always, in exchange for what? In the end, it is not about how much can be conceded but about how much control can be retained. In line with the theme of our reflections on our text, the powerful oppressor is thinking: how far should we let them go? Perhaps it is also this: how much of the revolutionary spirit of the oppressed, sitting around the negotiating table, can be captured by the trappings of the taste of power, so that, alienated from the revolutionary longings for freedom and justice in the hearts and sacrifices of their own people, we can remake them in our own image? In this sense, South Africa's white politicians have proved themselves masters of the game. They negotiated, and as Conrad Koch puts it, for white people the end result is "apartheid without the guilt."[6]

A Site of Struggle?

By the time we get to Exodus 8, there is wide scholarly agreement that Moses and the pharaoh are indeed negotiating. However, might it not be that the negotiations have already started in chapter 3, with Moses' reported reluctance to accept God's charge to go tell Pharaoh that Yahweh was ready to bring the people out, and all Pharaoh had to do was let them go? Might it be that what we have always read as reluctance on Moses' part was in fact Moses already negotiating with Yahweh? That first "but," followed by the question "Who am I that I should go to Pharaoh…?" (3:11 NRSV), is not reticence, humility, or uncertainty. That is negotiating. Yahweh's response, "I will be with you…it is I who sent you…" (v.

12), is quickly swept aside by Moses' "What is [your] name?" (v. 13). The "Who am I?" from 3:11 is neatly counterbalanced with the "Who are you?" in 3:13, as Moses anticipates the people's response that he cannot be sure of but nonetheless throws into the scale as an argument Yahweh has to respond to.

Yahweh does respond, declaring, "I AM WHO I AM" (Ex. 3:14, NRSV), strengthened by the reminder that this God is the God of their ancestors and of the covenant who has "given heed" (v. 16) to the people's suffering and is resolute to bring them "out of the misery of Egypt" (v. 17). I am the One who fights for you, liberates you, maintains you, protects you, leads you. Yahweh is confident: "They will listen to your voice..." (v. 18), and if Pharaoh initially refuses, ultimately he will let you go, for "I will stretch out my hand and strike Egypt" (v. 20). Yahweh goes even further and assures Moses that the Israelites shall not leave Egypt empty-handed. There shall be reparations: "each woman shall ask [demand from?] her neighbor...for jewelry of silver and gold, and clothing...and so you shall plunder the Egyptians" (v. 22). Moses, however, does not share Yahweh's confidence. Another "but" is on the way. "But suppose they do not believe me or listen to me, but say, 'The LORD did not appear to you'" (Exod 4:1, NRSV).

Notice how Moses now shifts the argument. The issue now is not whether Yahweh has *spoken* to him. He must now have proof that Yahweh has appeared to him. Words are not enough—Moses needs an appearance, something visible. In ancient Israel's theology, Moses is asking for the impossible. He knows that, but he presses on regardless. If there is no image to be seen and reported, there should at least be a sign of God's presence. He knows the rules, but, as modern negotiators would say, he is pushing the envelope. Moses talks as if that miraculously burning bush is not enough "proof" that Yahweh has *appeared* to him. This is a game Moses can play all day, it seems.

In exasperation, Yahweh gives in and resorts to something God thinks Moses can understand, something he clearly needs, even though Moses presents it as if it is the people who need it. "Signs" and wonders—magic, in other words. It does not require the long speeches he thinks he should be making, forgetting it really is only four words he has to say: "Let my people go." "What is that in your hand?" God asks (4:2, NRSV). The staff in Moses' hand is turned into a snake, his hand put inside his cloak turns leprous, and the water from the Nile turns into blood. Still, though Yahweh has given him what he asked for, Moses remains sceptical. In the New Revised Standard Version, which I am using here, the caption above Exodus 4:1-17, put there by the translators as their understanding of the contents of the passage, is "Moses' Miraculous Power." But clearly, Moses only does what Yahweh instructs, no, *empowers* him to do. It is therefore, strictly speaking, not Moses' "miraculous powers" but Yahweh's power on display here. But is this Freudian slip from our translators also a window into how the human mind works, an inadvertent but accurate understanding of the mind of Moses? It wants to say that in this negotiating game Moses is playing, he is gaining the upper hand. Thus, it's quite natural that those magic powers now become *his* miraculous powers. Can we then, at this point, consider this: the burning bush is not enough as "proof of life" of Yahweh because Moses has no control over it? The staff, however, is in Moses' hand and in his control. For those watching, there would be no argument as to whose power is at work here. Negotiating is intoxicating.

It is as if every round is giving Moses more confidence. Now that he's got his signs, which will do as proof that Yahweh has "appeared" to him, Moses ups the ante. Every instruction from Yahweh is met with a new "but" from Moses and a new counterargument. "I have never been eloquent…" (4:10). Working with the supposition that Yahweh really needs him for this mission, and based on the fact that Yahweh has already invested all this time pleading and negotiating with him, burning bush and all, Moses plays the refusal card: "O my Lord, please send someone else" (v. 13). His stammering is an impediment, but Moses turns it into a trump card. It is a bold move, and whether he means it or not, it does not really matter. He is negotiating, after all.

"Then the anger of the LORD was kindled against Moses," says verse 14. "It's about time!" the reader would think, expecting something dramatic. Moses, however, keeps his cool. Moses does not want to face the pharaoh on his own, and even though Yahweh repeatedly assures him, "I will be with you," "I will be your mouth," Moses goes for the tangible rather than the intangible. A good negotiator knows that a profession of good faith is never enough. Moses does not stop until Yahweh gives in: "What of your brother, Aaron?" (v. 14). The end result is great for Moses. Aaron, his younger brother who looks up to him, will go with him, be at his side every minute, speak for him, and consider him "like a god" (see v. 16). And on top of that, Moses will have some tricks up his sleeve: his magic staff, his hand, and the water from the Nile. It is a resounding victory for him. The burning bush, it turns out, is more than just the place of Moses' calling. It is what South Africans call "a site of struggle" and one that Moses wins. Whatever else Moses is, he is one supremely skilled negotiator.

A Son of Pharaoh's Daughter

Where does it all start, though? Where does Moses get all this from? Surely not from the isolation of his desert years in the land of Midian. I suggest that in order to understand this better, we do not look at Exodus 3 and 4 but rather at Hebrews 11:23-28. There we find a glowing tribute to Moses' faith, where he is placed in that row of venerable heroes of the faith for his role in the liberation of his people. The author of Hebrews completely omits the women of Exodus 1 and 2 from this gallery despite their faith and commitment. Seeing that he does mention Rahab, one has to wonder why, unless that author is so intent on Moses because of the point he makes in verses 24 and 25: "By faith Moses, when he was grown up, refused to be called a son of Pharaoh's daughter, choosing rather to share ill-treatment with the people of God than to enjoy the fleeting pleasures of sin" (NRSV). It is meant as high praise.

That point is a reminder of something else as well, however. Moses grew up in the house of Pharaoh. He was, for most of his life growing up, a child of the palace. Better than any Hebrew except Joseph, the man this current pharaoh "did not know" (Ex. 1:8), Moses understood the Egyptians, the grand politics of the empire, and the petty politics of the palace. He understood that military readiness and power were not the only arrows in Egypt's quiver. Military conquest was not by any means all they knew and sought. The pharaohs knew when and how to negotiate, always to their own advantage. These are skills that would have been part of the education of the sons of pharaohs, and sometimes the daughters, passed on from generation to generation, and it is not at all implausible that Moses, growing up in the palace as "a son of Pharaoh's daughter" (Heb. 11:24), would have been schooled in all these skills.

In my reading of the text, Moses emerges more as a skilful negotiator than a reluctant liberator, although he certainly is that too. In negotiating so fiercely with Yahweh, and getting his way, Moses prepares Yahweh for the reality that he will go to Pharaoh, not with a blunt command to let the people go but to negotiate their way to freedom. In his contest with Yahweh, Moses prepares *himself* for what he, knowing what he knows, expects to be a difficult task. Moses not only reveals what his political strategy is going to be but also reveals his politics, and the difference between the politics of Moses and the politics of Yahweh becomes clearer. That is why, earlier, Moses does not want Yahweh, whose politics he can't control, "to be his mouth" (see Exod 4:12-16). He wants someone more pliable, one who shares his politics, into whose ears he can whisper, and who will listen. Aaron fits the part perfectly. The politics of Moses is the politics of accommodation and incrementalism, what some would call "realism," without asking *whose* realities are really determining the course of events here. The politics of Yahweh is the politics of *now!* That is the urgency in the words "Let my people go!"

The politics of this God is the politics of resistance, which is revolution, where the people's suffering, their struggles, their legitimate expectations, and their right to freedom are the realities that count. The politics of the palace turns on the realities as the empire sees them: what is to the benefit of the empire. When Martin

Luther King Jr. talked incessantly about "the fierce urgency of now!" and spelled out the reasons "why we can't wait," he was driven by the politics of God. When Barack Obama chastised young people about their impatience and insisted on the virtues of gradualism, he was captured by the politics of the palace.[7] That is the fundamental reason why four little words become twelve chapters.

In one of my most beloved quotes from John Calvin, the reformer makes the point that it is God's self who implants the longings for justice in the hearts of the oppressed.[8] Our longings for freedom, justice, and dignity are not mere instinct. They are there by divine, creational intention. That is how God created us. Our natural state of being should be living with dignity in freedom and with justice, in harmony with ourselves, with those around us, and with creation. That is what God saw when God pronounced our creation as "very good." Thus, as a result of this creational impulse, tyranny and oppression cannot be long endured by people created in the image of God and called to freedom as their natural state. This point, too, Calvin makes with great emphasis. Then Calvin goes on to make another point. The cry, "How long?" that always bursts forth from the heart of the oppressed, that cry for freedom, is in fact a cry from God's own heart. "It is as if the LORD hears Godself cry, when the oppressed cry."[9] That is exactly what I am seeing here in the exodus story. In that repeated "I have heard, seen, know...," we hear the cries of the oppressed coming from God's own heart.

And in essence, that is the difference between the politics of God and the politics of Moses. Between the politics of heaven and the politics of the palace. Yahweh hears the "groanings" of the people; Moses hears the counterarguments from Pharaoh. Yahweh shares the impatience of the oppressed. Moses seems to have all the time in the world. Yahweh's is a revolutionary impatience driven by God's revolutionary love for freedom, by God's compassionate justice and outrage at injustice. The people have to go. Now! Delay means continued injustice. Freedom is always a matter of the fiercest urgency. Ponder the way the many words for "liberation" rush from the mouth of Yahweh as that impatience grows: "I am the LORD, and I will free you...and deliver you...I will redeem you...I will take you as my people..." (Ex. 6:6-7, NRSV). The words with which Yahweh starts, "I am the LORD," are a declaration of authority, of power, of firm intent. I am the Guarantor of freedom, God says, the Bringer of justice, the Deliverer of my people. No one will stand in my way. The repeated references to "burdens of the Egyptians" and "the misery of Egypt" is a way of emphasizing God's hatred for slavery, domination, and oppression. In verse 7, Yahweh speaks as if the act of deliverance has already been accomplished: "I am the LORD your God who *has freed you* from the burdens of the Egyptians." Yahweh speaks as the God of the oppressed. Moses speaks as the child of the palace.

The Politics of the Hardened Heart

Scholars are right about the layers of tradition in the exodus story and the confusion it sometimes causes. That strange passage in 4:18-31, with the quite baffling verse 24 in the middle, is but one example. Likewise, one is not sure which appearance before Pharaoh comes first, the one in chapter 5 or in chapter 7. In Exodus 7, Moses and Aaron are not yet before Pharaoh, and they are told by Yahweh to anticipate Pharaoh's response, which is not a flat-out "no" but rather a request to prove their bona fides by performing a wonder. It is only by verse 10 that they are standing before Pharaoh and immediately begin to "perform a wonder" (v. 9, NRSV) as Pharaoh requested. Now all that preparation in the desert comes into play, though it is not Moses' but Aaron's staff that becomes a snake. This has all the signs of an opening gambit in negotiations, and subsequently, Pharaoh calls in his magician/priests, who do the same.

The fact that Aaron's snake swallows all the others is apparently not very impressive; Pharaoh does not listen, his "heart [is] hardened" (Ex. 7:13), the people are not freed. The first plague, water turned to blood, follows immediately. But this, too, Pharaoh's magicians/priests imitate, and Pharaoh is not persuaded (vv. 17-22). Does it matter that whatever Moses and Aaron do in this round is a death-inviting trick, senselessly repeated by the priests of Egypt? And to prove what? No one really knows, and the text does not say. Death upon death can hardly be "proof" that Yahweh lives. No liberation here, no signs of life-giving hope, only death upon death. It does Egypt no good, but neither does it bring the people their freedom. The first round of negotiations ends quickly and inconclusively.

Not so in Exodus 5. Moses and Aaron come before Pharaoh and tell him what Yahweh desires: let the people go. It is clear that Pharaoh has no intention of giving in at all, and the negotiations immediately become utterly serous. They begin with the pharaoh's derisive response: "Who is the LORD [who is this new god, unknown to me], that I should heed him...?" (Ex. 5:2, NRSV). They tell him that this God is "the God of the Hebrews" who demands that the people be free to go "a three days' journey into the wilderness" to worship (v. 3), exactly as Moses was told in 3:18b. Curiously, though, Moses does not repeat God's words in 3:19 and 20, namely that God knows that the pharaoh will refuse and that therefore Yahweh will "strike Egypt with all my wonders." The risks of uttering those threatening words to the face of the king of Egypt are too great. So Moses, clever negotiator that he is, omits those words but adds words of his own: "...or he will fall upon us with pestilence or sword" (5:3). Moses turns Yahweh's threat to the pharaoh into a threat to the Israelites. Will that little embellishment soften the tyrant's heart?

Apparently not. Pharaoh dismisses the revelation of who this God is as easily as the threat to the people. He could not care less. He is the pharaoh, the king of Egypt, the man-god of the empire. It is he who holds the power of life and death in his hands. A god who takes pleasure in killing for no good reason is a god he can live with. So without missing a beat, Pharaoh changes the subject. "Moses and Aaron…" (v. 4). He is indignant, even enraged, an emperor who sees his power challenged; a slave owner who smells a rat, who sees the day go by in idle chitchat while the empire's work needs to be done. "Why are you taking the people away from their work?" Notice that now the subject under discussion is no longer freedom and the rights of the people; it is about enslavement and the rights of the enslaver.

In the next twenty verses, the pharaoh firmly asserts control: "Get to your labors!" (Exod 5:4, NRSV). Pharaoh issues new commands to the taskmasters and the supervisors. Straw for the making of bricks shall no longer be provided. "Let them go and gather straw for themselves" (v. 7). However, the demand for the number of finished bricks remains the same. That's another lesson the pharaoh will teach his son. With slaves, leniency does not work. It creates the wrong impression, namely weakness. Hence, it is not recommended. In slaves, it only encourages rebelliousness. The slaves will complain, the pharaoh knows, but coming up with that old, tired slave master's trope, he orders his men to pay no heed: "they are lazy" (v. 8). He knows how the psychology works: poison their minds with ideas of "freedom" and you have a fight on your hands. But double the workload and they won't have time to "pay…attention to deceptive words" (v. 9). Teach them the most important lesson of imperial *realpolitik*: freedom is deception. None of this "Woke up this morning with my mind stayed on freedom" nonsense. Double the workload, double the punishment. Beat that foolishness out of them!

Pharaoh hopes that the outcome of all this will be as expected, that in the face of this overwhelming show of power and cruelty, the slaves will turn on the one who brought them those foolish dreams of freedom in the first place. And so they do. "The LORD look upon you and judge!" they say to Moses and Aaron. "You have brought us into bad odor with Pharaoh and his officials, and have put a sword in their hands to kill us" (5:21). And Moses, with nowhere else to go, turns to Yahweh with something like an "I told you so." "O LORD! Why have you mistreated this people?" (v. 22). Notice that now it is not the pharaoh who has mistreated the people; it is Yahweh. And Moses reminds Yahweh of their long and difficult negotiation sessions: "Why did you ever send me?" (v. 22). That is, when I told you to send someone else, you got angry. But look at us now, "and you have done nothing!" (v. 23). The people fight with each other, they fight with their leader, and their leader fights with God. Not a bad day's work. The politics of the palace, tried and tested, is working once again. Yahweh will have to start from scratch, and so we get Exodus 6:1-13.

But the politics of the palace is also the politics of the hardened heart. What in the palace passes for the politics of negotiations is in God's eyes no more than the politics of the hardened heart. Yahweh has known this from the start, and told Moses so. "I know, however," Yahweh said way back in 3:19, "that the king of Egypt will not let you go, unless compelled by a mighty hand." Yahweh knows the mind of the oppressor, as will Frederick Douglass, as we have witnessed. Pharaoh will resist, as all oppressors do. He will cling to his slaves, as he must cling to his power. He will think of losing face as he loses his chattel. There will be arguments about the blow to Egypt's economy and about the blow to Egypt's ego. He will think of the political fallout at home and the geopolitical consequences for the empire. He will consider his standing with his armies. He, their commander-in-chief, and they, the people's heroes, one and all. He will think of his standing with his priests and the gods of Egypt, the gods of conquerors and slave owners, losing the battle against an unknown, unseen God of slaves and underlings. So he will harden his heart. God knows the ways of tyrants, slaveholders, and oppressors. They will resist the people's cry for freedom by any means necessary, and if outright suppression no longer works that well, they will try negotiations. Also, while the oppressions continue, negotiations open a new front, and that's all to the good, for as the Rolling Stone song says, so the pharaoh thinks: "Time is on my side...."

There is a bit of a conundrum here. In 4:21, it reads that Yahweh warned Moses, "I will harden his heart." In other places, it reads that Pharaoh hardened his own heart. The conundrum is that where it reads that Pharaoh hardened his heart, it is sometimes explicit. Where it reads that God hardened Pharaoh's heart, the tense used is passive: the heart of Pharaoh *is hardened*. The ambiguity causes great debate, and some conclude that it really means that nowhere is it God who hardens Pharaoh's heart. It is all his own doing. The punishment he and his people draw from Yahweh in those fearsome plagues is all his doing. These scholars point out that the story also makes clear that Yahweh gives the pharaoh ample chance to repent, and sometimes it looks as if he does, only to recant and refuse to let the people go. Every time he rejects the opportunity for repentance and obedience, his heart is hardened.

The hardened heart of the pharaoh might also be the narrator's way to describe the pharaoh's politics of negotiation. You may go, Pharaoh says at one point but offer your sacrifices here in the land, close by, where I can keep an eye on you. Or go, but don't take your little ones, as if it is thinkable that the people should leave their children behind. But then perhaps he does not find that strange: since when do slaves have real feelings for their children? Since when do they have a right to something called a "family"? Isn't that why it was so easy for slaveholders of all kinds throughout the centuries to separate enslaved families on the auction block? As easy as it was for apartheid to break up Black families with their Pass laws, "migrant labour" laws, "influx control" laws, and their "Population Registration Acts"? Besides, I need to replenish my numbers, Pharaoh might be thinking. You take the old folks, and I'll keep the younger ones. You may go, he promises at one point but then wonders aloud, "But which ones are to go?" At another, you may go, but leave your livestock here. Then, in an afterthought, as if his magnanimity deserves great praise, "Even your children may go with you" (10:24, NRSV). Abusive power brings false pride, and false pride brings a false sense of reality, which brings a distorted sense of generosity; even after nine plagues, Pharaoh still thinks he is in charge. He still thinks it is in his power to define freedom.

But perhaps the hardened heart may tell us something else, and perhaps the ambiguity is the narrator's purpose, and that is why we are told as early as 4:21, "I will harden Pharaoh's heart." We should read this together with the repeated claims and pronouncements from Yahweh, "I am the LORD," "I am the God of your ancestors," "I AM WHO I AM," and the seven-fold "*I* will" in 6:1-13 that we have mentioned before. In the end, this is not a fight between slaves and slave owners. It is not even a fight of the empire against rebellious underlings. It is a battle between the gods of Egypt and the God of Israel, between the man-god and slaveholder, Pharaoh, and the Liberator God who loves justice and proclaims freedom. And in the end, Pharaoh will discover that this is a fight he cannot win. In the end, he will have to submit and let the people go. In the end, every knee in Egypt, including his, shall bow, and every tongue shall confess that this God is indeed the God of justice and freedom. This is a parable for oppressors and for peoples in struggles for freedom.

Only Don't Go Too Far

What Pharaoh offers in Exodus 8:28 comes right in the middle of the devastations of the fourth plague. There are six more plagues to come, but this is, in my view, the most significant and cleverest of his concessions. It is also the one that makes this aspect of the exodus story such a powerful parable for our times. You can go, only do not go too far.

As I write, the African National Congress's elective conference has come to an end. With depressing predictability, Cyril Ramaphosa was reelected as its president, thus remaining the president of the country until national elections in 2024 if the criminal acts he has been accused of and still has to answer for do not catch up with him before then. Elected along with him, and just as predictable, was the coterie of shady, questionable, and incompetent characters that have passed for "the leadership" in the past five years. The elections might be challenged, since accusations of corruption and bribery are rife, but they were elections by the ANC delegates, and the country will bow down to this reality, a painful reminder of the relevance of the parable of the bramble we discuss in chapter 11 below. At the time of this writing, the situation has worsened, and South Africa's leadership crisis has deepened.

It is, however, an equally painful reminder of our parable under discussion, taken from the exodus story. Among the many issues surrounding President Cyril Ramaphosa, one of the most disturbing is his captivity to white monopoly capital, here in South Africa and in the West, and the ways in which he has led South Africa further along the destructive path of neoliberal capitalism. That South Africa is today the country with the greatest socioeconomic inequalities in the world is the result of an economic trajectory chosen by the ANC government since 1994, much to the satisfaction of world bodies like the IMF and the World Bank.[10] So while the dire situation in this country is not solely his fault, there is no dispute that in Ramaphosa's reign this process of neocolonialist enslavement of South Africa's generationally impoverished masses has been both accelerated and exacerbated. No South African leader has become so much the darling of those international financial institutions, the G-7, and the capitalist West in general, especially after the hiccup of the Zuma years. One supposes that his billionaire status has to be part of the reason, but still, in some spectacular ways, Cyril Ramaphosa, more than anyone before him, has become the personification of South Africa's captivity to neoliberal capitalism and all its ills.

Critical analysts such as Patrick Bond[11] and Sampie Terreblanche[12] have seen this from the start and have been ringing the alarm bells ever since. Eugene Cairncross offers scathing, but entirely on point, critique in what he calls "the triumph of capital" in South Africa's "post-Apartheid" economy.[13] He mentions how tax concessions by the "new" government, especially to the gold-mining industry, have been preserved and how privatization and commercialization of state assets like the fuel producer Sasol, "for a song," has benefited it as a private company with the post-apartheid state foregoing these profits. Under Ramaphosa, with South African Airways, parts of Transnet, and Denel already gone, and with Eskom, the electricity provider, and the rest of Transnet on the chopping block, the list has grown alarmingly.

Cairncross gives a perfect description of how far the pharaoh of our negotiated settlement was willing to let South Africa's people go—not too far at all. He explains how ownership and control of lands, mines, and major industries remain concentrated "in the hands of a handful of capitalists" exactly as it was in the past. And not only that: ownership of major economic activities has been "systematically transferred to foreign capital, either directly or through the stock exchange." It seems nothing was left to chance. Under the ANC government, exchange control became another tool of enrichment of the few, albeit that "the few" now included the few Blacks from the new elite and the political aristocracy.

> During the period of 1998 to 2002, the six largest corporations—Anglo American, Gencor/BHP Billiton (mining conglomerates) Old Mutual, SAB (South African Breweries) and Liberty—moved tens of billions of Rands off-shore, and listed as "foreign" companies. Two major consequences of these actions are initial movement of the vast amounts of capital offshore, *out of the control of present or future South African governments, and the future profits made in South Africa would be exported to the now externally listed and domiciled companies.* [South Africa's] current balance of payment deficit is to a significant extent attributable to the continued export of profits and dividends to these (and other) now "foreign" companies.[14]

One should perhaps highlight just three further issues related to this state of affairs. First, those exported profits, though created here in South Africa from the minerals taken from our soil, should have benefited the development of the people of South Africa, who instead have to carry the loss of these benefits through the taxes they have to pay. Second, one need not look too far for the relationship between the continued impoverishment of South Africa's Black majority and the sudden, spectacular enrichment of the few. Third, consider some of the personalities involved. Trevor Manuel, who was the Minister of Finance presiding over these events, is today Chairman of the Board of that same Old Mutual, now linked to that same Liberty, and Cyril Ramaphosa is also part of Gencor—the same companies, among others, that benefited so handsomely from these decisions. They are, of course, not the only ones, but they are two of the most prominent who came to their wealth through their political positions and choices. And that wealth is legendary. It is the reward empire offers its minions at the cost of justice for the masses, but that is what the elites call South Africa's "rapid deracialization of capital."

The rest of the African continent does not fare much better, and, in the case of the so-called "independent" Francophone countries, the former French colonies, things are even worse. The successful negotiation gambit, offered by France, is outrageously scandalous. Africa was allowed to go, but not too far. Pastor Barry

Wugale, in his aptly titled booklet *Africa in Captivity*, quoted before, pointed to this situation, but it is well worth finding and reading the original article by socio-economic analyst Siji Jabbar.[15]

Jabbar describes the utterly fraudulent independence France negotiated with all its former colonies in Africa. Under the overall title "The Colonial Pact," it is a system designed for the complete benefit of France and its economic and political interests, called, fittingly perhaps, although stunningly cynically, "a system of compulsory solidarity." The word "compulsory," preceding "solidarity" and encompassing wholesale, premeditated fraud, already blows the mind but is perhaps fitting for what France has designed and what those African countries have conceded to. This system of "compulsory solidarity," Jabbar explains, obliges former colonies to put 65 percent of their currency reserves into the French Treasury, plus another 20 percent for financial liabilities. This means that these African countries have access to only 15 percent of their own money. Furthermore, France has first right of refusal for all government contracts, even if better deals could be secured elsewhere. On top of that, France also has first right to all and any natural resources found in those African lands. As I write, former French colony Niger has overthrown President Bazoum in a military coup. It has since become clear that the coup is widely supported by the population, because for the people of Niger, it is a step toward decolonization, toward ending the fierce grip of France on Niger and its mineral wealth. Niger is rich in gold, but is still one of the poorest countries in the world, while France, which owns no gold mines, is the fourth largest holder of gold in the world. Niger's uranium is owned almost exclusively by France. One in every three light bulbs in France is lit by the uranium France steals from Niger, while at the same time 80% of Nigerien households are without electricity. And that is on top of the fraudulent and exploitative financial arrangements mentioned above. Finally, the people of Niger are not only saying "enough is enough!", they are, despite the threats of military intervention by France and the US via ECOWAS (the economic and military cooperative states of West Africa), bluntly calling for France "to go." What they are calling for is the end of French neo-colonialist exploitation backed by US military intervention.[16] "You can go," said France, "only do not go too far away."

The Democratic Republic of the Congo is another scandalous example. After the decades of colonialism by Belgium—in which King Leopold II treated the country like his own personal fiefdom, a century of slavery, colonial exploitation, and death-dealing politics that claimed the lives of more than 10 million Congolese in what has become known as "the hidden holocaust"—the DRC's fabulous mineral wealth has become its curse. From the moment the Congo took its first breath as an independent country, the West made it known that it would not allow an independent Congo to go too far. And its first move lacked even the courtesy of subtlety: Congo's first, promising leader, Prime Minister Patrice Lumumba, scarcely into his first term, was abducted, tortured, and brutally murdered by a combination of Belgium, the CIA, and the forces of their puppet in Katanga, Moïse Tshombe. Today, there is constant civil war in that country, especially in those mineral-rich areas in the east. The central government has not been able to assert control or any kind of authority there, peace effort after peace effort has failed, and while the manufactured instability remains, the country is being looted by corporations from the West and Israel. Professor Hannes Swoboda of the Centre for Peace Studies and the Sir Peter Ustinov Institute in Vienna bemoans this very situation in the DRC and exposes the ruthlessness of today's pharaohs, as he writes, underscoring the point we are trying to make here.

> There is so much interconnection between the past horror of colonialism, the ongoing one-sided exploitation of natural resources and people, tribal disputes, regional interference, and lack of determination to stop the wars. Unfortunately, there seems not much hope for an end of this multi-layered conflict and people will continue to be killed.[17]

We could leave our ponderings here but for one small, though not insignificant, detail. As Moses leaves Pharaoh's presence, the king says, "Pray for me" (Exod 8:28, NRSV). Is this a genuine request, a heartfelt desire from a man who knows his people are staring death in the face, or is this yet another condition: I will let you go, but only if you promise to pray for me? The *New Interpreter's Bible* comments that this is "astonishing," for it is "a reluctant, but necessary, admission on the part of the pharaoh that Yahweh holds the power for life and that Pharaoh must finally submit to Yahweh's requirements." The prayer is for the removal of the plague. Prayers to Yahweh "are among Moses' few bargaining chips," and he intends to use them wisely. "The plagues are the result of social abuses, and the flies will be removed only when those abused are removed." Moses knows "what comes before what. First comes the exodus, the departure. Then, only then, comes prayer."[18]

But does Moses know "what comes first"? Knowing prayer is one of his "few bargaining chips," as the NIB puts it, Moses prays for Pharaoh before the people have been let go. The plague ends. So not too surprisingly, the narrative ends the account "with a twist that violates everything negotiated. Moses had been right to be suspicious, but he had not been fearful enough." Moses had shrewdly sequenced matters in this agreement with Pharaoh: first exodus, then prayers. But Moses had promptly disregarded his own condition and had prayed for Pharaoh before there was exodus. So, unsurprisingly, the NIB concludes, "One more time, Pharaoh has triumphed and bested Moses. One more time, Pharaoh refuses to listen. One more time, Pharaoh acts with a hard heart. One more time, Yahweh is refused, and the slaves stay in bondage."[19] This is how the politics of the palace trips one up and blocks the freedom of the people.

This, remember, is a parable on the perils of negotiating with Pharaoh. I, Pharaoh, will give "permission" so that it is I who gave my permission, not Yahweh who demanded, who will get the glory. It is my magnanimity, my wisdom, my impeccable timing, so I get to set the parameters of your freedom. It is all in my power, so I will set the conditions. Of course I deserve that Nobel Peace Prize. You can go, but not too far, and while you are at it, pray for me. We have to ask: Where does the pharaoh get the gall to demand prayers for him and his people? The answer is devastatingly simple. Because he is the pharaoh, and Moses just showed that he does not have his priorities straight. What Pharaoh is in fact saying is this: you will not have your freedom, but I will let you have your religion, only that religion should be practised on my behalf as well. Imagine that: while God is punishing the pharaoh for holding us enslaved, we pray to God to have mercy on the pharaoh and his people, so that our enslavement can continue.

Even now, knowing he is losing the battle but because he has bested Moses in this round of negotiations, Pharaoh, as befits every slaveholder and every colonizer, lays claim on everything: the people's bodies and their souls, their hearts and their minds, their freedom and their faith. Pray for me. What for? we should be asking. For our God to sanction and bless your enslavement of us? So that our God, who just a moment ago demanded our freedom and called us "my people," should now confirm your claims of ownership? Pray to keep you and your people safe from the plague; save you and your people from the one thing right now that can force you to let us go? Pray that God save your life, keep you strong and healthy, so you can continue with business as usual?

Pharaoh is preying on the spirituality and faith of the people. This arrogance is astonishing but not at all surprising. South Africans should know. "Pray for me" means appease your God with your worship, but please me with your submission. Go practice the rituals of your faith, but forget the dreams that inspired your revolution. Go worship your God, tell God all your sorrows, let God know all your sufferings and pain. Share it all with the nation and the world if you think it will help, but pray for me, forgive me, and then come back to me and be my slaves once more. Pharaoh shows no remorse, no repentance, no desire for justice or freedom, and forget about the reparations and restitution Yahweh wanted in Exodus 6. Don't go too far, and don't forget to pray for me. That is why Africans regale the well-known saying ascribed to Kenya's first democratically elected president, Jomo Kenyatta, pertaining to the work of Western missionaries in Africa. Kenyatta was reported to have said, "When the missionaries came to Africa we had the land, and they had the Bible. They asked us to pray. When we opened our eyes, they had the land and we had the Bible." That is why we had a Truth and Reconciliation Commission.

Still, this part of the exodus narrative does not end here. The struggles go on until they reach the Red Sea and beyond. In the beginning, Yahweh promised that they would worship the God of their liberation "in the wilderness"—in other words, away from the enslavement, the power, and the violent control of the pharaoh. But at that Red Sea, that decisive crossing from the land of slavery into the land of freedom, the story ends as it began, with the suppressed, ignored, marginalised, revolutionary women who refuse to be marginalised, suppressed, or ignored. With Miriam in the lead, they take up their rightful place in the revolution and in history, towards freedom, dignity, and full humanity. This is what M. M. Thomas understood: power as the dignity of the people, their full and rightful participation in the shaping of their history and their future.

This is a parable of struggle and strife, of oppression and suppression, of rising up and marching on, of the righting of the wrongs, of the last who shall be first. The powerless shall be empowered, the weak shall be girded with strength; the hopeless shall find new hope, and those with might shall not prevail. For it is not Moses but Miriam, with tambourine in hand, who first sings the song of praise and freedom, dancing before the LORD, leading the whole crowd of women and men, Israelites and those other slaves who toiled and suffered with them and have now been freed with them:[20]

> I will sing to Yahweh, for Yahweh has triumphed gloriously;
> horse and rider Yahweh has thrown into the sea.
> Yahweh is my strength and my might,
> Yahweh has become my salvation;…
> Sing to Yahweh, for Yahweh has triumphed gloriously;
> Horse and rider Yahweh has thrown into the sea.
> (Exod 15:1-2, 21, NRSV)[21]

There is still much to fight for, but there is much to look forward to.

Chapter 10

Missing Micaiah

On Prophetic Integrity about Haiti

Wendell Griffen

In September 2021, disturbing news coverage of US Border Patrol agents on horseback chasing asylum seekers from Haiti who tried to enter the United States at Del Rio, Texas, left a lasting memory of a time when white slave patrols used horses and dogs to capture enslaved Africans who tried to escape the brutalities suffered from white capitalists who stole their bodies and labor to produce the wealth that funded the United States. The deeper history of white people to the people and place now called Haiti is even worse.

Haiti is about the size of Maryland. It is found on the western third of Hispaniola in the Caribbean. The eastern two-thirds of Hispaniola is the Dominican Republic. Hispaniola was home to Taino/Arawak people for thousands of years before Christopher Columbus stumbled upon it in December 1492.

Spanish colonizers enslaved their Taino hosts and forced them to work in gold mines. Hunger, violence, disease, and harsh working conditions decimated the indigenous enslaved people, so King Ferdinand and Queen Isabella of Spain licensed the colonizers to enslave Africans to replace the work force. The enslaved Africans worked on plantations to grow sugar cane, coffee, tobacco, and other raw crops for export to Europe. French colonizers replaced the Spanish in the western part of Hispaniola and continued the plantation system until San Dominque (the name the French gave that part of Hispaniola) became the most profitable French colony in the world.

Enslaved Africans waged a violent revolution against French colonizers that forced France to abolish slavery in 1794. Napoleon Bonaparte responded by invading San Dominique with the largest fleet then assembled and thousands of French soldiers. However, African resistance to the French invasion over the next ten years was so fierce that Napoleon lost over fifty thousand soldiers, including eighteen generals. The Africans defeated the French invaders in 1804. The war also led Napoleon to negotiate the Louisiana Purchase in 1803, a land deal that covered what is now all or part of the states of Louisiana, Arkansas, Missouri, Kansas, Nebraska, Oklahoma, Iowa, Colorado, Wyoming, Minnesota, the

Dakotas, and Montana. That successful revolt made Haiti the first Black republic, the only nation where enslaved people overthrew their oppressors and the second nation in the Western Hemisphere (after the United States) to declare independence from its colonizers.

However, the United States refused to recognize Haiti until 1862. Politicians from pro-slavery states opposed recognizing and having a harmonious diplomatic relationship with a nation that had overthrown white enslavers. White Americans worried that the existence of Haiti challenged the slave-driven US economy and would encourage slave revolts in the US. Instead of being a good neighbor to Haiti, the United States sided with France and Britain in imposing an economic embargo against Haiti. The US supported France in its demand that the government of Haiti pay reparations to the white enslavers covering the cost of land, the value of enslaved persons, livestock, commercial properties, and services the enslavers claimed were lost due to the successful revolt. Even Haitian officials were assigned a monetary value—as former enslaved persons—that the French (with US support) demanded be repaid. However, no reparations were paid by the enslavers to the formerly enslaved persons.

The US sided with the French to force Haiti to take out a loan for 150 million gold francs with a designated French bank to cover the cost of "reparations" to French enslavers for the loss of their "property." The value of that loan was ten times that of Haiti's total revenue in 1825 and twice the price the United States paid France for the Louisiana Purchase, which covered seventy-four times more land than Haiti.

In 1915, the United States invaded and began a military occupation of Haiti that lasted until 1934—almost two decades. Over the years, the US has supported insurrections against Haitian political leaders, propped up corrupt and ruthless Haitian leaders, sponsored the assassination or forced removal of Haitian leaders, and been complicit in fomenting greed and discord among Haitians. Also, Haiti—the most impoverished nation in the Western Hemisphere—has suffered earthquakes, hurricanes, and other catastrophic natural disasters.

Now the US refuses to welcome Haitians who seek asylum from atrocities, inequities, poverty, disease, catastrophic natural disasters, centuries of white supremacist-sponsored and -financed internal strife, and other hardships. Instead, in 2021 Border Patrol agents on horseback chased and brutalized Haitian asylum seekers. In addition to that despicable conduct, the Biden administration forced asylum-seeking Haitians onto planes and returned them to Haiti rather than process their petitions for asylum.

Haitians who trek across Central America to seek asylum in the United States are survivors of a failed state, gang violence, and a US military coup and kidnapping of former President Jean-Bertrand Aristide and his wife in 2004. Their most recent president, Jovenel Moïse, was assassinated at his residence by foreign mercenaries on July 7, 2021, and his wife was shot several times and suffered critical injuries. Natural disasters including earthquakes, tropical storms, landslides, and flooding have occurred repeatedly in recent years. Added to this list of horrors, Haitians have suffered centuries of white supremacist schemes to punish their nation for overthrowing white enslavers. They have the right, under US law, to seek asylum in this country. And they have the right to protection from abuse and oppression—in the United States—when they seek asylum.

Instead, Haitian asylum seekers are now experiencing the latest instance of more than two hundred years of white supremacy, brutality, greed, hypocrisy, disregard for the rights of Black, Brown, indigenous, and other people of color, and deliberate US policy decisions. The suffering produced by those decisions, past and present, is worse than despicable. It is worse than outrageous. It is damnable. No sensible person who believes in justice should expect a just God to bless a nation that behaves this way. A nation that mistreats vulnerable Haitians and other desperate people who seek asylum does not deserve to be blessed. That nation deserves to be damned as an enemy to God and justice.

So why haven't people who profess to be followers of Jesus said so? We seem to lack the prophetic integrity of Micaiah, the Hebrew prophet (and disciple of Elijah) mentioned in 1 Kings 22. Micaiah, unlike other religious figures who were popular with King Ahab of the northern kingdom of Israel, refused to predict a favorable outcome for Ahab's plan to invade and retake Ramoth-gilead from the king of Aram (Damascus-Syria). Instead, Micaiah endured political disfavor and physical abuse by first mocking Ahab and his plan and then boldly predicting that the plan would lead to Ahab's demise. For doing so, Micaiah was publicly slapped by Zedekiah, a religious leader popular with Ahab.

> [1]For three years Aram and Israel continued without war. [2]But in the third year King Jehoshaphat of Judah came down to the king of Israel. [3]The king of Israel said to his servants, "Do you know that Ramoth-gilead belongs to us, yet we are doing nothing to take it out of the hand of the king of Aram?" [4]He said to Jehoshaphat, "Will you go with me to battle at Ramoth-gilead?" Jehoshaphat replied to the king of Israel, "I am as you are; my people are your people, my horses are your horses."
>
> [5]But Jehoshaphat also said to the king of Israel, "Inquire first for the word of the LORD." [6]Then the king of Israel gathered the prophets together, about four hundred of them, and said

to them, "Shall I go to battle against Ramoth-gilead, or shall I refrain?" They said, "Go up; for the LORD will give it into the hand of the king." [7]But Jehoshaphat said, "Is there no other prophet of the LORD here of whom we may inquire?" [8]The king of Israel said to Jehoshaphat, "There is still one other by whom we may inquire of the LORD, Micaiah son of Imlah; but I hate him, for he never prophesies anything favorable about me, but only disaster." Jehoshaphat said, "Let the king not say such a thing." [9]Then the king of Israel summoned an officer and said, "Bring quickly Micaiah son of Imlah." [10]Now the king of Israel and King Jehoshaphat of Judah were sitting on their thrones, arrayed in their robes, at the threshing floor at the entrance of the gate of Samaria; and all the prophets were prophesying before them. [11]Zedekiah son of Chenaanah made for himself horns of iron, and he said, "Thus says the LORD: With these you shall gore the Arameans until they are destroyed." [12]All the prophets were prophesying the same and saying, "Go up to Ramoth-gilead and triumph; the LORD will give it into the hand of the king."

[13]The messenger who had gone to summon Micaiah said to him, "Look, the words of the prophets with one accord are favorable to the king; let your word be like the word of one of them, and speak favorably." [14]But Micaiah said, "As the LORD lives, whatever the LORD says to me, that I will speak."

[15]When he had come to the king, the king said to him, "Micaiah, shall we go to Ramoth-gilead to battle, or shall we refrain?" He answered him, "Go up and triumph; the LORD will give it into the hand of the king." [16]But the king said to him, "How many times must I make you swear to tell me nothing but the truth in the name of the LORD?" [17]Then Micaiah said, "I saw all Israel scattered on the mountains, like sheep that have no shepherd; and the LORD said, 'These have no master; let each one go home in peace.'" [18]The king of Israel said to Jehoshaphat, "Did I not tell you that he would not prophesy anything favorable about me, but only disaster?"

[19]Then Micaiah said, "Therefore hear the word of the LORD: I saw the LORD sitting on his throne, with all the host of heaven standing beside him to the right and to the left of him. [20]And the LORD said, 'Who will entice Ahab, so that he may go up and fall at Ramoth-gilead?' Then one said one thing, and another

said another, ²¹until a spirit came forward and stood before the LORD, saying, 'I will entice him.' ²²'How?' the LORD asked him. He replied, 'I will go out and be a lying spirit in the mouth of all his prophets.' Then the LORD said, 'You are to entice him, and you shall succeed; go out and do it.' ²³So you see, the LORD has put a lying spirit in the mouth of all these your prophets; the LORD has decreed disaster for you."

²⁴Then Zedekiah son of Chenaanah came up to Micaiah, slapped him on the cheek, and said, "Which way did the spirit of the LORD pass from me to speak to you?" ²⁵Micaiah replied, "You will find out on that day when you go in to hide in an inner chamber." ²⁶The king of Israel then ordered, "Take Micaiah, and return him to Amon the governor of the city and to Joash the king's son, ²⁷and say, 'Thus says the king: Put this fellow in prison, and feed him on reduced rations of bread and water until I come in peace.'" ²⁸Micaiah said, "If you return in peace, the LORD has not spoken by me." And he said, "Hear, you peoples, all of you!"

²⁹So the king of Israel and King Jehoshaphat of Judah went up to Ramoth-gilead. ³⁰The king of Israel said to Jehoshaphat, "I will disguise myself and go into battle, but you wear your robes." So the king of Israel disguised himself and went into battle. ³¹Now the king of Aram had commanded the thirty-two captains of his chariots, "Fight with no one small or great, but only with the king of Israel." ³²When the captains of the chariots saw Jehoshaphat, they said, "It is surely the king of Israel." So they turned to fight against him; and Jehoshaphat cried out. ³³When the captains of the chariots saw that it was not the king of Israel, they turned back from pursuing him. ³⁴But a certain man drew his bow and unknowingly struck the king of Israel between the scale armor and the breastplate; so he said to the driver of his chariot, "Turn around, and carry me out of the battle, for I am wounded." ³⁵The battle grew hot that day, and the king was propped up in his chariot facing the Arameans, until at evening he died; the blood from the wound had flowed into the bottom of the chariot. (1 Kings 22:1-35, NRSV)

In this narrative, Ahab (ruler of the kingdom of Israel) sought a military alliance with Jehosophat (ruler of the kingdom of Judah) to retake the important city of Ramoth-gilead in Transjordan from the ruler of Aram. Although Jehosophat expressed support for the military offensive, he wanted to be sure that it had prophetic endorsement. Even after hundreds of prophets loyal to Ahab, led by one named Zedekiah, endorsed Ahab's intention, Jehosophat seemed dubious of their integrity as shown by his question, "Is there no other prophet of the LORD here of whom we may inquire?" (1 Kgs 22:7). So Ahab, who sought Jehosophat's support and recognized that one prophet—Micaiah—might not endorse the invasion idea, was forced to summon that prophet from where he was being detained despite the fact that Ahab considered him politically uncooperative, to put it mildly (see v. 8).

Unlike the prophets who attended Ahab's court, Micaiah stood in disfavor with Ahab's imperial ambitions. Unlike those prophets who predicted success for the proposed venture to retake Ramoth-gilead, Micaiah's response that the venture would succeed was an outright sneer, followed by an unequivocal prediction that Ahab's military campaign would be disastrous (1 Kgs 22:15-18). In doing so, Micaiah not only refused to give Ahab a prophetic endorsement but also declared that Ahab was being misled by prophetic sycophants as part of a divine decree for the downfall of his reign (vv. 19-23). For that boldness, Micaiah was publicly assaulted by Ahab's prophetic puppet (Zedekiah) and then sentenced to even more harsh imprisonment (vv. 24-28).

Micaiah's prophetic integrity and dissent in the face of Ahab's imperial ambition and Zedekiah's persecution stand in direct contrast to religious silence about US and Western European conduct towards Haiti. Although he did not mention Haiti, the following except from the speech Martin Luther King Jr. delivered at Riverside Church in New York City on April 4, 1967—exactly a year before he was murdered in Memphis, Tennessee—during his call for the United States to end its military occupation and aggression in Vietnam and Southeast Asia seems equally applicable.

> It is a sad fact that, because of comfort, complacency, a morbid fear of communism, and our proneness to adjust to injustice, the Western nations that initiated so much of the revolutionary spirit of the modern world have now become the arch anti-revolutionaries. This has driven many to feel that only Marxism has the revolutionary spirit. Therefore, communism is a judgment against our failure to make democracy real and follow through on the revolutions that we initiated. Our only hope today lies in our ability to recapture the revolutionary spirit and go out into a sometimes-hostile world declaring eternal hostility to poverty,

racism, and militarism.... This call for a world-wide fellowship that lifts neighborly concern beyond one's tribe, race, class and nation is in reality a call for an all-embracing and unconditional love for all men [humanity].... We must move past indecision to action. We must find new ways to speak for peace in Vietnam and justice throughout the developing world—a world that borders on our doors. If we do not act we shall be dragged down the long dark and shameful corridors of time reserved for those who possess power without compassion, might without morality, and strength without sight.[1]

It was hard to find evidence of such "neighborly concern" about Haiti and about its history, French imperialism, and two hundred years of French and US disregard for—and outright hostility toward—Haitian suffering. When French President Emmanuel Macron paid a state visit to the United States in 2022, he and US President Joe Biden faced no prophetic criticism about the role their nations have taken toward Haiti. The prophetic integrity of Micaiah was either missing or invisible concerning Haiti, once the richest source of colonial wealth to France and now the poorest, sickest, and most disregarded nation in the Western Hemisphere.

Where are congregations hearing about the deliberate unconcern for Haiti? The question Jehosophat asked Ahab applies: "Is there no other prophet of the LORD here of whom we may inquire?" Is the spirit of Micaiah lost concerning God's Haitian people? How is it that day after day, week after week, month after month, year after year, and decade after decade prophetic truth-telling has not been done by pastors, religious educators, religious authors, and the mission entities of faith groups? Have we become court prophets to the interests of US and French imperialism, white supremacy, and indifference about suffering descendants of enslaved Africans? If so, why? What spell has been cast over us? What sums have been paid to purchase our silence or willful indifference?

TransAfrica Founder and Black activist lawyer Randall Robinson was not silent or indifferent. Despite being ignored by corporate news media, most US politicians, Black civil rights organizations, and human rights organizations, Robinson was bold and blunt in interviews with Amy Goodman of *Democracy Now* after former Haitian President Jean-Bertrand Aristide and his wife Mildred were kidnapped by US forces on February 29, 2004, in what Robinson and Aristide termed a "US military coup."[2] Although US policymakers in the George W. Bush, Obama, Trump, and Biden administrations, most members of the US Congress, the United Nations, human rights groups, and faith groups have imitated Ahab's court prophets concerning the overthrow of a democratically elected leader of a Black nation in the Western Hemisphere by the nation that boasts of being "the land of the free and the home of the brave," Randall Robinson often denounced that action as well as the long history of US involvement in Haitian suffering.

Robinson is not a theologian. He was not a member of the clergy. He was not an elected official. Nevertheless, he was prophetic regarding Haiti, reparations for descendants of formerly enslaved Africans, and US imperialism for decades. One wonders how the history of Haiti might have been different if followers of Jesus had exercised the Micaiah-like prophetic integrity of Randall Robinson.

Jesus offered a perspective on the "Missing Micaiah" issue in his lesson about a needy neighbor who knocked at midnight seeking food to entertain unexpected guests:

> [5] And he said to them, "Suppose one of you has a friend, and you go to him at midnight and say to him, 'Friend, lend me three loaves of bread; [6] for a friend of mine has arrived, and I have nothing to set before him.' [7] And he answers from within, 'Do not bother me; the door has already been locked, and my children are with me in bed; I cannot get up and give you anything.' [8] I tell you, even though he will not get up and give him anything because he is his friend, at least because of his persistence he will get up and give him whatever he needs. [9] So I say to you, Ask, and it will be given you; search, and you will find; knock, and the door will be opened for you." (Luke 11:5-9, NRSV)

Clearly, people would rather not think and talk about the centuries-long abuse, mistreatment, and calculated neglect shown by the United States and France for Black children of God in Haiti. Judging from the silence on this subject from pulpits, from lecture podiums, in classrooms, and among faith-based missionary societies, it appears that many people think Haitian suffering, systemic racism, and imperialistic indifference have nothing to do with the gospel of Jesus. Our unwillingness/avoidance of the issue of reparations for Black people in the United States is dwarfed by the refusal of prophetic people (including Black people) to complain about the way Haiti and Haitians have been treated for more than two centuries. People who are up in arms about the plight of Ukrainian men, women, and children freezing, starving, and being raped, robbed, murdered, and otherwise traumatized by war have not given Haitians a thought as that society is threatened by cholera, has suffered two devastating earthquakes, and reels from successive episodes of political upheavals.

The plight of Haiti has rarely been raised by a US legislator. Senator Raphael Warnock, pastor of the congregation served by Dr. Martin Luther King Jr., hasn't mentioned Haiti. Senator Cory Booker of New Jersey hasn't mentioned Haiti. Vice President Kamala Harris hasn't mentioned Haiti. House Minority Leader Hakeem Jeffries of Brooklyn, New York, hasn't mentioned Haiti. The Congressional Black Caucus doesn't demand help for Haiti. Churches that send aid and mission groups to Haiti have not pressured politicians concerning Haiti. Religious groups that boast about loving the world have not shown enough interest—let alone love—for Haiti even to make the plight of that nation a meeting agenda item.

In the lesson about the friend who sought to borrow bread from a neighbor to feed an unexpected overnight guest in Luke 11, we read about people needing help. Today the Black descendants of children of God in Haiti who suffered centuries of deliberate racial injustice and oppression need help. But as Jesus observed, people we count as friends often refuse pleas for help. The lesson from Luke 11 about the friend who refused a nighttime request for bread shows how people refuse because helping requires them to move outside their zones of comfort and convenience. The friend denied the nighttime request because he did not want to get out of bed and risk disturbing his children. The fellow could have gotten out of bed. Children can go back to sleep. But those are the types of excuses people in need get from others they consider "friends."

The point is clear. Unhelpful "friends" and unconcerned people in power are reasons for longstanding injustice suffered by Haiti. Too many of us are like the neighbor who did not want to be bothered when it comes to Haiti. Too many of us have refused to use our power to make a just difference in the lives and fate of Haitian people. Too many preachers, Sunday school teachers, and Bible study leaders have spoken about these passages and avoided applying them to demands for racial justice, including reparations for Haiti. Too many of us have been unlike Micaiah and Randall Robinson.

Yet the point Jesus emphasized about persistence in Luke 11 is pertinent to Haiti. And in this context, we should remember that Jesus commended disruptive persistence in working for justice and dismantling injustice! Think of the needy neighbor standing outside a house knocking loudly at night. Freedom Riders were persistent. The sit-in demonstrations in segregated restaurants and stores were acts of holy persistence. Preaching again and again sermons about reparations is an act of holy persistence. Protesters who show up at shopping centers and in front of public buildings are engaged in acts of holy persistence. Demanding meetings with politicians and business leaders concerning the plight of Haiti and Haitians is in keeping with the persistent nighttime neighbor. Jesus did not condemn the disruptiveness of the needy neighbor. He mentioned it to illustrate what faithful people must do.

In the same way, integrity about Haiti requires that we become faithful people who make what former US Congressman John R. Lewis frequently termed "good trouble." We must disturb the false sense of peace that is actually political quietism, manufactured consent, and manufactured contentment. We should disrupt the processes and practices of systemic racism and indifference concerning Haiti. We must make noise like the nighttime neighbor. And like Micaiah, we must be willing to suffer displeasure from religious people who are friends of empire. We must be willing to be branded "enemies of the state." We must stop expecting justice to happen because people feel right about doing justice. Justice happens because "friends" and powerful people get to the point that they are worn down by our asking, seeking, and knocking.

May we be people with the kind of faith that works, pounds, demands, and disrupts racist systems and processes. May we, as children of God, understand that God will work through our protests. God will work by our agitation. God will work even when "friends" and the powerful would prefer to be left alone.

This is the faith we must demonstrate to obtain reparations for Haiti. We must petition, demonstrate, boycott, protest, and disrupt those who are comfortable with injustice and unconcerned about the continuing debt this society owes Black children of God who are the descendants of the first group of Black people to overthrow a European empire and take their freedom. Haitians await evidence that we will be people of Micaiah-like prophetic integrity who ask, seek, and pound doors until they receive the justice they deserve.

Chapter 11

Paying Homage to the Bramble
On Democracy Born of Disastrous Decisions[1]

(Judges 9:7-21; Daniel 2:17-23; 1 Samuel 8:1-22)

Allan Boesak

"Power to the People!"

The South African struggle cry, *"Amandla ngawethu!"*—"Power to the people!"—is now known across the world. The image is always fist in the air, face uplifted, mouth wide open—vividly defiant, vividly confident. It is the people claiming their right to be governed by those chosen by themselves. It is the shortened version of the Freedom Charter's bold assertion that "no government can justly claim authority unless it is based on the will of all the people...." It is a universal claim, valid everywhere, a truth that wherever it is denied brings that country to ruin.

One learns from experience, of course, so our experience in South Africa in the last thirty years has taught us some painful lessons. We have also come to discover just how truthful and accurate are the Bible's insights into human nature and our propensities for evil. So I, at least, have come to be more and more precise about that wonderful, vibrant, yet so easily orphaned phrase. In doing so, I have turned once again to the wisdom of India's M. M. Thomas, who, watching the slow and painful demise of India's historic liberation movement The Indian National Congress, saw how the arrogance of power, entitlement, and self aggrandizement can bring down not only a liberation movement but the entire nation. All this despite its noble history and historic leadership. Those great and noble names—B. R. Ambedkar, Jawaharlal Nehru, Mahatma Gandhi—strong as these were, would eventually crumble under the weight of their political party's inability to keep faith with the people. With prophetic discernment and bold truth telling, M. M. Thomas helped us clarify the issues. This is a revolution, Thomas wrote, but is in no way a bourgeoise political parlour game, and it is "the new sense of dignity and historic mission" that is the driving force of the people's revolution.

It is not to grab the reins of power in order to manipulate the people's dreams and aspirations, to turn the nation's purse into a trough, to have unfettered access to the nation's treasures, and to make of governance the misrule of the totally inept and the fatally misguided. It is not to make the laws that control and manage the people's legitimate expectations while putting no limitations to their own selfish expectations at all, as we are seeing tragically unfolding in South Africa as I write this. Central to it all, Thomas says, is "the new sense of dignity" of a people too long oppressed, too long reviled, too long despised, too long exploited. The dignity of the people is the key. And central to *that is power, but power "as the demand of the people."* That means power "as the bearer of dignity and for significant and responsible participation in society and social history."[2]

This is how I have more and more come to understand it as I watched our struggle cry, "Power to the people!" become more and more the joke at the overloaded tables of the rich and powerful, the economic elites and the political aristocracy. Their arrogance and greed know no bounds, and their abuse of power is of the most casual kind because they need fear no consequences. They hold power firmly in their view, but accountability is never in their purview. The illustrious names that once stamped their movement with nobility—Pixley ka Isaka Seme, John Dube, the Mandelas, the Tambos, the Sisulus—they are dragging from one bottomless pit of shamefulness to the other. Their politics is a feeding frenzy of recklessness, an orgy of self-satisfied aggrandizement, and always, always, whatever else they gobble up, on their menu is the dignity of our people.

For people of faith, it is clear. South Africans need to return to the wisdom of Daniel, as we need to return to the wisdom of M. M. Thomas. We need to pray to God to show who is in control of history, even as we pray for the power to, once again, take up the revolution that will change the fate of our nation and put our people on the path God has destined for us. God is in control, so we are called to build, challenge, and shape our societies until, as Jesus taught us to pray, God's will is done on earth as it is in heaven (Matt 6:10).

Almost forty years ago, at a time in South Africa depressingly similar to our times today, I wrote in a short commentary on John's Apocalypse,

> During the time of Hitler's Germany, Pastor Walter Lüthi, one of the witnesses from the Confessing Church, spoke a word of warning to those Christians in Germany who did not seem to understand the signs of their time. They did not understand that in Hitler the beast had once again taken shape, and not for the first time but once again. And they did not understand that the first duty of the church was to recognise this beast for what it was and to resist. Lüthi's message was clear: Hitler ought to be resisted; he was not to be played with, or ignored, or argued

away. "The Apocalypse is upon us," he said, "Daniel is an active volcano."

I continued to say, "We are seeing it again, and not only in South Africa. The church must know, as the beasts must know, for the Apocalypse speaks not only of the suffering of the faithful. It speaks also of the destruction of evil and the victory of the Lamb. Indeed, Daniel is an active volcano."[3] Oppressed people in life-and-death struggles for justice, freedom, and dignity, need to know this.

The Daniel Dilemma

The book of Daniel begins with a fairly prosaic announcement—even though nothing about war and sieges and conquest is ever prosaic—about the siege of Jerusalem. There is no historic explanation, no telling of how events unfolded, no heart-rending prose, as in the book of Lamentations, about the results of this disaster. Just the statement. Names of power are dropped: King Jehoiakim of Judah, the vanquished; King Nebuchadnezzar of Babylon, the conqueror. Then, immediately, a name of greater power puts things in perspective: it is Yahweh, the God of Israel, who let King Jehoiakim fall into the hands of Nebuchadnezzar (see Dan 1:2). And that, from beginning to end, is the point of the whole story of Daniel. As that NAME is mentioned, all other names, however powerful they are conceived to be, must know their place. With the mentioning of that NAME, the drama begins.

King Nebuchadnezzar's nights are wrecked by dreams that leave him profoundly disturbed. So bad is this that "his sleep left him." He calls in "the magicians, the enchanters, the sorcerers, and the Chaldeans" (Dan 2:1-2, NRSV). The Chaldeans are especially mentioned because they were renowned for their powers of interpretation of events and phenomena and supposedly saw themselves as a kind of master race because of that reputation. Nonetheless, they apparently were in service to the Babylonians, underscoring the power of King Nebuchadnezzar. True to their reputation, the Chaldeans are confident: "Tell your servants the dream," they said to the king, "and we will reveal the interpretation" (v. 4). The king, however, is far from being assuaged. So anxious is he that he issues a decree that promises a threat of death should they fail: they "shall be torn limb from limb" (v. 5).

Even this does not help. No one can interpret the dream. The Chaldeans seek to cover themselves and save their lives. This thing is too difficult, they tell Nebuchadnezzar: "There is no one on earth who can reveal what the king demands! …except the gods…" (vv. 10-11). This is the wrong thing to say to a man with such great power living with such great fear. "Because of this the king flew into a violent rage" and ordered the executions, verse 12 tells us. In desperation, all those wise and famous men from the master race run to Daniel for help, who, understanding not only that the lives of the Chaldeans are in danger but also that, in his violent rage, the king will kill Daniel and his friends, "responded with prudence and discretion" (v. 14). The gods behind whom the Chaldeans sought refuge cannot help, but Daniel knows who can. Seeking the companionship of faith in the company of his three friends, Daniel turns to that Power higher than the power of the king, the Chaldeans, and their gods. He and his friends pray to the One to whom belongs all wisdom and power.

Yahweh responds by giving Daniel a vision, and the very first, and eternally fundamental, thing Daniel is given to understand is summed up in Daniel 2:21: "[God] changes times and seasons, deposes kings and sets up kings; [God] gives wisdom to the wise, and knowledge to those who have understanding" (NRSV). The New Living Translation puts it even better: "[God] controls the course of world events; [God] gives rulers their power, [God] takes it away." Daniel is talking about the NAME that puts all other names in their place. To people oppressed, powerless, and in distress, these are powerful, comforting words. This is wisdom for the ages. This is sustenance for struggle. God appoints kings, and God brings them down. God has the greater power.

But how does this square with our modern times, with our democratic elections, where it is not God but the people, through their vote, who determine whom shall rule us? In places like England, some may still believe that their monarch is appointed by God, rules by divine decree determined ages ago and inherited by their offspring no matter how fit or unfit those offspring may be for rule. And even if they profess to be a "constitutional monarchy," and even though England has elections, the belief that their monarch has some divine appointment and enjoys special favour from God, giving them the right to call themselves "Head" of the Church of Christ, is still rampant enough to keep that institution going. All the splendour, the pageantry, the pomp and circumstance are supposed to reflect that unique position of power and cow the rest of us into submission. It is meant to reflect some kind of earthly, godlike power that awes us even as it elevates them. Such foolishness boggles the mind, and I have no time for it. I am glad that in South Africa we fought for a different kind of democracy caught up in just four words from that immortal document, the Freedom Charter: "The People Shall Govern!"

But is that not the heart of our dilemma, a direct contradiction of what Daniel confesses? When it is not God through some miraculous intervention but people through their votes and electoral systems who appoint rulers and depose them by voting them out? It is not really a contradiction, for that is why Daniel, coming out of the vision, says not one but two things. First, lest we fall into constant despair, God is in control of human events. Second, lest we become complacent, it is God who gives wisdom and discernment to human beings. The first does not cancel out the second. Daniel is talking about the wisdom to know when those who rule abuse the power given to them, whose rule does not serve God in serving the people and ruling with justice and compassion. He means the discernment to see, understand, and interpret the signs of the times, to discern when rulers are not shepherds of God's flock but the fake shepherds the prophet Ezekiel rails against, those wolves Jesus exposes who come only to steal, kill, and destroy, and those hirelings who take bribes and forsake the flock, who run away when danger comes. Daniel means the discernment to see and understand that the time to act has come, to use the wisdom God is the source of, to rise up and protect God's people, to rescue the rule of justice from the hands of those who use their power, entrusted to them by the people, to do injustice and to aid and abet those who thrive on injustice.

People of faith know that beyond their actions, there is God, in power and in control. That is why, in 1985, we called for a day of prayer for the downfall of the apartheid regime and why churches across the world joined us in those prayers on that day. We were in a struggle against apartheid, on the streets of confrontation every single day. We prayed without ceasing, and we prayed in faith, because we knew Daniel was right: God is in control of human events. We fought without resting, we struggled without pause, because we knew Daniel was not wrong: it is God who gives wisdom and understanding, it is God who gives us the discernment to read the signs of the times, to know it is time to rise up against what is evil. We took our prayers into the streets to glorify God in our sacrifices for what was right.

That is also why, thirty years into the new democracy, South Africans who are aware of Daniel's wisdom are so angry at what is happening right now. They have the wisdom to discern that South Africa today, despite the sacrificial struggles for the rule of the politics of decency, trustworthiness, honesty, and virtue, is being ruled by what Church Father Augustine called "a gang of robbers" because they do not know justice. They have the wisdom to know that despite the mind-numbing propaganda of the colonialist media, they are being ruled by an elite class that have sold out their dreams, hopes, sacrifices, and legitimate expectations in a devil's pact with the old, white, capitalist class. They have the wisdom to know that their revolution has been stolen, but they have the discernment to understand that it is still a revolution, and a revolution can reclaim itself. They know they have entrusted the people's power to these abusers and usurpers, but they also know that they can take that power back. They understand too, that "taking back" involves a new struggle, calling for self-sacrificial love. And besides and above all that, they know that the God they prayed to in their struggles against apartheid is the same God Daniel prayed to. They remember Rev. James Calata, a man who, in those dark days of 1937, with colonialism metamorphosing into official apartheid, himself understood Daniel: "The handle that turns the wheels of the universe is in the hand of God, and because of that hand, a new world is about to be begotten."

But it is not as if Daniel were speaking only of the future, of times he could not know of, of systems of government he would never experience. After all, he knew the history of ancient Israel. He knew the stories of how the kings of Israel and Judah, one after the other, betrayed Yahweh and the people, turned justice into wormwood, oppressed the weak and the vulnerable, and exploited the poor, all the while enriching themselves and bringing the people to ruin. He knew what it meant to have rulers who turned out to be the opposite of what Yahweh had intended. He knew also about Samuel, how Samuel had tried to warn the people not to follow their desire "to be like the other nations" (see 1 Samuel 8), abandoning the politics of trust in God, justice and equality among the people, and peace in their world. Daniel knew how God dealt with such rulers. He also knew though, how God told Samuel to let the people have their way, make their own choices, assert their own will, even if it meant abandoning Yahweh as their ruler, because the rewards of greed were so rich and the lure of self-aggrandizement was so great.

In 1 Samuel, "the monarchy" is code for the politics of the established, elite classes pitted against the longings, desires, and legitimate expectations of the people. Samuel's warning is a warning against the politics of power for power's own sake, not, as M. M. Thomas of India reminded us above, power "as the bearer of dignity and significant and responsible participation in society and history." Thomas means power as the heartbeat of politics for the sake of the people, representing and driving the politics of decency, honesty, integrity, courage, and virtue—to quote yet another prophet, but from our own times, African American intellectual giant W. E. B. Du Bois.

It is with this kind of power and this kind of politics in mind that the prophet Samuel speaks, for the people confronting Samuel are the "elders," the elites, who by themselves, and coveting the power-hungry ways of the elites of other nations, now pressure Samuel. They do not speak for the people. Samuel, in speaking for Yahweh, also speaks for the people, entirely excluded from this conversation. Here, as always, Yahweh's concern is for the people. The phrase "Yahweh is your king" means the politics of God is the politics of freedom, justice, inclusion, equity, and peace. The ruler who knows, acknowledges, and engages that is one who understands what it means when the Bible says, "Yahweh is your king."

It is not what some have called "theocratic politics," where, as in Dominion Theology, "the Bible" replaces the democratic Constitution and God rules directly through God's "chosen agents," all "Bible-believing," "born-again" Christians, to the exclusion of everyone else. That is a neocolonialist, white Christian Evangelical, imperialist theology chasing world dominion, the kind of Christian fascism we reject completely.[4] It is, rather, the essence of the best of genuine democratic politics for our times, when the politics of the common good is also the politics of common sense. This is what the parable we are about to discuss is all about. It is also about the perils of democratically made disastrous choices.

"So All the Trees Said to the Bramble…"

In the middle of the book of Judges, we come upon a parable, a story, a fable if you will. This is the first and oldest parable in the Bible. We know from the Gospels that Jesus almost always taught the people through parables, stories that aimed at bringing home some powerful truth about life, about God, about the reign of God, and about faithful living before God in the world. But, as we learn from New Testament scholar William Herzog II, and the theme of these reflections, Jesus' parables were not just stories; they were "subversive speech."[5]

This parable, recorded in Judges 9:7-15, was told by Jotham, son of a great leader, the deeply respected Gideon, after one of his half-brothers by the name of Abimelech, having massacred seventy of Gideon's sons, proclaimed himself king. Besides the massacre, this in itself was scandalous since Gideon, the father, had refused the title and the throne, even when he was at the height of his popularity. But that is another story.

In a fascinating little book, pastor Barry Wugale, a Nigerian human rights and ecojustice activist who now lives and works in South Africa, uses this parable to illustrate what he thinks is the dilemma of Africa and her people, her politics and her political leaders.[6] The problem is not just Africa's politics, Wugale says; it is also Africa's churches. Africa is in captivity, he writes, and the call is for "a second liberation" after the end of colonialism. From outside, Africa is kept captive by imperialism and neocolonialism, which assure the ongoing exploitation and appropriation of Africa's resources by others. From the inside, our captivity is caused by the creation of new political aristocracies, a sense of false patriotism, and the manipulation of Africa's citizens. For Barry Wugale, Jotham's parable of the trees reflects Africa's situation precisely. Pastor Wugale is not wrong. But it also fits South Africa's current situation after almost thirty years of democratic life, and it, as it is, even as I write, describes the dilemma of world politics.

Abimelech's action was a murderous, bloody power grab, shocking even in its day, but as always with these things, there were some people ready to embrace the new situation—some out of fear, some with a sense of resignation, and others with an eye keenly open for new opportunities, political position, social standing, and economic benefit. The surviving son, Jotham, found an occasion to speak to an assembled crowd. The new king was present. From the story, it seems that Jotham made his speech just after the coronation, so this was a loud and clear protest, a call for rectification of a deeply wrong situation, a call for justice. It was also courageous. It was a brave speech in which Jotham reminded those present of the struggles for freedom his father had led, the example he had set, and the sacrifices he had made. "My father," he told the crowd, "fought for you, risked his life, and rescued you from the hand of Midian" (Judg 9:17, NRSV). He was forthright in his condemnation of their betrayal, and he called their evil by its name: "but you have risen up against my father's house this day, ...[murdered] seventy men on one stone, and have made Abimelech...[your] king..." (v. 18). Jotham tried to taunt them into shame. If you think, he told them, that you have acted with honour, then rejoice in your deeds and in your king, but if not, he added, shading the taunt with a veiled threat, "let fire come out from Abimelech, and devour [you] the lords of Shechem, and Beth-millo" (v. 20). These are the cities that supported Abimelech. Jotham then added, "let fire come out from the lords of Shechem, and from Beth-millo, and devour Abimilech" (v. 20). In Jotham's view, the "lords"—the leaders—as well as "the people" bear responsibility for the current crisis.

Jotham was brave, but he was wise enough not to be reckless. Just after he spoke, he "ran away" (v. 21). His last sentence was a clever oratorical device. Basically, he said that he hoped they would never know peace, that in their betrayal, greed, and dishonesty they would turn against each other and "devour" one another. Dishonourable people might make convenient pacts and deals, Jotham was saying, but they will never be able to trust each other. You may have the power now, he said, but you have no future. You can't ever look towards the future; you will have to spend too much time looking over your shoulder. The politics of betrayal, forgetfulness, and expedience is doomed to live forever with the politics of fear and mistrust. That is why South African billionaire Barry Herzov, once one of Ramaphosa's most fervent backers, is now on YouTube with a video called *Voertsek Cyril!*[7]

Jotham's last words slotted in neatly with the parable he had just told them, which he placed in the middle of his speech. Here is the parable, summed up from the ten verses devoted to it in the biblical story known as "the parable of the trees."

"The trees," Jotham began, "once went out to anoint a king over themselves" (Judg 9:8, NRSV). This is as democratic as one could get. No unilateral declarations, no self-proclamations, no bending to traditions of hereditary kingship. The trees had choices. They called on the olive tree, the vine, and the fig tree. "Reign over us," they said. "Sway over us," says the Hebrew original text, a powerful politically suggestive phrase. Each one of those declined. Said the olive tree, "Shall I stop producing my rich oil by which the gods and mortals are honoured and go to sway over the trees?" (v. 9). Those words, "to sway over the trees," were used by every tree that was approached. Keep them in mind. They are the way the parable describes having power, though not power to serve others but instead power over others. It is the power that exploits, manipulates, and intimidates; the power that tends to corrupt; the power that rules without justice and compassion. It is the politics of authoritarianism and exclusion. It is politics at its worst because it is the politics of self-interest, self-aggrandisement, and control. It is fearful and therefore resentful of the power of the people. It is politics without vision. The trees would have none of it. The fig tree protested that it could not give up its sweet, delicious fruit. Should the vine give up producing its wine, which "cheers gods and mortals," to "sway over the trees?" (v. 13). No, said the vine. The olive tree was just as resolute. What it was doing was too precious to give up for the dubious choice of going into politics.

So finally, the trees went to the bramble bush, and only the bramble, useless as it is, accepted (vv. 14-15). It is important to cite the bramble tree's response in full: "And the bramble said to the trees, 'If in good faith you are anointing me king over you, then come and take refuge in my shade; but if not, let fire come out of the bramble and devour the cedars of Lebanon'" (9:15, NRSV). The bramble's first words should already make the skin tingle—not yet crawl (that will surely come later) but tingle, as they should make every alarm bell ring. The one who has no good faith at all, no integrity, no history of trustworthiness—no struggle credentials, we would say—demands "good faith" from others. This does not spell any good for anyone. What it shows, though, is the bramble's political acumen. It may not be trustworthy, but it knows the game. As an opening gambit, this is a masterstroke, putting everyone else on the defensive and putting the bramble in charge of the negotiations.

This parable is a story about politics and power, the usurpation of power, and the abuse of power. It is a story about wilfulness and wrong choices, about the politics of desperation reaching for the politics of delusion. About groping in the dark, the blind asking the blind to lead them. It's a story about South Africa, I keep on saying, about democracy and its decisions that lead to disasters, as it is a story about the state of politics in our world today.

In Jotham's parable, the various samples of trees insist that they are too important and worthwhile to be king. Thus, for those "noble" trees, kingship is not seen as "worthy" enough, certainly not on a par with their elevated status. The olive with its luxuriant oil, the fig tree with its sweet fruit, and the vine with its new wine to gladden the heart of God and of humankind consider themselves all too worthy to be king. The bramble is a useless tree, the most "unworthy" of all, but it becomes the choice of the trees. Politics, the other trees are saying, is for the useless and the shiftless, the charlatan and the con artist. The beautiful flowers the bramble sprouts in the spring are a fleeting phenomenon and not of much value, since the thorns always get in the way. It is some promise of potential good, but that potential is never really fulfilled. It remains metaphoric of the politics of empty promises, lies, and meaningless intentions. Are the trees, here always the image for the people, so bedazzled by those fleeting flowers that they do not see or mind the thorns? The flowers will wither soon. The thorns will stay. But they come and bow down nonetheless, eager to show their "good faith." So they come, pledging "good faith and honour" (v. 16), making an alliance. It is an expression of trust and confidence.

The bramble's response drips with irony and arrogance, at the same time a reflection on the politics of power and expedience. If you really, truly, "in good faith" want me to be king, it says—in other words, it has to be your clear and willing choice, *your* decision—then I will welcome you. Note the overturning of the situation, revealing the political and moral bankruptcy of the moment and of the people. To the most unworthy, the people must show "good faith," and the most unworthy "welcomes" them, because the people have come to the bramble, willingly giving it that power. It offers "shade" that its meagre branches cannot possibly give (v. 15). Empty promises, but not as if the people did not know that. They walk into this situation with eyes open. Welcoming the bramble means welcoming the meaningless promises they know the bramble has no intention of keeping because it cannot—there is a scarcity of shade, that is, of the justice, peace, and dignity that they crave or the politics of integrity, humility, and courage that they long for and deserve.

Still one of the best, and in my view unsurpassed, commentaries on the book of Judges, though written over thirty years ago, is the brilliant work of Italian Hebrew Bible scholar J. Alberto Soggin.[8] Born in 1926, he lived through the years of Benito Mussolini's fascist Italy, and in Mussolini, the pacts with Adolf Hitler, the authoritarianism, the suppression and the violence, Soggin doubtless recognised the politics of the bramble. Soggin saw the destruction of the politics of decency and integrity, the disregard for truth and honesty, and the consequent and inevitable disrespect for human life from right up front. That is why his reading of the parable is so stark, his critique so unequivocal, so fiercely critical of politics. Of all the trees, only "the worst" is willing to accept political responsibility. "Shall I sway over the trees," writes Soggin, in a reminder of my remarks above, "is a phrase which seems to want to bring out both the general arbitrariness and the futility of power when it is confronted with real problems." The bramble is the symbol of those who are always eager for political power even though they are the least fit for it.

The moral of the parable is decidedly negative and polemical: not only does someone who successfully pursues an autonomous and recognised productive activity refrain from seeking political power; they even refuse when it is offered. Not only does political power offer too many opportunities for corruption, "occasions for licence and illicit actions which are not to be found elsewhere, but it also distracts from honest and productive work." Probably the vast majority of Cyril Ramaphosa's cabinet would be totally at sea outside of politics, not prepared or qualified for any other honest work or position. Soggin reads verse 15a as the point of the story. "Come and take refuge in my shade," it says. The bramble promises "shade," that is, protection, and specifically the protection and security that justice provides, which it is unable to give. The offer the bramble makes to the other trees, that they can "come and take refuge" in its shade, is ludicrous. It is an absurd pretension of power. The point Jotham wants to make here is that the people know this full well. They are not unfamiliar with the bramble, with its lies and deceits, its predilection for violence, or its protection of the unjust. Yet in their desperation they believe the bramble, they choose it, they vote for it.

In a democracy, that is precisely what happens. We choose our political leaders. We willingly go to the bramble and ask it to rule over us. In the US, my friends talk about voting as a real, vexing political dilemma: the choice between the lesser of two evils. And truth be told, the US is by far not the only country facing that dilemma. So although our complaints after an election might be legitimate, we are not completely devoid of responsibility, and the tragedy is that our complicity undermines our right to complain. Unless we resist and fight for the restoration of justice and rights, our complaints will remain just that: complaints, moanings, and groanings about the things we should have known would happen because we knew full well to whom we were giving power.

Then comes the threat against those who refuse to bow down, to accede to the demands of the bramble, because if there is to be hope for resistance, there has to be dissent. "Let fire come out of the bramble and devour the cedars of Lebanon" (Judg 9:15, NRSV). In the Bible the "cedars of Lebanon" are considered the noblest of trees, desirable for their aromatic qualities as well as their resistance to decay and bugs. For Lebanon with its exceptional climatic suitability, cedars were a valuable export, a source of wealth. Associated with luxury, adorning the houses of the wealthy and powerful, they were indeed trees fit for nobility." They are exuberantly extolled in the Bible. Ezekiel 31:3-7 (NRSV) is as good an example as any:

> ³Consider Assyria, a cedar of Lebanon,
> with fair branches and forest shade,
> and of great height,
> its top among the clouds.
> ⁴The waters nourished it,
> the deep made it grow tall,
> making its rivers flow
> around the place it was planted,
> sending forth its streams
> to all the trees of the field.
> ⁵So it towered high
> above all the trees of the field;
> its boughs grew large
> and its branches long,
> from abundant water in its shoots.
> ⁶All the birds of the air
> made their nests in its boughs;
> under its branches all the animals of the field
> gave birth to their young;
> and in its shade
> all great nations lived.
> ⁷It was beautiful in its greatness,
> in the length of its branches;
> for its roots went down
> to abundant water.

These verses are the praise reserved for the ruler who does do what Yahweh requires, who knows, loves, and executes justice, who does not oppress the widow, the orphan, and the stranger; a ruler who is the protector of the weak and defender of the defenceless. In Ezekiel 31, however, these verses are spoken about Egypt's pharaoh. This, Ezekiel tells him, is what you *should* have been. But because you are an oppressor of people, a doer of injustice, and a warmongering imperialist who profits from destruction and misery, you have become the exact opposite. What was meant to be a cedar has turned into the bramble. Therefore, says Yahweh, you shall be cast down (vv. 10-11).

Still, if the cedar was this highly regarded, why then would the bramble direct its potential wrath against it so specifically, not even mentioning the other trees that were its "competitors" for kingship? Some commentators think the threat is therefore aimed at Israel's nobility, its elites, the "cedars of Israel," so to speak, from amongst whose ranks the most likely threat to the bramble's kingship is supposed to come. For once the people's eyes are opened, once they realise that the bramble's promises are absurd, would it not be natural to turn to the nobility of Israel, those who by their birth, status, and position would be best equipped, would *know* how to rule?

I do not think so. The threat is against those who will not bend, who dissent, who will not be afraid to speak truth to power. This is, after all, the book of Judges, remember? Those leaders come from among the people. They are the people's heroes. Those who, like Gideon, will not lead the struggle in order to claim kingship, positions for their own aggrandisement and self-enrichment. Those who will open the eyes of the people to their foolishness in choosing the bramble as their king. Those who will rise up and with their charisma and courage and visionary leadership lead the people in resistance against the tyranny that the bramble represents. Their aim is not to restore kingship and the rule of the elites. Their aim is to restore justice and power and dignity to the people.

Because they are from among the people, they understand the people, what they need but especially what they deserve, and what they do not deserve is the bramble as their king. Because these leaders are from among the people, they understand that sometimes the people make mistakes. Sometimes the people are so desperate for hope that they believe promises brambles are not able to keep, while in fact the only promise the bramble will keep is the "fire," the promise of oppression, of retribution against those who dare to stand up on behalf of the people.

No, the nobility of the cedar should not be sought in the so-called nobility of the elites. Nobility lies in the willingness to struggle, to stand up against oppression, to sacrifice for beliefs and ideals that matter against all odds. It lies in those who struggle for justice, who lead lives of self-sacrificial love for the people, and who discern the truth from deceit. It is these "cedars of Lebanon" that the bramble fears so much that even as it promises false protection for those who pay fealty to it, it swears vengeance against those who dare question and resist its rule.

Haunted by Du Bois

Then Soggin makes an extremely important point. Whereas these types of parables about animals and plants are common in the ancient Near East and are always used favourably, he argues, the parable here in Judges 9 is resolutely and fundamentally negative. There is a decidedly negative judgement on politics as a whole, about political power and those who seek it, it seems. No exceptions. This is what politics, under any circumstances, looks like. That should give us pause, for it raises the question: is this what politics *per se* always is? Does it have to be like this always?

The Bible offers another possibility. Psalm 82, Psalm 146, and Romans 13, for example, have a very different expectation of those who are given political power. If they are to be rulers who deserve honour, the psalms proclaim, and if they are to be considered servants of God "for your good," as Romans 13 testifies, then they *will* do justice, protect the weak, rescue from the hands of the wicked the poor and the vulnerable. In the New Testament, we learn, this is precisely the politics of Jesus, so brilliantly captured in Obery Hendricks's excellent study.[9] For that reason, the prophet Ezekiel calls those given positions of authority "shepherds" of the people (see Ezek 34). The prophet's indictments are so scathing because Yahweh has set the bar for rulers so high, and the expectations of the people are therefore entirely legitimate. "Ah, you shepherds of Israel who have been feeding yourselves!" he cries (Ezek 34:2, NRSV). Ezekiel could have been talking about South Africa's politicians whose slogan has become "It's our time to eat!" which means gorging themselves on that which belongs to the people.

> [3]You eat the fat, you clothe yourselves with the wool, you slaughter the fatlings; but you do not feed the sheep. [4]You have not strengthened the weak, you have not healed the sick, you have not bound up the injured, you have not brought back the strayed, you have not sought the lost, but with force and harshness you have ruled them. [5]So they were scattered, because there was no shepherd; and scattered, they became food for all the wild animals. [6]My sheep were scattered, they wandered over all the mountains and on every high hill; my sheep were scattered over all the face of the earth, with no one to search or seek for them.
>
> [7]Therefore, you shepherds, hear the word of the LORD: [8]As I live, says the Lord GOD, because my sheep have become a prey, and my sheep have become food for all the wild animals, since there was no shepherd; and because my shepherds have not searched for my sheep, but the shepherds have fed themselves, and have not fed my sheep; [9]therefore, you shepherds, hear the word of the LORD: [10]Thus says the Lord GOD, I am against the shepherds; and I will demand my sheep at their hand, and put

a stop to their feeding the sheep; no longer shall the shepherds feed themselves. I will rescue my sheep from their mouths, so that they may not be food for them. (Ezek 34:3-10, NRSV)

The "shepherds," those whom Jesus in John 10 calls "the hired hands," who do not have the courage to protect the sheep when the wolves come to steal, kill, and destroy, are the false shepherds who rule without justice and who have therefore lost all authority and credibility. They do not care, except for themselves. So they run away, are bribed into complicity or intimidated into acquiescence, or are simply too cowardly to stand between their flock and the wolves. In utter derision, Jesus calls them "hired hands." To such people, the most terrifying words in Ezekiel 34 are "I am against the shepherds; and I will demand my sheep at their hand" (v. 10). For the people, though, these are the most comforting words. They now know: we are not forgotten, our cause is not lost; our dreams may be shattered, but they are not scattered to the winds. It is not true that all hope is gone. Yahweh, the God who loves justice, is our shepherd, and our lives are precious in God's sight. It is in this prophetic reminder that our resilience lies, and it is through this truth that our perseverance is resurrected.

These expectations of politics for the good of the people are not what Jotham's parable portray. This is deep wisdom, Professor Soggin tells us, but it is wisdom that comes from the wells of the experiences of the people. Soggin is emphatic: the wisdom here is not the wisdom of the court. In other words, this wisdom is not from the circles of the elites, the powerful and the privileged, who boast of wisdom not because they know and understand better but are assumed wise because they have power and privilege. This wisdom is from the people, from the bottom up. It is the bitter experience of the people with politics and those with political power. It is suffering and struggle and faith that birth wisdom, not power and privilege.

This parable sees politics through the eyes of those who suffer, who are neglected and pushed to the outer edges of the margins of life. This is what the people now expect from politics and political leadership after centuries of subjection to power: oppression, arbitrariness, and irrationality. To "sway over the trees" is not only the symbol for authoritarian power. It is also a sign of Jesus' depiction of Herod in Matthew's Gospel (11:7) as "a reed shaken by the wind," without steadfastness, without principle—the politics of bending to the highest bidder. It is to be thoroughly mistrusted. This is politics that cannot survive without those threats of reprisal and punishment against anyone who dares to speak up and does not accept the rules of the game as they are set and imposed by those in power.

This is what I hear in the daily lament of South Africans, looking at our situation today: "Is this what we fought for? Are these the fruits of our struggles?" This is what I hear in the daily lament of our siblings in the US as they have to fight for those fundamental rights they have fought so hard for before, and won, and are now in danger of losing again—from voting rights to the protection of women's rights over their bodies to the administration of justice in the courts.

In our struggles, every victory, however small, is a victory over the machinations of evil. It is a stride toward freedom. Every time we speak up for those made voiceless or step into the breach for the vulnerable, every time we stand up for the truth by exposing the lies of empire, it is a stand against the bramble, a step towards our greater nobility. These are to be cherished, revered, and held on to. Under the rule of the bramble, we have found, here and everywhere in the world, that the bramble is intent on reversing every single step we made in righteousness, undoing every deed of justice, unmaking every stride towards real and lasting freedom. That is the fire, the bramble promises, that it will rain upon those who resist, who continue to believe in justice and humanity, in dignity and equity. It is the fire that seeks to destroy the very things that make and keep us noble.

"Thus here we have a deliberate rejection of the institution of the monarchy as such, and not just some of its worst aspects," Soggin concludes. A rejection of politics as a whole, not just some aspects of it, in other words. This is how deep the disillusionment, the disappointment, and the anger run. But the point Soggin makes, that the critique is *from below*, also means that the politics rejected here is the politics of the elites, of control by the few for the benefit of the few. Hence the prominent role ancient Israel gives to the judges and the prophets, the fighters for justice and the liberation of the people, and all *from among the people*. They are all in search of the politics of justice and freedom, of peace and dignity—the politics of life, in other words. They fight because they know such a politics is possible. W. E. B. Du Bois's politics of decency, honesty, integrity, courage, and virtue is not a dream fashioned out of thin air or a fairy tale cut from whole cloth. It is the wisdom gathered from the politics of struggle of our people throughout the centuries, anchored in our spirituality of struggle, purified by the selflessness of our sacrificial love, uplifted by the indestructability of our hope.

There is a point Soggin does not make but I think is well worth pondering. Once, Israel knew that its strength, its hope, and its future did not lie in military might and the power of clever but unscrupulous politics. Hence the utter significance of the Song of Miriam (Exod 15:1-2 and 21) that I have previously alluded to. For the same reason, the Miriamic tradition, though suppressed, has survived, especially as put forth in the book of Numbers where Miriam stands up to proclaim, in opposition to Moses, an entirely different kind of leadership, holding up entirely different expectations of liberation and its character. That is also why the Song of Miriam is so different from the Song of Deborah (Judg 5:2-31) and at the same time echoed so longingly, but strongly, in the Song of Hannah (1 Sam 2:1-10) and in the Magnificat of Mary (Luke 1:46-56).[10]

Once—and this is a point I made before in the first three chapters of this book—ancient Israel knew that it was not military might and unbridled power that formed its core identity. Neither was it what made Israel "great." The prophet Elisha, successor to Elijah, knew it when, at the sight of Elijah ascending up into the heavens in a whirlwind, he spoke the truth closest to Yahweh's heart: "Father, father! The chariots of Israel and its horsemen!" (2 Kgs 2:12, NRSV). In other words, it is the prophetic presence, the prophetic witness, the prophetic truth spoken in prophetic boldness, the prophetic faithfulness in standing up for what is right and just, that is the life and strength of Israel. Not the love of abusive power, mendacity, and corruption that was Ahab's reign. Not the worship of violence and the dependence on those who know only violence to "prove" their worth. It is not the cold, calculated cynicism that passes for what is called "*realpolitik*" that shows strength; it is the fire of compassionate justice that shows the fibre of a nation's character. That is why the prophetic tradition, especially as held up so relentlessly by the eighth century prophets, is such a resilient tradition in the Bible. In these times, as at every time, that should be the enduring message of the prophetic church.

Just as in ancient Israel, there was a time when oppressed people everywhere knew exactly what we were striving for in our politics. We articulated those ideals the Hebrew prophets were talking about for ourselves, and we held them high as we fought for justice and freedom. We had those God-sent prophets in our midst, from Sojourner Truth and Harriet Tubman to Ella Baker and Claudette Colvin. From Krotoa and Charlotte Maxeke to Albertina Sisulu and Winnie Mandela. From Nat Turner and David Walker to Frederick Douglass and Martin Luther King Jr. From Pixley ka Isaka Seme and A. B. Xuma to Albert Luthuli, Steve Biko, and Nelson Mandela.

We knew what we fought for—not just freedom and democracy in general but, as that incomparable intellectual giant from Black America, W. E. B. Du Bois, put it, for the politics of decency, honesty, integrity, courage, and virtue, standing up against the politics of brute force. And because we fought for it and sacrificed for it, bled for it and died for it, we knew that there were things, when freedom came, that we would not give up. That is what made us noble and free. Knowing this, we gave all of it up in bowing down and paying homage to the bramble.

So, haunted by the wisdom of Du Bois, we return to the issues I raised in the beginning. For people of faith, it is clear. South Africans need to return to the wisdom of Daniel and to the wisdom of M. M. Thomas. We need to pray to God to show who is in control of history, even as we pray for the power to once again take up the revolution that will change the fate of our nation and put our people on the path God has destined for us. God is in control, so we are called to build, challenge, and shape our societies until, as Jesus taught us to pray, God's will is done on earth as it is in heaven.

I remain entirely convinced that what Black liberation theologian Allen Dwight Callahan writes for African Americans, their choices, and their prophetic calling is true for all of us:

> As Esau sold his birth right for a bowl of stew, African Americans [and all of us] may forego asking the tough questions of our time and instead choose to savor the hand-me-down emoluments of wealth and power acquired at their ancestor's expense. They would close this deal with the Devil as second class citizens of an imperious imperial nation. Such is the present lot of slavery's children in the land of their birth. The electoral process illegally disenfranchises them. Both major political parties regularly neglect them. The criminal justice system unjustly arrests, incarcerates and executes them. The military disproportionately dispatches them to the front in its many and unjust wars. The executive branch of the federal government refuses to hear them, the judiciary branch refuses to protect them, and the legislative branch refuses to represent them. African Americans may choose to sell their birth right to the descendants of a master class that had proven itself as crafty and unscrupulous as the young Jacob. A century and a half after the fall of the slave regime, these heirs to ill-gotten gains still rule the United States as did their forebears—with scripture and injustice. Or, with the collective critical consciousness that is their heritage, slavery's children may call both scripture and injustice into question.[11]

Chapter 12

Briers, Scorpions, and Thorns

On Prophetic Perseverance and Hope for a Desperate World
(Ezekiel 2:3-7)

Wendell Griffen

¹He said to me: O mortal, stand up on your feet, and I will speak with you. ²And when he spoke to me, a spirit entered into me and set me on my feet; and I heard him speaking to me. ³He said to me, Mortal, I am sending you to the people of Israel, to a nation of rebels who have rebelled against me; they and their ancestors have transgressed against me to this very day. ⁴The descendants are impudent and stubborn. I am sending you to them, and you shall say to them, "Thus says the Lord GOD." ⁵Whether they hear or refuse to hear (for they are a rebellious house), they shall know that there has been a prophet among them. ⁶And you, O mortal, do not be afraid of them, and do not be afraid of their words, though briers and thorns surround you and you live among scorpions; do not be afraid of their words, and do not be dismayed at their looks, for they are a rebellious house. ⁷You shall speak my words to them, whether they hear or refuse to hear; for they are a rebellious house. (Ezekiel 2:1-7, NRSV)

"See, I am sending you out like sheep into the midst of wolves; so be wise as serpents and innocent as doves." (Matthew 10:16)

¹Then Jesus told them a parable about their need to pray always and not to lose heart. ²He said, "In a certain city there was a judge who neither feared God nor had respect for people. ³In that city there was a widow who kept coming to him and saying, 'Grant me justice against my opponent.' ⁴For a while he refused; but later he said to himself, 'Though I have no fear of God and no respect for anyone, ⁵yet because this widow keeps bothering me, I will grant her justice, so that she may not wear me out

by continually coming.'" ⁶And the Lord said, "Listen to what the unjust judge says. ⁷And will not God grant justice to his chosen ones who cry to him day and night? Will he delay long in helping them? ⁸I tell you, he will quickly grant justice to them. And yet, when the Son of Man comes, will he find faith on earth?" (Luke 18:1-8)

We live in a world that is desperate for messages of hope. But messages of hope must be delivered by hopeful messengers, and messengers of hope seem to be in short supply.

The whole world has spent years wrestling with novel coronavirus, and the United States has the most cases. Climate change is affecting every place. People disheartened by the killings of George Floyd, Breonna Taylor, Ahmaud Arbery, and Rayshard Brooks and countless videotaped episodes of abusive behavior by law enforcement agents against law-abiding and unarmed people are still waiting for federal, state, and local laws that stop those abuses almost three years after those persons were killed.

Our desperate world hopes for change because it is full of hellish situations. But why are our situations hellish? What are faithful people to do in the face of so many evils that oppress the world? Let's consider a passage from Ezekiel 2.

Ezekiel was a Hebrew priest taken into exile in Babylon after the Babylonians conquered Judah. In Babylon, he sensed the Spirit of God calling him into the different role of prophet. The passage from Ezekiel 2 is an excerpt from his call from God. Several important terms stick out:

Mortal (or "son of man" in the KJV): the term used by the Spirit of God to describe Ezekiel. It reminded Ezekiel that he was human, not divine.

I am sending you...: words that explain how and why Ezekiel said what he said and did what he did. Ezekiel understood that he was God's agent.

I am sending you to the people of Israel, to a nation of rebels who have rebelled against me...: words that identified the audience Ezekiel was to address and described the moral and ethical character of that audience.

Ezekiel was commissioned as God's prophet to people who came from his homeland. He was not a prophet to strangers but to people with whom he was culturally and politically related. He knew their stories and shared the anguish of their exiled situation, including separation from their homeland, loss of their religious shrine, military conquest, and being a defeated minority community in a society that was culturally, politically, and religiously alien to everything they knew.

Yet the Spirit of God stressed that Ezekiel's fellow Israelites were in Babylon as divine judgment for being "a rebellious house" (Ezek 2:5, NRSV). They were "a nation of rebels...against [God]" (v. 3), for "...they and their ancestors have transgressed against me to this very day. The descendants are impudent and stubborn. I am sending you to them..." (vv. 3-4).

It was important for Ezekiel to understand that his mission from God was to deal with people whose hellish situation as exiles in Babylon was the result of their long and stubborn history of defying divine imperatives of love and justice. Ezekiel needed to understand that he was not being sent to God-obeying people, God-honoring people, and God-trusting people. He was not being sent to repentant people. Allow me to paraphrase:

> Ezekiel, you're accustomed to thinking of your people as religiously devout and God-loving. So let's get something straight about "your people." "Your people"—because they don't act like they are "my people"—are rebels. They are rebels against divine authority. They are rebels against divine instruction. They are rebels.
>
> Whenever you see them, whenever you speak to them, and however you deal with them, know that you are dealing with impudent, stubborn, arrogant, and hypocritical rebels. Know that you are dealing with people who behave wrongly toward God and one another because they are wrong-headed and wrong-hearted people.
>
> Understand that they didn't become rebellious due to recent events. Their ancestors were the same way. Their moral and ethical DNA is disobedient and unloving.
>
> Know that "your people" aren't rebellious against divine authority and imperatives because of the Babylonian conquest. They are conquered and displaced as a divine judgment on their rebellious character against divine authority.
>
> Don't let the fact that you share history with them mess you up. You represent me. These people are rebellious against me! Know this, always! You need to know what I know about "your people" so you won't get messed up when they don't do right.
>
> You need to know and remember this to avoid going off the deep end. This knowledge will keep you from thinking your work is for nothing when people don't heed your messages.
>
> Whether or not they listen to you—remember, Ezekiel, "your people" are a rebellious house—you are my prophet. Whether or

not they like you, *when you speak my truth to them, they will know that you are my prophet.*

Our world faces hellish situations because people have persistently and deliberately defied divine imperatives of love and justice. Systemic racism against immigrants, Black people, indigenous people, and people of color exists because of rebellion against the divine imperative that we love God and love our neighbors as ourselves. The same is true about income inequality; genocide; land theft; discrimination against Palestinians; bigotry, misogyny, and discrimination against women, girls, and people who are LGBTQI; and disparities in health care. These hellish situations have the world in what amounts to a state of exile.

The world needs prophetic people who aren't afraid to speak truth to power. The world needs people who can't be bought off, bullied, and bossed out of standing up for what is loving and fair and true.

The world needs people who talk boldly and plainly about what Howard Thurman called the "hounds of hell"—meaning hate, hypocrisy, unbelief, and deceit.

The world needs people who challenge racism and white supremacy, hateful nationalism (whether it is based on religion, ethnicity, or political chauvinism), and imperialism.

The world needs prophetic people who aren't afraid to challenge militarism (whether it is disguised as "law enforcement" or national security or it masquerades as the hateful faith of religious evangelism).

The world needs prophetic people who will challenge the capitalist greed responsible for manifest destiny, chattel slavery, income inequality, and the technocentrism that allows people to profit and get tax breaks for poisoning the creation and our fellow creatures.

The world needs prophetic people who challenge sexism, misogyny, and patriarchy (including homophobia and transphobia).

The world needs prophetic people who challenge xenophobia and denounce people who treat sojourners, migrating people, and strangers as aliens to be feared, distrusted, and mistreated rather than neighbors and siblings in the family of God.

This is not only true concerning the world. It is also true about specific unjust situations around us. If it matters to God how "nations" treat vulnerable people—if God assigns labels of "righteous" or "wicked" based on how "nations" treat hungry, thirsty, impoverished, frail, incarcerated, and immigrant people—then what label fits us?

Can a society that boasts of being the economic leader of the world be "righteous" when it will not feed hungry people, will not house unsheltered people, and will not provide medical and mental care for sickened people?

Can a society that boasts of being "a nation of immigrants" be "righteous" when its leaders call immigrants "illegal," separates immigrant infants and children from their parents, refuses to welcome immigrants seeking asylum from violence, poverty, and national calamities, and blames immigrants for crime, poverty, and disease?

Can a society that calls itself "the land of the free" be "righteous" when it holds 2.5 million men, women, and youth in prisons, jails, and other places of detention every day?

Do we see what God sees? Do we hear what God hears? Do we recognize that God knows the difference between religiousness and righteousness? God knows that systemic poverty is a sign of national wickedness, not national wealth. God knows that systemic refusal to provide healthcare, nutrition, clean water, clean air, and hospitality to migrating people is a sign of national wickedness, not proof of national health.

It is a wickedness that also operates behind state-sanctioned and financed walls disguised as punishment, as illustrated by the case of Mumia Abu-Jamal, a Black journalist and activist now serving a life sentence after his 1982 conviction for first degree murder and death sentence was reduced—following thirty years of litigation—to life without parole because of sentencing irregularities. Abu-Jamal has always declared that he did not kill Philadelphia police officer Daniel Faulkner in 1981.

Abu-Jamal was convicted in a trial where the presiding judge was overheard by a court stenographer saying that he was "going to help them fry the nigger." He was convicted in a trial where prosecutors used racist reasons for striking Black prospective jurors. And in 2019, Philadelphia prosecutors discovered and revealed—for the first time—six boxes of documents that supported Abu-Jamal's innocence, including a letter from a key prosecution witness to prosecutors asking when he would get his money.

For forty years, judges in the Commonwealth of Pennsylvania and in US federal courts have played the part of the unjust jurist that Jesus spoke about in Luke 11. Judges discounted proof that prosecutors engaged in racially discriminatory conduct during jury selection. Judges also belittled evidence that Judge Albert Sabo, the trial judge in Mumia's murder trial, told another judge he was "going to help them fry the nigger." A court stenographer overheard Judge Sabo, who died in 2002, make that statement. According to a *New York Times* obituary published after his death, Judge Sabo presided over thirty-one criminal cases that resulted in death sentences, the most in Pennsylvania history. Nevertheless, judges refused to set aside Mumia's conviction and sentence in the face of evidence of Judge Sabo's blatant racial bigotry and judicial prejudice.

Recently a different Philadelphia trial judge—Judge Lucretia Clemons—heard arguments from Mumia Abu-Jamal's legal team that his 1982 conviction and current life sentence should be overturned because concealment of the exculpatory information before his trial was fundamentally unfair based on a 1963 decision by the US Supreme Court (*Brady v. Maryland*). Judge Clemons is a Black woman who grew up in Mississippi and whose grandfather was lynched by white racists. However, she strangely refused to follow the ruling in *Brady v. Maryland*. Rather than grant the relief dictated sixty years ago, Judge Clemons directed that defense lawyers go search the six boxes of concealed evidence and persuade her that the 1982 conviction and sentence should be overturned.

Mumia Abu-Jamal's wife was later found dead, unexpectedly, by a family friend. His spiritual advisor learned that Mumia, in prison, only had the right to view his wife's body via Zoom and was not allowed to view to view the December 30, 2022, public funeral service of the woman who loved him and supported his quest for freedom from prison for forty years. Mumia's thirty-minute viewing was strictly regulated, with two prison guards assigned to him and a third at the door.

The experience Mumia is enduring at the hands of the incarceration system as he fights an unjust conviction and life sentence, struggles with congestive heart disease, and grieves the death of his wife reminds us that the purpose of the criminal punishment system is not to accomplish justice. Rather, the criminal punishment system operates to validate cruelty. It exists not merely to make cruelty possible but to commend it in the name of criminal punishment so that cruelty is accepted on the excuse—no, the lie—that emotional, physical, environmental, social, moral, spiritual, and other cruelty is necessary. That is a lie. It is up to people who are righteous to say so.

That means it is up to Judge Lucretia Clemons to say so. As a jurist, it is her duty to say that it is not right for someone to be incarcerated for forty years based on a conviction obtained because prosecutors concealed evidence. As a jurist who knows what is right—based on the 1963 US Supreme Court decision in *Brady v. Maryland*—Judge Clemons knows that it is not right, meaning fair and just, for anyone to be convicted of any crime in such instances, let alone convicted of murder.

That is what Judge Clemons knows because she is a judge. It is what she knows and what any other judge should know, even as she knows that overturning the conviction and sentence of Mumia Abu-Jamal means she must confront the briers, thorns, and scorpions of a hostile law enforcement culture existing as the Fraternal Order of Police, corporate media that are beholden to the FOP, politicians who court FOP support to win elections, and Maureen Faulkner—the widow of the slain Officer Daniel Faulkner whose life mission is to ensure that Mumia Abu-Jamal dies in prison no matter that fundamental fairness (due process) requires that his murder conviction and life sentence be overturned.

In this sense, Mumia Abu-Jamal is like the widow who hounded the unjust judge seeking justice. Judge Clemons is the latest judge to whom he has appealed for relief from his murder conviction and life sentence. In the face of proof that prosecutors concealed six boxes of exculpatory information from Abu-Jamal's defense attorneys before his 1982 trial and for another thirty-seven years before notifying his lawyers and the court about it, the responsibility rests with Judge Clemons to declare that conduct unfair. It is up to her to rule that such prosecutorial concealment turned the 1982 murder trial into a sham proceeding. It is her duty to rule that the prosecutorial concealment violated well-known standards for due process of law that Pennsylvania and other courts have long recognized as grounds for overturning criminal convictions and sentences.

Thus far, Judge Clemons has not done those things. Unlike the Hebrew midwives Shiphrah and Puah, who defied an imperial edict to murder male Hebrew babies in Exodus 1, Judge Clemons has not acted to spare Mumia from continued unjust imprisonment. Unlike Jochebed and Miriam, the mother and sister of Moses, Judge Clemons has not defied the "rebellious house" of FOP and Maureen Faulkner's (the widow of Daniel Faulkner) bloodlust. Unlike the royal Egyptian princess who acted to protect the infant Moses from the infanticidal edict of her father, Judge Clemons has yet to act to protect Mumia Abu-Jamal.

In that sense, the ruling by Judge Clemons that defense attorneys present new arguments resembles that of Felix, the Roman governor of Palestine who heard the appeal of Paul and, according to Acts 24:25 (NRSV), "became frightened and said, 'Go away for the present; when I have an opportunity, I will send for you.'"

The pericope from Ezekiel 2 raises other, more disturbing possibilities. Perhaps Judge Clemons, like other judges who heard and disregarded Abu-Jamal's appellate challenges to his conviction and sentence due to the racist behavior by Judge Sabo, evidence of racial discrimination during jury selection, and prosecutorial racist closing arguments, is part of a "rebellious house" determined to defy moral and ethical imperatives of justice. Perhaps she is unwilling to denounce a corrupt judicial guild that "turn justice to wormwood, and bring righteousness to the ground!" (Amos 5:7, NRSV) and who "push aside the needy in the gate" (Amos 5:12).

One does not contemplate these possibilities lightly. Yet that is precisely what Ezekiel learned was his prophetic duty: "I am sending you to them, and you shall say to them, 'Thus says the Lord GOD.' Whether they hear or refuse to hear (for they are a rebellious house), they shall know that there has been a prophet among them" (Ezek 2:4b-5, NRSV). Ezekiel's duty was not to placate the operatives of systemic injustice. Rather, he was commissioned by the Spirit of God to courageously confront, denounce, and condemn injustice "though briers and thorns surround you and you live among scorpions…" (Ezek 2:6).

The venomous nature of scorpions makes it risky to be around them. The prickly nature of briers and thorns exposes one to be lacerated by them. Nevertheless, the prophetic mission is clear: "…do not be afraid of their words, and do not be dismayed at their looks, for they are a rebellious house. You shall speak my words to them, whether they hear or refuse to hear; for they are a rebellious house" (Ezek 2:6-7). An inherently corrupt and defiant society must be confronted and condemned, not cajoled. Doing so in that context will always be hazardous. That is why Jesus told his followers that they would be "like sheep into the midst of wolves…" (Matt 10:16).

Mumia Abu-Jamal languishes in state prison in Pennsylvania having been accused, tried, convicted, and sentenced to life imprisonment for murder of a white police officer by a corrupt prosecutorial and judicial system that is characteristic of the US mass incarceration empire. He and countless other captives of that empire are, like the widow mentioned by Jesus, pleading to judges for relief and liberation from their unjust imprisonment. Unlike the widow, however, Mumia is locked inside a Pennsylvania prison. He cannot spit in the face of judges who refuse to grant relief. He can only file appeals from prison. This requires the rest of us to view Judge Clemons as being like the "unjust judge" Jesus talked about. We must plead for the unjustly imprisoned. We must become their advocates and surrogates.

Like that unjust judge Jesus taught about, Judge Clemons knows that the holding in *Brady v. Maryland* requires that Abu-Jamal's conviction and sentence be overturned. She knows that holding has been US law since 1963. She knows that it was the law almost two decades before Abu-Jamal's conviction. She knows that it has been the law for the entire time Abu-Jamal has been imprisoned—including more than thirty years on death row and another decade since the death sentence was changed to life without parole. Judge Clemons knows that it is her duty to order Pennsylvania prosecutors to either retry Abu-Jamal or release him from prison. And Judge Clemons knows that Mumia Abu-Jamal will die in prison unless she orders him released pending retrial or released outright if prosecutors decide not to retry him. Her refusal to issue the ruling she knows is required by the holding in *Brady v. Maryland* shows that Judge Clemons, like the unjust judge mentioned by Jesus, is part of the "rebellious house" Ezekiel was commanded to confront and condemn. People who know the meaning of justice have a moral duty to expose those judges as being officials of what the Spirit of God had Ezekiel understand is "a rebellious house."

The colony that became the United States was "a rebellious house" when colonizers landed in the Western Hemisphere to claim its wealth for European monarchs. Those monarchs had papal and priestly approval for "rebellious house" land theft and human enslavement of indigenous and African people. Hence, US law is bottomed on "rebellious house" precepts. US politics bows to "rebellious house" greed, hate, hypocrisy, violence, and deceit.

This reality explains why policing in the United States is infested with white supremacy, violence against people of color, women, LGBTQI persons, and other vulnerable persons and populations since its inception. The reality also explains, for Mumia Abu-Jamal and the rest of us, why briers, thorns, and scorpions are fitting metaphors for the FOP, corporate media, complicit politicians and preachers, and Maureen Faulkner, widow of the murdered Philadelphia police officer Daniel Faulkner, whose bloodlust is its own prison.

God knows that we see the suffering caused by these and other briers, thorns, and scorpions, see the hardships vulnerable men, women, and children face every day across the world, and do nothing to interrupt the wicked causes of that suffering, let alone correct the harms produced by those wicked causes. God knows we ought to see. God knows we have many opportunities to see. And God knows we have no excuse for refusing to see Jesus in the plight of Mumia Abu-Jamal and every other unjustly imprisoned person. We have no excuse, as individuals and nations, for ignoring the hungry Jesus, dismissing the sickened Jesus, refusing to be concerned about the mass incarcerated Jesus, refusing to welcome the immigrant Jesus, and refusing to protect and provide for the impoverished Jesus.

Yet Jesus emphasized that the prophetic people the world needs must be both shrewd and loving as we confront "rebellious house" societies and operatives. That is what Jesus meant when he told his first followers to be "wise as serpents and innocent as doves" in Matthew 10:16. Dr. Martin Luther King Jr. termed this as being tough-minded and tender-hearted in *Strength to Love*.

The world of briers, thorns, and scorpions needs loving people who have a shrewd awareness about the threats, treats, and temptations of empire. The world needs people who are shrewdly aware of their own vulnerability and God's superabundant power despite the real and present threat of briers, thorns, and scorpions to our ambitions, our comfort, and even our lives. The world needs loving people who shrewdly understand the tragedy of human greed, cruelty, hate, hypocrisy, and other wickedness yet boldly proclaim and affirm the triumph of unconditional love.

Simply put, the world needs people of prophetic hope. The world needs people who know the tragic capacities and propensities of the "rebellious house" and its briers, thorns, and scorpions of hate, unbelief, hypocrisy, and fear, yet boldly live and love as children of God. The world needs prophetic agents with a shrewd and loving faith that is not afraid to hope and not ashamed to call people to embrace God's call to oneness and community. The world needs people willing to hope for justice and challenge people to do justice. The world needs people who believe in mercy and love enough to be merciful and loving. The world needs people who believe God deserves our reverence, people who are not ashamed to humbly revere God, and people determined to challenge their human siblings to be God's trustees and show reverence for the creation and our fellow creatures.

In 1980, the Jackson 5 released their fourteenth long-playing record, titled *Triumph*, for Epic Records. The album was certified platinum, sold three million copies on its first issue, and peaked at number 10 on Billboard's top 200. The first song on the *Triumph* album, "Can You Feel It," is my favorite workout tune. I love the way the group sings that question—"Can you feel it? Can you feel it? Can you feel it?"

Our desperate world needs people of prophetic hope.
Shrewd hope.
Loving hope.
Shameless hope.
Unflinching hope.
Down-side-up hope.
War-stopping and peace-loving hope.
Greed-fighting and justice-doing hope.
Good Friday and Resurrection Sunday hope.
Pentecostal hope.
John Lewis's "good trouble" hope.
I don't feel no-ways tired hope.
God is up to something hope.
We are marching in the light of God hope.

"Can you feel it? Can you feel it? Can you feel it?" If so, join the ongoing fight for love and justice, and continue to pray for the strength to carry on that fight.

O God of boundless love, we are your people.

O God of bold truth, we are your people.

O God of death-proof hope, we are your people in a world of briers, thorns, and scorpions.

Grant that we will challenge your world with prophetic hope.

We pray for strength to live in the power of that hope for you in every breath and heartbeat by the power of the Holy Spirit as followers of Jesus Christ, now and always. Amen.

Epilogue

We collaborated to write this book that views certain global realities as parables. We now ask readers to ponder and answer one question. Now what?

What will people do who believe that humans are accountable to our Creator for how we treat one another, other creatures, and the creation?

What will followers of Jesus do about the issues we highlighted?

The problems mentioned in this book have moral and ethical importance. They exist as political, fiscal, social, and other dynamics associated with how humans use and abuse power.

We hope readers will reimagine the religion of Jesus as a moral and ethical commentary on how humans use and abuse power. Humans never use power in a moral and ethical vacuum. What is happening around us involves moral and ethical issues.

We believe that the gospel of Jesus teaches that humans have moral and ethical power to influence what happens in our world. We have moral and ethical power to challenge and overcome imperialism, racism, capitalism, authoritarianism, sexism, militarism, technocentrism, religious nationalism, and xenophobia, individually and collectively. We have the moral and ethical power to condemn disregard for the divine imperatives that humans love God and others, including the planet that is our home.

That is why we wrote this book. Now that you have read it, what will you do?

Allan Aubrey Boesak, Cape Town, South Africa
Wendell L. Griffen, Little Rock, Arkansas

Notes

Introduction

[1] Reported by AP News, 15 December 2022.

[2] Quoted in Zizek, "Disorder Under Heaven," 29 June 2016, https://criticallegalthinking.com/2016/06/29/disorder-under-heaven/).

[3] See, e.g., Sachs, "Reaching a Lasting Peace with Ukraine," *International Peace Bureau*, 24 October 2021. See also several discussions on YouTube, e.g., "Reaching a Just and Lasting Peace in Ukraine," 25 January 2023, youtube.com/watch?v=zFaMVZzueEU&tab_channel=IBPInternationalPeaceBureau; "Jeffrey Sachs on the Path to Peace in Ukraine," *Canadian Foreign Policy Institute*, 4 May 2023, https://www.youtube.com/watch?v=k_uyfb6OyZ8; "Noam Chomsky and Vijay Prashad on Ukraine," *Democracy Now!* 3 October 2022, https://www.youtube.com/watch?v=EGZyj-_T6hQ.

[4] See "Adam Schiff: We're Using Ukraine to Fight Russia," *Useful Idiots*, 1 March 2022, youtube.com/watch?v=4d4rcoPulY4&tab_channel=usefulidiots. On Senator Graham see Laco and Gordan, "Russia issues warrant," *Daily Mail*, 29 May 2023, https://www.dailymail.co.uk/news/article-12136213/Russia-issues-warrant-Lindsey-Grahams-ARREST-Ukraine-released-edited-video-him.html.

[5] The remark about regime change in Russia was not in Biden's text. He slipped it in, and officials afterwards tried to "walk it back." See "Biden walks back Putin regime change comment," *CBS News*, 28 March 2022, https://www.youtube.com/watch?v=7HhOD3fcyHw.

[6] See Osang, "A Year with Ex-Chancellor Angela Merkel," *Spiegel International*, 1 December 2022, https://www.spiegel.de/international/germany/a-year-with-ex-chancellor-merkel-you-re-done-with-power-politics-a-f46149cb-6deb-45a8-887c-8aa37cc9b3c3; Prouvost, "Hollande: 'There will only be a way out,'" *Kyiv Independent*, 28 December 2022, https://kyivindependent.com/hollande-there-will-only-be-a-way-out-of-the-conflict-when-russia-fails-on-the-ground/.

[7] "Problems of War and Strategy," 6 November 1938, *Marxists Internet Archive*, https://www.marxists.org/reference/archive/mao/selected-works/volume-2/mswv2_12.htm.

[8] Barakat and Cochrane, "How can we end the hunger pandemic?" *Al Jazeera*, 17 December 2022, https://www.aljazeera.com/opinions/2022/12/17/how-can-we-end-the-hunger-pandemic.

[9] "Inequality Kills," *Oxfam*, 16 January 2022, https://www.oxfamamerica.org/explore/research-publications/inequality-kills/.

[10] See "Kabul suicide bombing," *CBS News*, 30 September 2022, https://www.cbsnews.com/news/afghanistan-school-suicide-bombing-attack-kabul-deaths-injuries/.

[11] See "Contaminated medicine kills at least 10 children in Yemen," *Al Jazeera*, 14 October 2022, https://www.aljazeera.com/news/2022/10/14/at-least-10-children-died-from-contaminated-medicine.

[12] As this book goes to print, the world seems to be changing in front of our very eyes. In the Middle East, Russia and China have taken diplomatic initiatives that have brought peace and the resumption of diplomatic relationships between Iran and Saudi Arabia. The war in Yemen is finally coming to an end. Syria has been welcomed back into the Arab League. The West African country of Niger has, through a military coup overthrown the pro-Western government of Mohammed Bazoum, making it clear that this is a political action taken to "break the bonds of French neo-colonialism."

Niger is being backed by Burkina Faso, Mali, and Guinea, but also by Algeria. But even more remarkable is the astonishing public support for the coup leaders—all on the basis of "freedom from neo-colonialist France." Across the continent, a new wave of anti-colonialism is overtaking Africa. Not since the 1960s has the continent seen such fundamental political shifts. This, plus the outcomes and progress of the BRICS+ alliance (Brazil, Russia, India, China, South Africa) having just added Argentina, Iran, Egypt, Ethiopia, Saudi Arabia, United Arab Emirates with over 40 other Global South nations on the waiting list, is totally unprecedented. The geo-political and geo-economic consequences for the world are going to be enormous.

[13] See Walter Brueggemann, *The Prophetic Imagination* (Minneapolis: Fortress, 2011).

[14] Obery M. Hendricks, *The Politics of Jesus, Rediscovering the Revolutionary Nature of Jesus' Teachings and How They Have Been Corrupted* (New York: Doubleday, 2006), 5.

[15] William R. Herzog II, *Parables as Subversive Speech: Jesus as Pedagogue of the Oppressed* (Louisville, KY: Westminster John Knox, 1994).

Chapter 1

[1] Since this chapter turned out to be exceptionally long, it was decided to offer it in three parts. The reader should read Parts II and III as the continuing unfolding of the same narrative.

[2] Helmut Gollwitzer, *The Way to Life: Sermons in a Time of World Crisis* (London: T&T Clarke, 1981), xii.

[3] "Kleptocatic rule": rule by persons totally corrupt, and robbing the nation of its treasures, intent only on self-enrichment. "Kakistocratic rule": rule by incompetent and dishonest persons devoid of intelligence, political insight, and wisdom. Tragically, that is precisely the situation in South Africa as I write this.

[4] See, e.g., Martin Gilens and Benjamin I. Page, "Testing Theories of American Politics: Ethics, Interest Groups, and Average Citizens," *Cambridge University Press*, September 18, 2014, https://www.cambridge.org/core/journals/perspectives-on-politics/article/testing-theories-of-american-politics-elites-interest-groups-and-average-citizens/62327F513959D0A304D4893B382B992B; Saskia Brechenmacher, "Comparing Democratic Distress in the United States and Europe," *Carnegie Endowment for International Peace*, June 21, 2018, https://carnegieendowment.org/2018/06/21/comparing-democratic-distress-in-united-states-and-europe-pub-76646; and "The State of Democracy in Europe 2021," *International IDEA*, November 22, 2012, idea.int/gsod/sites/default/files/2021-11/state-of-democracy-in-europe-2021.pdf.

[5] See Walter Brueggemann, *1 and 2 Kings*, Smyth & Helwys Bible Commentary (Macon, GA: Smyth & Helwys Publishing, 2000), 216–17.

[6] See also Brueggemann, "The Liturgy of Abundance, The Myth of Scarcity," *Christian Century*, March 24–31, 1999, available at Religion-online.org/the-liturgy-of-abundance-the-myth-of-scarcity/. There, Brueggemann highlights the Bible's persistent theme of God's overflowing goodness, from the creation story in Genesis to the ministry of Jesus. Brueggemann writes, "In an orgy of fruitfulness, everything in its kind is to multiply the overflowing goodness that pours from God's creator heart." Jesus must have often heard his mother sing that revolutionary song we know as the Magnificat. Brueggemann says Jesus "enacted his mother's song well. Everywhere he went he created new life. Jesus' example gives us the mandate to transform our public life."

[7] *1 and 2 Kings*, 217.

[8] *1 and 2 Kings*, 221.

[9] *1 and 2 Kings*, 226.
[10] H. H. Rowley, "Elijah on Mount Carmel," https://www.escholar.manchester.ac.uk/api/datastream?publicationPid=uk-ac-man-scw:1m2856&datastreamId=POST-PEER-REVIEW-PUBLISHERS-DOCUMENT.PDF, 201. For a more complete treatment of this story, see also H. H. Rowley, *Elijah on Mount Carmel* (Manchester: Manchester University Press, 1960).
[11] Rowley, "Elijah on Mount Carmel," 195.
[12] See Mordechai Cogan, *I Kings*, Anchor Bible, vol. 10 (New York: Doubleday, 2001), 444.
[13] President Obama said, "At the dawn of history [war's] morality was not questioned...." Over time though, "philosophers and clerics and statesmen [sought] to regulate the destructive power of war," seeking to "control violence within groups." See "Remarks by the President," *The White House: President Barack Obama*, December 10, 2009, obamawhitehouse.archives.gov/the-press-office/remarks-president-acceptance-nobel-peace-prize.
[14] In D. H. Lawrence, *Studies in Classic American Literature*, vol. 2 (New York: Penguin, 1990), 65.
[15] See Walter Brueggemann, "Trajectories in Old Testament Literature and the Sociology of Ancient Israel," *Journal of Biblical Literature* 98, no. 2 (1979): 161–85.
[16] These terms were introduced by the work of sociologist Robert Redfield in his classic *The Little Community and Peasant Society and Culture* (Chicago: Chicago University Press, 1960). These terms have since been very usefully appropriated by biblical scholars to apply to our reading and interpretation of the Bible and in understanding the life and ministry of Jesus.
[17] See Allan Aubrey Boesak, *Children of the Waters of Meribah, Black Liberation Theology, the Miriamic Tradition, and the Challenges of 21st Century Empire* (Eugene, OR: Cascade, 2019), 74–88 and chapter 4.
[18] See Walter Brueggemann, *The Prophetic Imagination* (Minneapolis: Fortress, 2001).
[19] See my argument on the contrast between Moses' leadership and that of his sister Miriam as depicted in the exodus story in *Children of the Waters of Meribah*, chapter 4.
[20] See Nelson Mandela, "I Am Prepared to Die," April 20, 1964, available at http://law2.umkc.edu/faculty/projects/ftrials/mandela/mandelaspeech.html. Mandela refers to the Manifesto of Umkhonto (pub. December 16, 1961), which stated, "The time comes in the life of any nation when there remain only two choices—submit or fight. That time has now come to South Africa. We shall not submit and we have no choice but to hit back by all means in our power in defence of our people, our future, and our freedom."
[21] Mandela, "Prepared to Die."
[22] Rowley, "Elijah on Mount Carmel," 218.
[23] Rowley, "Elijah on Mount Carmel," 196n2.
[24] Rowley, "Elijah on Mount Carmel," 195–97.
[25] *1 and 2 Kings*, 229.

Chapter 2

[1] See H. A. Brongers, *I Koningen* (Prediking van het Oude Testament, Nijkerk: Callenbach, 1967), 173.
[2] Rowley, "Elijah on Mount Carmel," 191.
[3] Brueggemann, *1 and 2 Kings*, 221.
[4] Brongers, *I Koningen*, 179.

[5] Brongers, *I Koningen*, 181.
[6] See Brueggemann, *1 and 2 Kings*, 443. My emphasis.
[7] See Brueggemann, *1 and 2 Kings*, 444.
[8] Rowley, "Elijah on Mount Carmel," 216.

Chapter 3

[1] Rowley, "Elijah on Mount Carmel," 219.
[2] See Boesak, *Children of the Waters of Meribah*, chapter 4.
[3] See Kelley, "Last Year Obama Reportedly Told His Aides that He's 'Really Good at Killing People,'" *Insider*, 2 November 2013, https://www.businessinsider.com/obama-said-hes-really-good-at-killing-people-2013-11.
[4] See Edward S. Herman and Noam Chomsky, *Manufactured Consent: The Political Economy of the Mass Media* (New York: Pantheon, 1988).
[5] For more information, the most dependable resource—disputed but never disproven—is Seymour Hersh, "How America Took Out the Nord Stream Pipeline," *Substack*, 8 February 2023, https://seymourhersh.substack.com/p/how-america-took-out-the-nord-stream.
[6] See Paul Lehmann, *The Transfiguration of Politics* (New York: Harper & Row, 1975).

Chapter 4

[1] Allan Aubrey Boesak and Curtiss Paul DeYoung, *Radical Reconciliation: Beyond Political Pietism and Christian Quietism* (Maryknoll, NY: Orbis Books, 2012), 66.
[2] See "Resolution on Racial Reconciliation on the 150th Anniversary of the Southern Baptist Convention," June 1, 1995, https://www.sbc.net/resource-library/resolutions/resolution-on-racial-reconciliation-on-the-150th-anniversary-of-the-southern-baptist-convention/.
[3] See "Resolution on Racial Healing and Justice," *Baylor University*, June 26, 2020, https://boardofregents.web.baylor.edu/news/story/2020/enews-resolution-racial-healing-and-justice.
[4] Randall Robinson, *The Debt: What America Owes to Blacks* (New York: Dutton [Penguin Group], 2000), 206–208.

Chapter 5

[1] Robert P. Jones, *White Too Long: The Legacy of White Supremacy in American Christianity* (New York: Simon & Schuster, 2020).
[2] See Bob Allen, "Southern Seminary leadership nixes idea of reparations for historically black college," *Baptist News Global*, 4 June 2019, https://baptistnews.com/article/southern-seminary-leadership-nixes-idea-of-reparations-for-historically-black-college/. See also Wendell Griffen, "Baylor Doesn't Need Commission to Know Its Racist History," *Good Faith Media*, 13 July 2020, https://goodfaithmedia.org/baylor-doesnt-need-commission-to-know-its-racist-history/. Readers might also benefit from the observation of Brian Kaylor, a white Baptist writer. See "Baylor, White Churches Must Bare Racist Pasts before Reparations," *Good Faith Media*, 17 July 2020, https://goodfaithmedia.org/baylor-white-churches-must-bare-racist-pasts-before-reparations/.

Chapter 6

[1] Cornel West, *Democracy Matters: Winning the Fight against Imperialism* (New York: Penguin Press, 2004).

[2] West, *Democracy Matters*, 146–46.

[3] West, *Democracy Matters*, 150.

[4] West, *Democracy Matters*, 150.

[5] West, *Democracy Matters*, 171–72.

Chapter 7

[1] See Allan Aubrey Boesak, *Children of the Waters of Meribah: Black Liberation Theology, the Miriamic Tradition, and the Challenges of 21st Century Empire* (Eugene, OR: Cascade, 2019), 193–99.

[2] See Allan Aubrey Boesak, *Children of the Waters of Meribah*, Chapter 7

[3] See Steve Biko, *I Write What I Like* (Johannesburg: Picador Africa, 2017), 34, 104.

[4] Andries van Aarde, "Jesus's Affection Toward Children and a Tale of Two Kings," *Acta Theologica* 24 (2004): 150-175, Niddah 4:1.

[5] Helmut Gollwitzer, *The Way to Life: Sermons in a Time of World Crisis* (London: T&T Clarke, 1981).

[6] Dietrich Bonhoeffer, "The Things That Are Above," https://www.sermoncentral.com.the-things-that-are-above.

[7] "Dignity Not Destitution: An 'Economic Rescue Plan for All' to tackle the coronavirus crisis and rebuild a more equal world," *Oxfam*, April 9, 2020, https://oxfamilibrary.openrepository.com/bitstream/handle/10546/620976/mb-dignity%20not%20destitution-an-economic-rescue-plan-for-all-090420-en.pdf.

[8] Biko, *I Write What I Like*.

[9] From the text of his address sent to the author: Barney Pityana, "A better South Africa shall only be realised when inequalities dease to exist," NADEL Annual Conference, November 2019.

[10] John Calvin, *Commentaries*, Acts 5:29.

Chapter 8

[1] Mitri Raheb, *Faith in the Face of Empire: The Bible through Palestinian Eyes* (Maryknoll, NY: Orbis, 2014), 11 (italics in original).

[2] Samuel DeWitt Proctor, *The Substance of Things Hoped For: A Memoir of African American Faith* (New York: Putnam, 1995), 123.

[3] Miguel De La Torre, *Decolonizing Christianity: Becoming Badass Believers* (Grand Rapids, MI: Eerdmans, 2021).

[4] De La Torre, *Decolonizing Christianity*, 28–29.

[5] De La Torre, *Decolonizing Christianity*, 30.

[6] De La Torre, *Decolonizing Christianity*, 31–32.

[7] Rev. Dr. Martin Luther King Jr.'s "Beyond Vietnam: A Time to Break Silence" is among the writings of Dr. King compiled by James Melvin Washington and published under the title *A Testament of Hope: The Essential Writings of Martin Luther King, Jr.* (San Francisco, Harper and Row, 1986).

⁸ For reactions to "Beyond Vietnam: A Time to Break Silence," see http://www.milestonedocuments.com/documents/view/martin-luther-king-jr-beyond-vietnam-a-time-to-break-silence/impact.

⁹ Margalit Fox, "Vincent Harding, 82, Civil Rights Author and Associate of Dr. King, Dies," *New York Times*, May 21, 2014, http://www.nytimes.com/2014/05/22/us/vincent-harding-civil-rights-author-and-associate-of-dr-king-dies-at-82.html?_r=0.

¹⁰ Daniel Trotta, "Iraq War Costs US more than $2 Trillion: Study," *Reuters*, March 14, 2013, https://www.reuters.com/article/us-iraq-war-anniversary/iraq-war-costs-u-s-more-than-2-trillion-study-idUSBRE92D0PG20130314.

¹¹ "Human and Budgetary Costs to Date of the U.S. War in Afghanistan, 2001–2022," *Watson Institute*, https://watson.brown.edu/costsofwar/figures/2021/human-and-budgetary-costs-date-us-war-afghanistan-2001-2022.

¹² Akhilesh Pillalamarri, "Why Is Afghanistan the 'Graveyard of Empires'?" *The Diplomat*, June 30, 2017, https://thediplomat.com/2017/06/why-is-afghanistan-the-graveyard-of-empires/.

¹³ See, Jimmy Carter, *Palestine: Peace Not Apartheid* (New York: Simon & Schuster, 2006).

¹⁴ Jonathan Tran, "The Audacity of Hope and the Violence of Peace: Obama, War, and Christianity," Inaugural Ethics Lecture, Truett Seminary, January 31, 2012, in TBMaston Foundation e-Newsletter, no. 3 (March 2012), https://www.baylor.edu/content/services/document.php/184801.pdf.

¹⁵ Michelle Alexander, *The New Jim Crow: Mass Incarceration in the Age of Colorblindness*, (New York: The New Press, 2010).

¹⁶ Trayvon Martin was a seventeen-year-old Black male who was shot to death by George Zimmerman as Martin was returning to his father's residence from a convenience store in Sanford, Florida, the night of February 26, 2012. Zimmerman was acquitted by a jury on the charge of manslaughter.

¹⁷ Oscar Grant III was fatally shot in the back at point-blank range by Bay Area Rapid Transit (BART) police officer Johannes Mehserle during the early hours of New Year's Day 2009 in Oakland, California. Mehserle was eventually convicted by a jury of involuntary manslaughter and served two years in the Los Angeles County Jail, minus time served.

¹⁸ Amadou Diallo was a twenty-three-year-old Guinean immigrant who was shot and killed by four New York City Police officers who fired forty-one bullets, nineteen of which struck Diallo, outside his apartment in the Bronx. All four police officers were later acquitted of criminal charges related to Diallo's death.

¹⁹ See Raja Razek, "Missouri Police Officer who Killed Michael Brown Faces No Charges," *CNN*, July 30, 2020, https://www.cnn.com/2020/07/30/us/ferguson-missouri-michael-brown-darren-wilson-no-charges/index.html.

²⁰ See "'I Can't Breathe': Eric Garner Put in Chokehold by NYPD Officer," video, *The Guardian*, December 4, 2014, https://www.theguardian.com/us-news/video/2014/dec/04/i-cant-breathe-eric-garner-chokehold-death-video.

²¹ See Holly Bailey, "Officers Charged in George Floyd's Killing Had Been Taught to Intervene," *Washington Post*, January 28, 2022, https://www.washingtonpost.com/nation/2022/01/28/officers-charged-george-floyds-killing-had-been-taught-intervene-police-trainer-testifies/.

²² See Lucy Tompkins, "Here's What You Need to Know about Elijah McClain's Death," *New York Times*, January 18, 2022, https://www.nytimes.com/article/who-was-elijah-mcclain.html.

23 "Letter from Birmingham City Jail," in *A Testament of Hope: The Essential Writings of Martin Luther King Jr.* (San Francisco: Harper and Row, 1986), 298–300.

24 Obery Hendricks Jr., *Christians against Christianity: How Right-Wing Evangelicals Are Destroying Our Nation and Our Faith* (Boston: Beacon Press, 2021), 1.

Chapter 9

1 For the sake of clarity, I should make the point here that in a previous work I have, in agreement with growing consensus among many Hebrew Bible scholars, argued that there are multiple traditions on which the exodus story is built. I have, convinced mostly by feminist and Womanist scholars, chosen for the Miriamic tradition, the tradition that places the women from Exodus 2, and especially Miriam, at the centre. In such a view, the Mosaic tradition is a later, much more patriarchal tradition. For the purposes of this reflection, I take the Mosaic tradition as presented to the reader in this part of the exodus narrative at face value and engage with it as such. See my *Children of the Waters of Meribah: Black Liberation Theology, the Miriamic Tradition, and the Challenges of 21st Century Empire* (Eugene, OR: Cascade, 2019), especially chapters 2, 3, and 4.

2 See the much wider discussion in Allan Aubrey Boesak, *Pharaohs on Both Sides of the Blood-red Waters: Prophetic Critique on Empire Resistance, Justice, and the Power of the Hopeful Sizwe* (Eugene, OR: Cascade, 2017), 54–60.

3 See *Children of the Waters of Meribah*, 44–46.

4 See Frederick Douglass, "If There Is No Struggle, There Is No Progress," a "West India Emancipation" speech delivered at Canandaigua, New York, August 3, 1857, https://www.blackpast.org/african-american-history/1857-frederick-douglass-if-there-no-struggle-there-no-progress/.

5 See M. M. Thomas and J. D. McCaughey, *The Christian in the World Struggle* (Geneva: WSCF, 1951), 19.

6 Cited in Siya Khumalo, *You Have to be Gay to Know God* (Cape Town: Kwela, 2018), 216.

7 See Lawrence D Bobo, "Obama and the Great Progressive Disconnect," scholar.harvard.edu/files/bobo/2010_obama_and_the_great_progressive_disconnect_pathways.pdf. The notion from King is pervasive throughout his writings.

8 Calvin, *Commentary on the Twelve Minor Prophets*, Hab. 2:6.

9 Calvin, *Commentary on the Twelve Minor Prophets*, Hab. 1:2.

10 See the fulsome praise for the ANC government from the IMF, for example: "In successfully navigating from apartheid to democracy, the government of South Africa has made impressive gains in stabilizing the economy and laying the foundations for higher economic growth and a broad-based improvement in living standards" (Michael Nowak and Luis Antonio, *Post-Apartheid South Africa: The First Ten Years* [Washington, DC: The IMF, 2005]). This is in stark contrast to the sharp critique by many South African scholars and analysts of the World Bank, IMF, WTO, and other international financial institutions regarding their role in Third World countries in general and in South Africa's transition in particular. See, for example, the book from the two University of the Witwatersrand economists Vishnu Padayachee and Robert van Niekerk, *Shadow of Liberation: Contestation and Compromise in the Economic and Social Policy of the African National Congress, 1943–1996* (Johannesburg: Wits University Press, 2019).

11 See Patrick Bond, *Elite Transition: From Apartheid to Neoliberalism in South Africa* (Pietermaritzburg: UKZN Press, 2005).

[12] Sampie Terreblanche, *Lost in Transformation: South Africa's Search for a New Future Since 1986* (Johannesburg: KMM Review Books, 2012).

[13] See Eugene Cairncross, "Post-Apartheid South African Economy: The Triumph of Capital," in *South Africa Today: how do we challenge the social (trans)formation?* ILRIG conference paper, 2011, https://www.ilrigsa.org.za/wp-content/uploads/2020/06/Cairncross-2011.pdf. The citations are all from the same paper.

[14] Cairncross, "Post-Apartheid South African Economy," emphasis added.

[15] See Siji Jabbar, "How France Loots Former African Colonies," *This Is Africa*, January 24, 2013, thisisafrica.me/politics-and-society/france-loots-former-colonies/. For yet another analysis, see M. Molapi, "The CFA Franc Zone: A Modern Reincarnation of a Colonial Relic," OpenUCT [University of Cape Town], 2021, https://open.uct.ac.za/handle/11427/33859.

[16] See e.g. Horace Campbell on Democracy Now! 8/11/23, YouTube.com/watch?v=LMiLz2BMmWE&t=1s&ab_channel=DemocracyNow%21

[17] See Hannes Swoboda, "Congo—Colonialism, Neo-colonialism and Continuing Wars," *International Institute for Peace*, January 15, 2021, https://www.iipvienna.com/new-blog/2021/1/14/congo-colonialism-neo-colonialism-and-continuing-wars.

[18] *Exodus*, New Interpreter's Bible, vol. 1 (Nashville: Abingdon, 2015), 337.

[19] *Exodus*, NIB, 338.

[20] For a detailed discussion of the Song of Miriam, in contradiction to "the song of Moses," both in Exodus 15, see Boesak, *Children of the Waters of Meribah*, 74–88.

[21] I have replaced "LORD" and masculine pronouns for God with "Yahweh" here.

Chapter 10

[1] Martin Luther King Jr., "A Time to Break Silence," from *A Testament of Hope: The Essential Writings and Speeches of Martin Luther King Jr.*, ed. James M. Washington (San Francisco: HarperOne, 1986), 242–43.

[2] Listen to the telephone interview "Randall Robinson on Haiti," *Democracy Now!* March 1, 2004, https://archive.org/details/randall_robinson/randall_robinson_mikeR.mp3. Also see "Randall Robinson on 'An Unbroken Agony: Haiti, from Revolution to the Kidnapping of a President,'" interview by Amy Goodman for *Democracy Now*, July 23, 2007, at *Third World Traveler*, https://thirdworldtraveler.com/Amy_Goodman/Haiti_RandallRobinson.html.

Chapter 11

[1] The portion in this chapter dealing with Jotham's parable was originally part of a short exposition of the book of Judges published in Allan Aubrey Boesak, *I Turn My Face to the Rising Sun*, vol. 3 of The Fire, the River, and the Scorched Earth Between (Pietermaritzburg: Cluster, 2022), introduction.

[2] See M. M. Thomas and J. D. McCaughey, *The Christian in the World Struggle* (Geneva: World Student Christian Federation, 1951), 19.

[3] See Allan Aubrey Boesak, *Comfort and Protest: The Apocalypse of John in a South African Perspective* (Philadelphia: Westminster, 1987), 39.

4 "But it is dominion that we are after. Not just a voice. It is dominion we are after. Not just influence. It is dominion we are after. Not just equal time. It is dominion we are after. World conquest. That's what Christ has commissioned us to accomplish" (George Grant, *The Changing of the Guard: Biblical Blueprints for Political Action* [Fort Worth, TX: Dominion Press, 1987], 50–51).

5 William R. Herzog II, *Parables as Subversive Speech: Jesus as Pedagogue of the Oppressed* (Louisville, KY: Westminster John Knox, 1994).

6 See Barry Wugale, *Africa in Captivity: It's Time for the Church to Stand Up* (Cape Town: Reach Publishers, 2021).

7 "Voertsek" is Afrikaans for the word in which one chases away a dog. The closest English translation, in tone and intent, would be a four-letter word followed by "off"!

8 J. Alberto Soggin, *Judges: A Commentary* (London: SCM, 1987).

9 See Obery M. Hendricks Jr., *The Politics of Jesus: Rediscovering the Revolutionary Nature of Jesus' Teachings, and How They Have Been Corrupted* (New York: Doubleday, 2006).

10 See Allan Boesak, *Children of the Waters of Meribah*, 74–88.

11 Dwight Allen Callahan, *The Talking Book: African Americans and the Bible* (New Haven: Yale University Press, 2006), 246.

The Authors

Allan Aubrey Boesak is a South African Black liberation theologian, global human rights activist, professor emeritus of Black Liberation Ethics at the University of Pretoria, and the Chair of the Sankofa Institute for Pan African Leadership and Prophetic Ministry. Inducted into the Martin Luther King Jr International Board of Preachers, he is the award-winning author of more than twenty books, including *Selfless Revolutionaries: Biko, Black Consciousness, Black Theology, and a Global Ethic of Solidarity and Resistance*.

Wendell Griffen is Pastor of New Millennium Church of Little Rock, Arkansas, CEO of Griffen Strategic Consulting, PLLC, a retired Arkansas jurist with a quarter century of experience as a state court appellate and trial judge, co-chair of the Samuel DeWitt Proctor Conference, author of *The Fierce Urgency of Prophetic Hope*, and a frequent commentator about faith, public policy, law, and social justice.